RISKY BUSINESS

RISKY BUSINESS

Why Insurance Markets Fail
and What to Do About It

Liran Einav,
Amy Finkelstein,
and Ray Fisman

Yale
UNIVERSITY PRESS
NEW HAVEN & LONDON

Published with assistance from the Louis Stern Memorial Fund.

Yale University Press books may be purchased in quantity
for educational, business, or promotional use. For information, please e-mail
sales.press@yale.edu (U.S. office) or sales@yaleup.co.uk (U.K. office).

Set in Yale and Alternate Gothic type by Integrated Publishing Solutions.
Printed in the United States of America.

Library of Congress Control Number: 2022934606
ISBN 978-0-300-25343-6 (hardcover : alk. paper)

A catalogue record for this book is available from the British Library.

This paper meets the requirements of ANSI/NISO Z39.48-1992
(Permanence of Paper).

10 9 8 7 6 5 4 3 2 1

CONTENTS

RISKY BUSINESS

Prologue

OVERLOOKED NO MORE

Many a prologue or author's note opens with a childhood obsession, a formative experience, a bolt-of-lightning epiphany. Not so for a book on the economics of insurance. A life devoted to the study of insurance is something one is more apt to stumble upon — like a pair of old brown socks at the bottom of a drawer — than dream about from an early age.

Liran loves data, and a friend of his had great insurance data. Besides, compared to the other sectors that economists in his field were studying at the time — yogurt, laundry detergent, cement — insurance *was* rather glamorous. So that's his origin story.

Amy's love affair with insurance began when her thesis adviser, Jim Poterba, introduced her to the esoteric world of annuity contracts (reverse life insurance contracts that pay out *until* you die). While you never forget your first love, she eventually branched out into health insurance because, as you probably know, health insurance in the United States is a very big deal, by some measure a fifth of the entire economy.

Ray doesn't actually study insurance at all. Amy somehow convinced him at dinner one night that writing this book would be a good idea, in the same way that buying the Brooklyn Bridge offers a good investment opportunity.

The initial pitch that Amy made also ended up being a very long distance from the book we came to write. Amy thought the wider world was itching to learn about some fairly technical details of her research with Liran. Needless to say, she was mistaken.

But a funny thing happened in the process of failing to convince Ray to write that version of the book. We realized that while most people might think that insurance is the brown socks of the nonfiction world, it's simply because most people – fine, pretty much all people – never think about insurance at all. It only enters their minds when they send off a check for home or auto insurance and think, "wow, that's expensive!" or open a hospital bill and think with relief that someone else is covering the cost (or wonder indignantly why their insurer refused).

They don't realize what they're missing.

Insurance has a long and storied history – the first insurance contracts date to ancient Mesopotamia, at least. And insurance has preoccupied some of history's greatest minds. Edmund Halley (yes, *that* Halley, the comet guy) painstakingly calculated mortality tables that listed the probability that people of various ages would expire within a year. These served as the basis for one of the first attempts at pricing life insurance and annuities (spoiler: he did them wrong). One of the lasting contributions of the distinguished seventeenth-century mathematician Abraham de Moivre was a formula for simplifying these calculations for insurance salesmen of the pre-computer era.

Insurance has also played a surprisingly prominent role in a number of pivotal events in world history – eighteenth-century European states financed their wars and monarchical indulgences by selling insurance products rather than issuing bonds. But they too often got the pricing wrong and ended up accumulating unpayable debts. In the case of France, this arguably cost Marie Antoinette her head.

Quite a few literary and cinematic masterpieces rely on the peculiarities of insurance as essential storytelling devices. Arthur Miller's iconic play *Death of a Salesman* is one such example – his tragic protagonist, Willy Loman, hopes to find redemption in the fine print of his life insurance contract. Insurance also makes cameos in many lesser-known masterpieces, including the Taylor Swift song "No Body, No Crime" and the Simpson's episode "Curse of the Flying Hellfish."

Instead of thinking about insurance as the annual contract you sign (but of course never read) from GEICO or Allstate, consider instead the circumstances in which insurance matters in people's lives. These are the stuff of legend: life and death; fortunes lost and disasters averted – human tragedy played out on a historic or personal scale. When insurance is doing its job right, it offers a measure of salvation – or at least security – in a dangerous and uncertain world.

The kicker: insurance often *can't* do its job right – that's where our book enters the story.

Without giving away too much of the plot, there is a feature of *all* insurance products that accounts for much of what makes insurance markets full of puzzles, frustrations, and – dare we say – intrigue. It is known as the problem of selection, and it is the focus of our book.

Insurance sellers care not just about how much they sell but *whom* they are selling to. They care, in other words, about which customers they select. And why do they care? Because some customers are much more expensive to insure than others.

As we'll explain in the pages that follow, selection lies behind the fine print in Willy Loman's life insurance contract. Selection explains why Edmund Halley's death-rate calculations were spectacularly wrong. Selection explains — at least in part — why the annuities sold by the French monarchy were a ticking financial time bomb, thereby costing Madame Antoinette her delicate and well-coiffed head. More relevant to your modern life, selection explains why dental insurance is so appallingly inadequate, and why it's impossible to get insurance to protect against a financially ruinous divorce battle or so costly to insure against the medical expenses of a fifteen-year-old dachshund.

The problem of selection introduces a two-sided game of cat-and-mouse in which insurers try to pick the right customers (and avoid the wrong ones), while the "wrong" types of customers do all they can to get insurers to believe they're actually the right ones.

Who comes out on top in this matchup of wits and information? You'll need to read on to find out. We won't give the answer here, in part because — as you'll see — it's not so simple as declaring one side the winner.

To complicate things further (and to mix up some metaphors), the cat-and-mouse game between insurers and their customers isn't a free-wheeling pickup game. The government frequently plays the role of information referee, deciding which secrets customers can keep and how nosy companies can get in digging into their customers' pasts. In some cases, the government even cuts out the middleman and provides the insurance itself. As we'll see, whether it's refereeing or playing the role of cat directly, the government can sometimes manage to stave off selection problems. At other times, it can make these problems even worse.

—

PROLOGUE

At the risk of potentially coming off as self-important (and certainly at least a bit melodramatic), this book will help you understand the way the world is and also the way it could be. We will open your eyes to why learning about selection is important for understanding when markets — insurance or otherwise — do and don't work in *your* interest and in the interests of society more generally. If you've ever wondered why insurance can cost so much and yet somehow deliver so little, whether you should add roadside assistance to your auto policy, and maybe even what to do during open enrollment next November, we're here to help you. If you've never wondered, we're here to try to help you, too.

Or perhaps you think the world needs changing. Maybe you are a would-be entrepreneur who has designs on disrupting the insurance business or a policy aficionado who sees a different — maybe larger — role for government in providing health (or other) insurance. We're here to tell you there's a reason why so many insurance ventures — also started by smart and well-intentioned would-be disruptors — end in failure. And why health insurance — one of the defining issues of American politics — defies any facile policy solution that can be crystallized in a five-second sound bite. We'll take you through the rock-and-hard-place choices that result — again and again — from the problem of selection.

By the end, we hope you'll be able to make more sense of some things in the world that have always puzzled you and even clear up some mysteries that would have puzzled you if you'd ever taken the time to think about them. Maybe we'll never convince our teenage children that insurance is cool, but perhaps we'll get you to agree that it is at least far more interesting and worthy of attention than its brown-socks reputation might suggest.

PART I

SETTING THE SCENE

Chapter 1

DEATH OF A MARKET

Back in 1981, American Airlines had what seemed like the bright idea of locking in its most loyal customers by offering a mileage pass that guaranteed unlimited first-class travel for life. The price: a quarter of a million dollars. (After accounting for inflation, that would be about three-quarters of a million today). It was like a day-pass wristband at an amusement park versus pay-per-ride, only for a lifetime of free cocktails and lie-flat seats, waited on (this being the 1980s) by an army of shoulder-padded, spiral-permed flight attendants.

The company presumed that its new AAirpass would appeal to "the business and professional person" like the George Clooney character in *Up in the Air* whose work life revolves around airports and company site visits. The plan "made no sense for leisure travelers," according to American's president at the time, Robert Crandall.

Crandall later admitted that when it came to the AAirpass, "it soon became apparent that the public was smarter than we were." One AAirpass holder booked a Nova Scotia–New York–Miami–

London–Los Angeles–Maine–Denver–Fort Lauderdale vacation in a single July, visiting several of the destinations multiple times during the one-month trip. Another customer took sixteen round-trip flights from Chicago to London in less than a month. Particularly on heavily booked routes like Chicago–London, AAirpass holders were taking seats that would otherwise be filled by paying customers—the sixteen Chicago–London flights alone would have cost $125,000 if they'd been ticketed.

The AAirpass was turning into an expensive proposition. So American did what you might expect and raised the price to cover its—ahem—sky-high costs. By 1990, the AAirpass price had gone from $250,000 to $600,000. That only made the problem worse. Now only those who were *truly* committed to an airborne existence were willing to shell out for the pass, and the cost to American of serving the customers who were still interested in AAirpass rose faster than its price. The price topped a million dollars just three years later; by 1994, American cut its losses and canceled the program.[1]

American learned the hard way that the customers who are willing to pay the most are sometimes the ones you want the least. That's too bad for American but great for us, as it provides a view from twenty thousand feet (so to speak) of how private information can lead to the slow-motion collapse of a market. It also shows how even savvy businesspeople—like the president of American Airlines—can fail to anticipate this breakdown of the market. What Crandall failed to appreciate was that most of the people who are willing to shell out $250,000 for unlimited first-class flights belong to that rare breed of traveler who will fly—and fly constantly—for the sheer joy of it.

You may not shed any tears for American Airlines' shareholders who lost money off this debacle or care much that AAirpass folded after a decade-long run of losses. But it is just one example of a much larger problem, one that afflicts any market in which sellers care not just about how much they sell but also about *whom* they are selling to. We call these *selection markets,* because sellers care about which customers select their products.

About a decade before American Airlines launched its ill-fated AAirpass, the future Nobel Laureate economist George Akerlof effectively foretold its demise. He laid out the basic framework for how private information—what a buyer knows that a seller doesn't, or vice versa—can destroy a market. His twelve-page argument appeared in a 1970 article titled "The Market for 'Lemons.'" Like many important ideas in economics, it is at heart fairly straightforward and is well illustrated by many simple, real-life examples, the AAirpass among them. A business unwittingly attracts customers who—unbeknownst to the seller—turn out to be expensive to serve. The company is forced to raise prices to cover its unexpectedly high costs, which in turn weeds out all but the most expensive customers. And so it goes, with ever-higher prices attracting an ever-worse pool of customers, which demands yet higher prices still, until the market collapses completely. This powerful insight won Akerlof a Nobel Prize in 2001 and launched the field of information economics that in turn is the foundation for our book.[2]

One reason why Akerlof's ideas have had such resonance is that markets with selection problems are hardly a rare specimen—they're anywhere that not all customers are created equal, which is to say in all sorts of places. When you apply to take out a loan, dine at an all-you-can-eat restaurant, or decide whether to accept a job offer or even a marriage proposal, you're participating in a selection market. The bank's profits depend on who uses its credit card or takes out a loan, and the restaurant's profits on how gluttonous its patrons are.

—

An employer's output depends on which workers it manages to hire. And your marriage's future certainly depends on whom you marry.

The bank, the restaurant, the employer, and yes, even the guy down on one knee all have to worry about what they don't yet know about their would-be "customers." Has the credit card applicant just lost his job and decided to run up his debts and then declare bankruptcy? Will that scrawny teenage boy consume his weight in all-you-can-eat sushi? Is this employee a slacker who's somehow managed to buff up his résumé? And what exactly will your marriage partner be like once you've both said "I do"?

Perhaps most of all, the problem of selection afflicts just about every insurance market. Sometimes, selection leads insurers to severely limit their offerings—like dental insurance that covers only predictable, routine cleanings and cavities but isn't there for you when the dentist unexpectedly recommends an expensive implant. Sometimes, selection drives up premiums, making insurance much more expensive than you'd think it has any right to be—a pet insurance policy on a twelve-year-old bulldog can set you back more than $4,300 a year for a policy that will pay out a maximum of just $5,000.[3] And sometimes, as with AAirpass, it causes the market to disappear completely, as you're all too aware if you've ever tried to find insurance to cover the cost of a messy divorce or the loss of a job.

Insurance markets suffer from the same problems as AAirpass, all-you-can-eat restaurant deals, and credit cards—there are more expensive customers and less expensive customers, and all too often the more expensive customers are the ones who actually buy. Indeed, at about the same time that American Airlines was being taken for a ride, selection destroyed an arguably much more important market, one that was literally a matter of life and death for the people it affected.

—

Death of an Insurance Market

At some point in the 1980s, it suddenly became a lot tougher for healthy young men living in West Hollywood to get health insurance. Even more surprising, had these young men lived in East Hollywood, they'd have been able to buy coverage without any problem. In fact, there was an insurer at the time who was willing to sell health insurance in every single zip code in Los Angeles County, except one, which was located within West Hollywood's boundaries. If this seems puzzling, here's a big hint: outside of West Hollywood, health insurance companies in the 1980s also often steered clear of customers who worked in certain businesses, including flower shops, interior design firms, and hair salons.[4]

What West Hollywood, hair salons, flower shops, and interior design firms all have in common is a relatively high concentration of gay men. And this being the early 1980s, with the AIDS epidemic ravaging the gay community, insuring a young gay man – even a healthy one – was potentially very costly. If he got the disease, it could drive the medical bills covered by his insurer into the hundreds of thousands of dollars per year.[5]

That some subset of West Hollywood's residents would end up with stratospheric medical expenses shouldn't by itself ruin their chances of getting health insurance. The whole point of insurance, after all, is to provide some protection when fate deals you an unlucky hand. Those who are unfortunate enough to contract AIDS – or diabetes or any other expensive-to-treat disease – will at least be able to afford medical treatment. The premiums of those who stay healthy help insurers pay the medical bills of the ones who fall ill. The idiosyncrasies of fate are supposed to average out across customers – some will be unlucky and some will not – providing them with protection against catastrophic expenses and providing the insurance company with enough of a profit to make the business worthwhile.

The difference between AIDS and diabetes is telling, however. A physical exam might provide blood-pressure readings and information on weight that could signal elevated risk for diabetes, and an application form could note a family history of the disease. An insurer may therefore have a reasonable guess, based on a customer's medical history, of how likely they are to have diabetes and perhaps can charge a higher premium to those whom they anticipate may have higher medical expenses. (Whether insurers should be allowed to do this is a more complicated question that we'll take up later.)

However, there wasn't much in a medical record in the 1980s that helped predict the risk of AIDS. As AIDS was a sexually transmitted disease, unprotected sex was the main risk factor.[6] An applicant's sexual behavior is harder for an insurer to discern. It might ask. But the applicant might not tell. And the insurer had no way to check.

It was the AAirpass story all over again, only this time the market's collapse froze an entire group out of health coverage. Whenever customers have secrets about whether they'll be expensive or cheap for a company to serve—whether the product is a flat-bed seat on a transatlantic flight or a life-saving medication—it can wreck the market.

These are big problems, economically speaking, and often demand commensurately ambitious solutions. Yet the problem of selection is less well understood and less often discussed than many other, more widely discussed shortcomings of the free market.

A Market That Doesn't Work on Its Own

The first lesson you learn in economics is about the glory of markets. Some people are good at baking cakes but don't like eating them; others like eating but not baking — the two counterparties trade cake for money, guided by the fabled invisible hand of the market, which sets prices so bakers are motivated to produce exactly as many cakes as the hungry public desires. Bakers then spend their money on whatever *they* value at prices that similarly bring supply and demand into balance and harmony.

The second lesson is that the market has its limits. The list of market failings is a long one. Monopolies — like Rockefeller's Standard Oil in the nineteenth century or Apple's lock on the high-end smartphone market today — exploit their dominant position in the marketplace to set extortionate prices. Bank runs create panics that can plunge the economy into a recession or even a depression. Mining companies release toxic sludge into rivers, poisoning wildlife and drinking water of nearby communities. The market economy can create extreme inequities in income and wealth.

Lesson three provides well-known government solutions: antitrust regulation, deposit insurance, limiting (or pricing) pollution, stimulus spending in a recession, and redistributive taxation, to name a few. These governmental responses let markets continue to perform their wonders, while trying to limit risk-taking that threatens the economy, to prevent exploitation by dominant firms or insiders, and to ensure that the less fortunate aren't left starving in the streets.

This is all standard fare. Even most left-wing progressives appreciate that markets boost prosperity — they just want to put some guard rails in place. In turn, most free-market advocates understand that markets can't be left entirely to their own devices to solve all

—

problems — there are few voices calling for national defense or local policing to be managed solely by the forces of supply and demand.

This book is about another form of market frailty and government intervention that should also be standard fare but isn't: selection markets. In selection markets, some customers are more expensive to sell to than others. The selection *problem,* as we'll see, occurs when the costly-to-serve customers know who they are but the seller doesn't. As with other market problems, here too the government tends to take a middle-ground approach — letting the market continue to do its thing, albeit with a guiding hand from regulators.

Insurance markets — which are what we'll focus on — are a prime example of selection markets, and one that looms particularly large in the economy and in public policy. Insurance companies naturally care about who their customers are — an accident-prone driver or homeowner is going to be more expensive to cover than their more cautious counterpart. Insurance customers often know things about themselves that are relevant to the costs of insuring them. The insurance company may not know about these traits and can't easily learn them — like how frequently the customer gets distracted while driving or whether they tend to leave pots cooking unattended on the stove.

Private information can wreak havoc on the function of unfettered insurance markets. When it does, it raises the same pressing issues that arise with all the other cases of market limitations — from monopoly power to polluting firms to bank runs to inequality. When and how much should governments get involved? Should the government regulate whom insurers sell to and at what price? Should government get into the business of offering insurance itself?

Economists have been obsessing about the problem of private

—

information in selection markets for half a century. Amy and Liran have been researching and writing about them for their entire professional lives (which, they hasten to add, is not yet approaching the half-century mark). Our profession has come a long way in understanding how private information affects insurance markets, as well as how governmental attempts to redress these problems do (or don't) work.

But we haven't done enough to get the message out. This became painfully clear to us in listening to the oral arguments at the Supreme Court in 2012 over whether it was constitutional for the government to mandate that Americans buy health insurance. We heard the conservative Supreme Court Justice Antonin Scalia ask, If a paternalistic government could force people to buy health insurance, could it also force people to buy broccoli?[7]

If the public policy distinctions between health insurance and broccoli aren't clear to Supreme Court justices, we're sure they are far from obvious to the general public as well. That was the moment we realized we had to write this book. The economics of selection markets are essential for thinking about whether the government should mandate that we all buy health insurance (or automobile insurance or homeowners insurance) or let businesses, customers, and market prices collectively decide. They do not, however, feature in broccoli markets.

A World with – and without – Insurance

Before we can begin, we need to get you fully on board – in case you aren't already – with settling into a book-length treatment of insurance markets. Filled as they are with stories of death, money, and deceit, they really are much more interesting than you think (admittedly a low bar, we suspect). They're also incredibly important—for your everyday existence and for society at large.

Try to imagine a world without insurance. As the Harvard grad student Holly Wood (yes, that's really her name) wrote on *Vox,* in that world, "every day without an emergency is a relief."[8] Wood was writing about what it was like growing up as the daughter of a single-mom waitress, without the financial wherewithal to buy health insurance, but her insight is also an apt description of what life would be like without many other forms of insurance as well.

Life without insurance isn't "just" a problem for those who are (barely) surviving paycheck to paycheck and have to choose between buying groceries and buying insurance. Without insurance, just one piece of bad luck—whether illness, accident, or property damage— can be all that separates each of us from financial ruin. Death of the primary breadwinner can leave a family destitute. A house fire can leave them homeless, without any resources with which to rebuild. Health insurance, life insurance, automobile insurance, homeowners insurance, and the like all offer hedges against eventualities that we sometimes hardly even register as risks until disaster strikes.

In many instances, you don't have to *imagine* a world without insurance. Insurance is often simply not available at all, at any price. And the reason for this missing coverage is the problem of selection. This exactly describes the plight of West Hollywood's men in the 1980s. In the chapters that follow, we'll describe other forms of insurance that, if only they existed, would make people's lives more stable, predictable, and dare we say, happier. There's no such thing as divorce insurance, for example, nor is life insurance available for anyone who's ever suffered a stroke. If you want a dental plan that will cover high-cost procedures, you're also almost certainly out of luck.

—

In other cases, selection doesn't completely destroy the insurance market. But it doesn't make it stronger either. Rather, selection can make insurers twist in contortions to design products with all kinds of unpleasant features—like a waiting period before you can use your new roadside towing plan, seemingly unjust limitations on what insurance pays for, or rigid limits on when you can and can't make changes to your policy. It can also drive up the price of insurance to the point where it effectively prices many people out of the market. (That's economist-speak for "Selection can help you understand why insurance can be so damn expensive.")

Perhaps you're tempted to think that it's not a big deal if people choose not to buy high-priced insurance. We choose not to buy expensive things all the time. None of us owns a Porsche. They're way too expensive. That's not a sign that a market is failing. It's a sign that it's really expensive for Volkswagen to build each Porsche. The resulting "market clearing" price is such that enough other customers are willing to pay for the number of cars Volkswagen makes, but not us: the value we'd get from driving a fancy sports car is less (far, far less, in fact) than the price we'd have to pay for one. (It may also be a sign that we haven't—yet—gone through our midlife crises.)

This same Porsche logic might lead you to think that the customers deterred from buying insurance coverage because of high prices are the ones who value insurance the least. That is, maybe the cushion that an insurance policy provides—and the peace of mind that comes with it—are most important for those who are prone to burning down their houses, crashing their cars, subsisting on a diet of French fries, or spending their weekends skydiving. Their cautious and health-minded counterparts are unlikely to need a bailout anyway, so what does it matter if they pass on high-priced insurance policies?

That wouldn't be the right way to think about insurance. Because the role of insurance is to be a buffer against the vagaries of fate. And those vagaries, when they occur, can be just as catastrophic for the low risk as the high risk. Even the healthiest and most prudent among us can end up with astronomical hospital bills owing to random, uncontrollable twists of genetic fate, or five-figure home-repair expenses due to equally random acts of God. And what if disaster never strikes? We'll let the *New York Times*' *Wirecutter* — a provider of consumer product reviews for items ranging from sheets to vacuum cleaners to coffee makers — answer that one. As *Wirecutter* concludes in its guide to pet insurance, "[Even] if you never have to make a claim, your premiums weren't wasted — they were the cost of predictability, and of sleeping easier with a pet at your feet."[9]

In other words, the value of insurance isn't just the payout you get when bad things happen. It's the peace of mind it provides before anything happens at all — when insurance is working properly, most policyholders pay their premiums year after year and seemingly have nothing to show for it. This can create the mistaken sense that greedy and rapacious insurers are essentially printing money at their customers' expense. It is this type of misunderstanding that, we suspect, would lead the premium-paying public to agree with the sentiment expressed by the Yale historian Timothy Snyder, who lambasts health insurers for "simply collect[ing] rents from disease, like trolls on a bridge demanding a toll."[10] It's precisely because, as *Wirecutter* so helpfully explained, insurance has value even when it doesn't pay out, so that even safe drivers and healthy people can benefit from insuring their cars and their lives.

To see this point more concretely, let's go through a specific example. Consider two automobile drivers: a reckless teenage boy with a 10 percent chance of crashing his car in the next year and a cautious middle-aged mom who has only a 1 percent chance of getting into an accident. Of course, there's a much greater chance that the teenager (or, more likely, his parents) will make use of an auto insurance policy. But even the safe-driving mom would appreciate some protection against her one-in-a-hundred chance of an accident and the legal, medical, and damage-related costs it could create. She'd probably rather pay a little bit each year to protect against catastrophe than simply hope that she's not among the unlucky 1 percent.

That's why both reckless teenager and prudent mother get value from insurance. In both cases, the insurance takes the risk and uncertainty off them and foists it onto an insurer. The teenage boy is ten times more likely to have an accident than the middle-aged mom is, so he (or, again, his hapless parents) should have to pay ten times more for his automobile insurance. But for both mom and teenager alike, insurance is valuable. Insurance saves them from having to worry about financial catastrophe. It allows them to pay a small (relative to the financial cost of an accident) and preset amount in return for having someone else shoulder the uncertainty of collision expenses. That someone else is the insurance company.

This should work out well for the insured and also the insurer. The customer benefits because most people don't like to bear risk.*

---

*You might be thinking that people actually *love* risk because they pay good money to fly to Vegas to feed money into slot machines and play blackjack or buy lottery tickets for the one-in-a-zillion chance that it'll make them a millionaire. These are indeed instances in which people willingly pay to take financial risks, but they are perhaps unusual cases, relative to the circumstances we face in daily life. It's fun (or so we're told) to go with the guys for a weekend of gambling in Vegas—playing blackjack is more fun than paying a mechanic to fix the dents in your car. Lottery tickets afford the possibility of picturing, however briefly, the Porsche you'll drive and other luxuries you'll indulge in if you're holding the winning ticket. For the most part, though, people prefer to avoid risk when possible.

As a result, they're probably even willing to fork over a little more than what they would expect an insurance policy to pay out. It's worth it to pay a bit to reduce life's uncertainties, to have the peace of mind of knowing they're not on the hook for a much larger expense in the event of an accident. Naturally, there's a limit to how much anyone would pay for that insurance — peace of mind is valuable but not priceless — but it's typically more than just the amount you can expect your insurance to pay out.

And so the insurer is happy to oblige. While each individual customer is the source of some risk to the insurer, good luck and bad luck tend to even out over its millions of policyholders. And the extra amount that customers are willing to pay for their peace of mind yields enough money to pay for the other expenses of providing insurance — the actuaries who develop their pricing models, the TV spots where companies advertise their products, and so forth — and still have a tidy profit left over.

It's not a problem if some drivers are more accident prone than others — as long as the insurer knows what the customer knows. If the insurer knows that teenage boys are higher-risk drivers than middle-aged moms are (and who doesn't?), it can set prices for each accordingly. The problem, as we'll see in this book, arises when customers have information that their insurers don't have about how expensive they are to cover. Amy's auto insurer, for example, didn't know at first that it had insured one of the worst drivers in the middle-aged-mom set (they soon learned). When customers have private information about how expensive they'll be to insure, insurers can end up selling in Lake Woebegone, so to speak — it may seem like all their customers are more expensive than average (or at least more than expected). This can make a mess of insurance markets, for everyone — high-risk and low-risk customers alike. If you want to understand why some insurance products – like divorce insurance – can't be bought for love or money and why others are "too damn expensive," you need to understand selection markets.

Of course, many insurance companies survive and thrive despite the problem of private information. The fact that both the company and its customers stand to gain when corporations shoulder risk on their behalf explains why, despite these selection problems, the insurance business is alive and well in the United States today.

Big Business and Big Politics

Insurance plays an outsized role in the economy. Health care takes up nearly one-fifth of the entire U.S. economy, and health insurance is at the center of some of the most divisive policy debates. Even if you forget about health care completely, insurance is still a huge business, accounting for an additional whopping 6 percent of the economy.[11] Insurance touches on nearly every aspect of life: there is insurance for fire, flood, earthquake, automobile accidents, death, malpractice, and pet health care, to name but a few of the many hedges you can buy against disasters large and small. And that's just the insurance that the private market provides.

A major part of what modern governments do is provide and pay for insurance for their citizens. Think, for example, of public programs such as unemployment insurance and disability insurance. The single largest federal program, Social Security, is a form of government-provided insurance; it guarantees a steady income stream in old age, no matter how long you live (we'll have a lot more to say about this type of insurance in chapter 3). Social Security is almost one-quarter of federal spending. Government spending on health insurance for the elderly and poor makes up another one-quarter.

Reflecting the outsized role of insurance in the federal budget, the Treasury official Peter Fisher recommended "think[ing] of the federal government as a gigantic insurance company with a sideline business in national defense."[12]

Nor is the government's involvement in insurance limited to acting as a provider for some of it. Not by a long shot. The government also heavily regulates the operation of many forms of private insurance — life insurance, automobile insurance, health insurance, homeowner's insurance, flood insurance — you name it. Its rules can dictate which insurance plans are available, how high their prices can be set, and how much prices are allowed to vary across different customers.

Not surprisingly given all of this policy activity, the insurance industry has long been one of the biggest-spending interest groups, in Washington, D.C., and also in state capitals. The extent of insurers' political-influence activities surprised even the three of us. According to OpenSecrets (a nonprofit devoted to tracking lobbying and money in politics), insurers have outspent all other industries in their political action committee donations to federal candidates since 2014. And that's really saying something. To put it in perspective, donations by insurers' political action committees were more than twice that of defense firms, which rely on Pentagon contracts to survive. Insurers also take the number-two spot in how much they spent on government lobbying, just behind pharmaceutical and health-product manufacturers.[13] If you want to have an informed view on whether it can make sense for the government to mandate that people buy some types of insurance products or for it to heavily regulate some private insurance markets — and what K Street lobbyists hope to insert into rules and legislation — you once again need to understand the nature of selection.

—

What's in Store

Before we get into all of that, we need to do an important gut check. The theory of selection markets is a nice theory — and won a fancy million-dollar prize for its pioneers — but perhaps it's just that: just a theory. We've told some intriguing stories of selection making trouble in some rather-specific niche markets — like health insurance in West Hollywood in the 1980s and American Airlines' failed business traveler's program. Maybe they're interesting but idiosyncratic anecdotes rather than general principles about the way the world works. After all — check your file drawers and look on Google — there are lots of insurance companies selling a lot of different insurance policies. Odds are you've bought at least a few of them and have the relevant paperwork tucked away somewhere. How can selection be such a big deal if insurance, as we mentioned, constitutes a sizeable fraction of the U.S. economy?

Beyond this type of "just look out the window" test of whether insurance markets can manage selection, there's good reason to wonder how selection can actually matter in the so-called real world. Selection is a problem only when prospective customers know more about their likely risk than insurers do. In a great many cases, there's an argument that the opposite may be true. Sure, you can hold back some dirty little secrets from insurers (if they don't ask, you don't have to tell). But companies have enormous financial incentives to try to predict how costly it will be to cover you on the basis of the information they are able to wheedle out of you. With their armies of actuaries and mountains of data on past customers' characteristics and subsequent insurance claims, it seems like insurance companies should actually be better than any given customer at predicting how expensive they'll be. How can the customer possibly know more?

—

In the rest of part 1 of the book, we'll show you that the selection problem is real and that it is pervasive. We'll show you how selection has manifested itself in insurance markets out in the world, even in settings in which you might have guessed that insurers, rather than their customers, have the upper hand. We'll describe markets that selection has driven out of existence and markets in which selection has driven prices into the stratosphere. And we'll discuss how this can occur, despite the insurance companies' aforementioned reams of data and armies of actuaries. To accomplish this, we'll take you on a whirlwind tour that covers everything from marital breakups to mighty Harvard succumbing to selection to market mayhem that in some cases dates back for millennia and has brought about the collapse of monarchies.

By the end, you will hopefully have learned a thing or two that you can put to use when thinking about buying insurance in your own life. You will understand why even good drivers, happily married couples, and healthy young men would all be well served by having automobile, divorce, and health insurance — but also why that insurance may not, unfortunately, be available for them. You will also realize why you should buy insurance coverage — when it is offered — *before* you're outed as the "bad type" of customer by insurance companies and not wait for your car to break down before trying to buy insurance for roadside assistance. Perhaps what you learn will prompt you to engage in some introspection the next time you try to decide whether an insurance policy is a "good deal" for you or not. If you're in the market for pet insurance, for example, you would do well to think about whether you will want to do whatever is necessary to let Fido live another day or are willing to say that he has had a happy and fulfilling life and let him have a quick and peaceful end. (If you're the former, get pet coverage and get it early; if the latter, probably don't bother—your premiums are just going to pay for the medical care of the pets of the do-whatever's-necessary customers.)

Having established that selection in insurance markets is a pervasive, real-world problem, in part 2, we'll dive into a description of some of the ways that firms have tried to combat this problem and some of the problems that in turn result from these business "solutions." We'll start with the most obvious response by insurers: collect more information. If you've ever filled out an application for life or automobile insurance, you probably know what we're talking about. Automobile insurers, for example, often collect a host of information—some of which seems naturally related to your accident risk (like your driving history) and some of which doesn't (like your grades in school or your credit rating—that's why you agree to a credit check when you apply). We'll show that these strategies don't completely solve the problem from the insurer perspective—surprisingly, they can't ferret out *all* your secrets. Worse, what information they *do* collect might make insurance markets work less well from a societal perspective: for example, someone born with a genetic condition that puts them at risk of debilitating illness in later life may be unable to get insurance against future health expenses, which is exactly the sort of protection that insurance is meant to provide.

We'll then turn to subtler strategies that businesses deploy, ones that can be used to get customers themselves to reveal who they really are. Our discussion will help you understand the reasons for some otherwise-puzzling and often-annoying features of insurance contracts you've signed—why it can feel like insurers are looking for every opportunity to screw their customers through exclusions, waiting periods, and other coverage limits that are buried in the fine print.

—

We'll explain why your employer only lets you change your health insurance plan in the fall and why some health insurance plans offer a discount on your premium if you have a gym membership (no, it isn't because working out will keep you healthy). Once again, as we'll see, these strategies can help insurers mitigate selection problems, but these "solutions" come with problems of their own. By understanding why the world of insurance is the way it is, perhaps you'll feel a bit more Zen about it, even if it doesn't get you cheaper, better coverage.

Or perhaps where others see only problems, you see possibilities — given the high prices and seemingly meager payouts — and imagine that the insurance business is ripe for disruption. If so, we hope that this part of the book will at least give you pause (and maybe some ideas), as you write up that business plan, to consider how exactly you'll go about getting the "right" customers to sign up and dissuading the "wrong" ones from doing so. That way, you won't end up like American Airlines' Bob Crandall or the hapless entrepreneurs we'll meet in chapter 2 who tried unsuccessfully to build businesses selling unemployment or divorce insurance.

Since the private sector can't fully resolve selection problems on its own, in part 3 we'll investigate whether governments can (or do) help. This last part of the book explains why selection problems frequently call for a response from government — why insurance is different from broccoli, for example — and what policy options are available to "fix" insurance markets. We'll discuss a range of possible tools the government can use, including mandates for coverage, fines for not purchasing insurance or subsidies for doing so, prohibitions on the kinds of insurance products companies can offer, and restrictions on how much leeway they're allowed in setting prices.

We will help you understand some of the trade-offs that policy makers face in setting these policies. If they decide to mandate coverage, for example, should they force everyone to buy comprehensive insurance plans or set more minimalist requirements? Or should they encourage enrollment by sweetening the deal with subsidies instead? What if the best way to save the market is to subsidize the *least* vulnerable customers? Sometimes good economics can make for bad politics. Policy makers also need to decide how much insurers can stick their noses into other people's business. Should the government prevent insurers from asking prospective customers about their credit rating or requesting results of genetic testing, or should it let the market decide how much information to gather? Restricting what insurers are allowed to use in setting prices may seem desirable from a fairness or privacy perspective. But it can also drive some insurance products out of the market or even cause the entire market to collapse. An understanding of selection markets is crucial for thinking about these types of trade-offs, which will only increase in importance as Big Data (and hence the availability of information) becomes an ever more dominant force in our lives.

And in the epilogue, for readers who haven't yet heard enough about selection markets, we'll offer a brief sampling of how they work (or don't work) outside the insurance industry, with examples ranging from credit card offers to job prospects.

———

We aren't in the business of providing quick fixes or easy solutions to the problems that afflict the insurance industry or other selection markets. Rather, we'll explain why the right way to think about selection roughly corresponds to the societal responses to other market deficiencies. Businesses — and markets — do a pretty good job of getting insurance to people who value it (and not offering it to those who don't) while putting enough patches over the various se-lection problems that arise to keep many (but not all) markets from falling apart. But their responses are decidedly incomplete, which is why — as with Standard Oil and banks and income distribution — markets still need the guiding hand of government to help them along.

Chapter 2

INTO THE WILD

In the Broadway classic *Guys and Dolls,* the hustler Nathan Detroit (played by Frank Sinatra in the movie version) offers the inveterate gambler Sky Masterson the chance to bet a thousand bucks on whether their regular hangout, Mindy's, had sold more cheesecake or strudel the previous day. Sky has survived and even thrived as a professional gambler precisely because, while he loves to take a bet, he doesn't do so indiscriminately. He knows when to play the game and when to walk away. And in this case, he declines Nathan's offer, explaining his decision by way of the following story:

> When I was a young man about to go out in the world, my father says to me a valuable thing. "Son," the old guy says, "one of these days in your travels, a guy is going to show you a brand-new deck of cards on which the seal is not yet broken. Then this guy is going to offer to bet you that he can make the jack of spades jump out of this brand-new deck of cards and squirt cider in your ear. But, son, do not accept this bet, because as sure as you stand there, you're going to wind up with an ear full of cider.

—

Sure enough, Sky was wise to steer clear of Nathan's bet. The fix was in. Nathan knew that Sky was partial to Mindy's cheesecake and would therefore take that side of the bet, thinking the world shared his preference. But before proposing the bet, Nathan had already checked with Mindy and knew that yesterday's tally was twelve hundred cheesecakes to fifteen hundred strudels.

Sky's father was ahead of his time. The old man's key insight about the dangers of private information came decades before economists got around to formalizing this concept in Nobel Prize–winning work. Whether conveyed through scholarly research or strudel, the lesson is the same: if someone's selling something—*especially* if it seems too good to be true—it probably is too good to be true. You'd do well to wonder what it might mean for what they know that you, the unsuspecting buyer, do not. It's a timeless message that warrants constant repetition to ward off temptation to respond to the too-good-to-be-true business propositions of the Charles Ponzis and Bernie Madoffs of the world.

It's also yet another reminder of the ubiquity of private information and the selection problems that result. They're everywhere, even on Broadway. In *Guys and Dolls,* Nathan Detroit was the "seller" proposing the bet to the prospective "buyer" Sky Masterson. But the informational advantage can be on either side of a transaction. And buyer-side information can, by the same logic, lead to a "seller beware" admonition against serving the too-good-to-be-true buyer who is willing to pay top dollar for your services. To return to an example from chapter 1, who, after all, is willing to spend the most on an all-you-can-eat spread? Varsity football players and teenage boys in the midst of growth spurts. You can bet that the all-you-can-eat spreads are priced high enough to still turn a profit even if the only customers are oversized high school boys (although if you've learned anything from the story we've just told, if we're offering that bet, you might do well to decline it).

Selection doesn't always spell death for a market. As we've already observed, we know this must be true from the "just look out the window" test for selection market survival. Sky Masterson doesn't take the bet that Nathan proposes – the market for bets on Mindy's dessert sales can't survive the problem of private information. But all-you-can-eat spreads do exist, as do lots of other markets in which one side knows more than the other. Sometimes private information can kill a market. Other times, it causes some unraveling but not (as they perhaps say in the British insurance business) the Full Monty. Instead, selection "just" makes the market small. And expensive.

Hopefully, we've already whet your appetite with a couple of examples of market collapses for which we've pinned the blame on selection. In this chapter, we'll explore the ubiquity of selection problems in insurance markets, to emphasize that it isn't a once-in-a-decade phenomenon. It's everywhere. And it even shows up in situations where you'd expect that an insurer would be more than capable of outguessing its customers on whether they are good or bad for profits. Sometimes, as happened with the AAirpass and health insurance in West Hollywood – and other examples we'll see in the following pages – selection destroys the market completely. In other cases, we'll see that the market survives but the policies insurers offer are terribly expensive (think pet insurance) or just plain terrible (think dental insurance). In the second half of the chapter, we'll go beyond examples in which we merely suggest or assert that selection is to blame for the market dysfunctions and disappearances we observe. We'll draw on research that can more decisively pin the blame on selection for a market's collapse (in fact, it brought mighty Harvard University to its knees) or for the limited products on offer and even in one case show exactly what it is that customers know that insurers can't figure out.

Missing Markets

Thus far, we've provided only a single example of selection-driven all-out collapse of an insurance market: the highly unusual confluence of circumstances that made it impossible for residents of West Hollywood to get health insurance at the onset of the AIDS epidemic. We can see that selection killed the market because the market had existed before the AIDS epidemic hit, then it didn't.

There are surely many more examples, though often they're hard to see—literally. If private information will kill a market, it probably never existed in the first place. Perhaps because they are the dog-that-didn't-bark of the economy, the absence of many insurance products goes relatively unnoticed, despite the improvements they might bring to people's lives. This might also explain why selection problems are, despite their economic importance, less well understood than are many other, more widely discussed shortcomings of the free market. To get a proper sense of the market-killing potential of selection problems, we need some way of finding the silent dog.

Here's one approach: try to think of some insurance product that you feel *should* be available but isn't. There's a decent chance that if it did exist, it would present exactly the sort of money-losing proposition that Nathan Detroit offered Sky.

When we tried this approach ourselves, the first thing that came to our economically minded brains was private insurance against the risk of being laid off. Millions of Americans lose their jobs every single month. While the government provides some assistance, there's often a very wide gap between what a job was paying and what the government offers for unemployment benefits. A private market could help fill that gap.

We apparently aren't the only ones who've had this thought. We can see the traces left behind by entrepreneurs who also thought, "Why isn't there insurance offering protection against downsizing?" and quickly found the answer the hard way.

Take SafetyNet, a now-defunct provider of layoff insurance, which offered a policy that paid out as much as $9,000 to help its customers survive financially while they looked for work. As the SafetyNet policyholder Roger Kamin put it in an interview with a local news station, "I wanted to make sure I had a backup plan."[1] Kamin felt that his job was secure, but he had felt the same way a few years prior, when, after eleven years of steady work, his previous employer laid him off without warning. SafetyNet's coverage would give Kamin a lifeline if he lost his current job, bridging the gap between his monthly expenses and the much smaller check he'd receive from the government.

SafetyNet's founders were apparently aware of the dangers of selection. Workers might wait until they learned that they were about to get pink-slipped before deciding to buy unemployment "insurance." So the policy came with a waiting period—if you were laid off within six months of signing up, you'd get your premiums back but nothing more. The terms were similar for IncomeAssure and Paycheck Guardian, two other unemployment insurance products that have also long since ceased to exist. The six-month wait, it was thought, would be far enough in the future that workers couldn't sign up when they noticed their employer had stopped paying its suppliers, found their position described as redundant in a corporate strategic plan, or saw other signs of their job's imminent demise. As

David Sterling — CEO of SterlingRisk, the seller of IncomeAssure — explained in 2016 to the *New York Times*' Ron Lieber, "Anyone who knows they are going to be laid off after six months, I am happy to sell them an insurance policy. . . . I'd like to buy some lottery tickets and stock tips from them."[2]

Perhaps Mr. Sterling should have read the comments section of the last time Lieber had written about the unemployment insurance business, back in 2009. He would have come across Jackson of Boston, who observed, "I looked high and lo for this kind of insurance 6 months before I was laid off because I could smell the blood in the water having worked at this particular firm for 8 years"; or the Reddit user who, around the same time that Sterling was interviewed in the *Times*, posted a query asking about whether anyone had had any experience with IncomeAssure — because the user, Relaxed_Meat, was very, very interested in buying, given that his company was in the process of moving its operations to other regions. There had been "no official notice," Relaxed_Meat said, "but I am 99% sure we will be impacted within a year." Relaxed_Meat was incredulous that anything like IncomeAssure existed because, given his situation, "it seems like a too good to be true scenario." Two years later, SterlingRisk shut down IncomeAssure. It turned out it *was* too good to be true.[3]

Love Story

To ferret out some more examples of missing insurance markets, we did a (nonscientific) Twitter poll of fellow economists on the question of "insurance that you can't get but wish you could." We won't run through the full litany of responses, which numbered in the dozens. They included some suggestions that were serious (insurance against a housing-market crash), some that were less so (first-date insurance), and some that were endearingly self-referential (tenure-denial insurance). The winner, in our opinion, was the nonexistence of insurance against divorce (with the inevitable caveat from the nominator that, of course, "It was not for me").

Why would it be helpful if divorce insurance *did* exist? Because however blissful a couple might be on their wedding day, people and circumstances change. Some unions will last, and some will end in acrimony. And when a marriage comes to an acrimonious (or even amicable) conclusion, divorce can be really, really expensive. While the basic cost of legally erasing a marriage is modest (a few hundred dollars tops, in most states), once the lawyers get involved — as they unfortunately often do — the average cost can rise to over $15,000.[4]

Although it's uncomfortable to think about — let alone discuss with your spouse — it would be helpful to have insurance against the possibility of very high expenses if happily-ever-after doesn't last forever. That way, the emotional toll of separation isn't magnified by the financial toll of potentially five-figure lawyers' fees.

Providing this marital peace of mind is exactly what motivated John Logan to start SafeGuard Guaranty in 2010, an insurance start-up focused exclusively on divorce coverage. The potential market was — and is — enormous. There are well over two million marriages a year in the United States alone.[5] If even one out of twenty decided they would benefit from divorce insurance (we'd suggest the fraction is a lot higher), that's over a hundred thousand customers every year. If Logan had pulled it off, he might have made a fortune.

But pull it off he did not. Again, selection problems seemed to be the Achilles' heel. The selection problem is pretty obvious: odds are that only couples involved in volatile or otherwise-unpromising relationships would apply, thus torpedoing what would otherwise have provided a way for couples to off-load some of the financial risk of a marriage breakup if they unexpectedly drifted apart.

Logan was not naïve on this point. He employed a similar strategy to that of the hapless purveyors of layoff insurance: his policies came with a waiting period of forty-eight months — if a couple split up during the first four years after buying SafeGuard coverage, there'd be no payout to cover divorce costs. The idea behind the waiting period was to hopefully ward off prospective customers who were already bickering on their wedding night (or, even worse, couples that staged short-term marriages simply to get an insurance payout). As we'll see in chapter 4, waiting periods are a common technique that insurers employ to deal with selection. In many cases, they do help the market to survive. The markets for insurance against layoffs or divorce, however, turned out not to be such cases.

Logan claimed that he'd run the numbers and it all checked out. But SafeGuard's flagship WedLock insurance offering was short-lived — it was taken off the market within two years of its introduction, long before he would even have had to make a single payout.[6]

We looked at some of the products Wedlock offered, and it was easy to see why. The prices were exorbitant. Let's take a sample policy that required a couple to pay a little over $1,900 per year in premiums. That level of coverage would provide up to $12,500 to cover the cost of a divorce in four years' time (recall that's the earliest a customer could make a claim). The maximum payout from the policy would increase by $2,500 for each year a couple stayed together (though they'd be paying $1,900 per year just to keep their coverage). So, for example, if a couple divorced after ten years of paying premiums, they'd get $27,500, more than enough to pay lawyers in even a relatively expensive separation. But they also would have paid in ten years' worth of premiums, which adds up to, well, a whole lot—around $19,000 in total.

The payout was sufficiently modest that a *New York Times* story on Wedlock suggested that couples would be better off putting the money they might have spent on divorce insurance premiums into a savings account instead.[7] It would yield just a bit less than divorce coverage to pay lawyers' fees if the need arose. But as a bonus, if the couple stayed married, they could keep their money, plus a little interest. In other words, at Wedlock's price, the coverage was only worthwhile if, on their wedding day, the couple was near certain that they weren't in it till death do them part. Perhaps it would be a worthwhile investment for the likes of Elizabeth Taylor (whose seven marriages all ended in divorce), or one of her hapless spouses, but not really for anyone else.

And why did Logan choose to set the price so high? Presumably because, when he'd run the numbers, he did it understanding full well that the customers he'd attract would be couples with the highest risk of divorce. If he'd cut his prices, the numbers would no longer "check out."

Pricey Insurance, for All Creatures, Great and Small (Except Maybe Fifteen-Year-Old Dachshunds)

In Wedlock's case, the price was so high that the product couldn't survive. In other cases, selection can lead to outrageously high prices without driving the market entirely out of existence. The runner-up in our Twitter poll of missing insurance products was pet coverage, which, going back just a few years, was largely nonexistent because it was assumed that the market would collapse under the weight of hidden information.

Recently, though, that's changed. Now pet owners can buy health insurance — but at very high prices and not for all pets. (And pro tip — if you do choose to insure your pet, you'd better check the fine print on exclusions, which may include some very common maladies.)

As industry lore has it, the pet insurance business was launched in 1981 by the veterinarian Jack Stephens, motivated by compassion rather than profit. He saw pet insurance (again, according to the industry's founding legend) as a way of helping families that couldn't afford to pay veterinary bills and would thus be forced to resort to what he called "economic euthanasia" of their beloved pets.[8]

Stephens was a visionary in his own way — seeing a viable business opportunity where others had foreseen failure — and pet insurance has grown to a $1.5 billion industry today. But that surely didn't mean he had a way of solving selection problems, which are still apparent in the pet insurance business. However beloved our animal companions might be, only about 1–2 percent of pets have insurance coverage.[9]

And that coverage is expensive — or so it seems to us. A seven-year-old dachshund? In 2020, Petplan charged nearly $100 per month for a policy. That's for a plan that only pays for 80 percent of a pet's medical costs and caps total payments at $15,000 for the year. Oh, and it also excludes routine care — the anticipated trips to the vet that, for humans, are also rolled up into the cost of a health insurance plan. The selection problems become even starker as your beloved Rover enters his golden years: a fifteen-year-old dachshund costs over $650 per month, with a 70 percent reimbursement rate (and yes, again, a $15,000 cap, no coverage of routine care, and all the rest of the fine print).[10] That is nearly $8,000 per year for an insurance plan that will never, ever, ever pay out more than $15,000.

We can't say for sure that selection is what's driving up the cost of pet coverage (rather than, say, insurers gouging their customers), but it looks awfully suspicious — all the more so because, unlike Petplan, many pet insurers won't take Rover as a new customer at all once Rover is as old as fifteen.[11] They've presumably found that the only dogs that sign up for coverage in their canine golden years are headed toward expensive end-of-life treatment — less sentimental owners take the "economic euthanasia" route. So companies that do offer coverage to elderly canines attract the very worst risks.

We suspect that part of the selection problem for pet insurance is that it's hard for an insurer to know which customers are going to want to pull out all the stops to try to save their pet and which ones are not quite so sentimental about their dogs, cats, and hamsters. A pet insurance company has good reason to worry that only people who plan to fight as hard to save their gecko as they do to save their grandma will buy coverage. The result is insurance prices that are "too high" for less sentimental pet owners.

Liran's wife, Shirit, it turns out, would happily and willingly empty their savings account to keep their four-year-old mutt, Shoco, alive. (Liran, however, is the less sentimental type when it comes to the family pets.) When Shoco came down with an expensive-to-treat autoimmune disorder and Liran realized how far Shirit was willing to go, he finally thought about getting pet insurance. But by then, Shoco's coverage would have excluded any expenses related to her already-diagnosed disease. (Humans may similarly face coverage exclusions for preexisting conditions or be rejected for coverage entirely. We'll discuss why selection prompts insurers to place these types of limits on coverage in chapter 5. The same forces are at work for people and their pets — even if the exclusion for "ingested object for [covered lives] who have a documented history of ingesting ob-

—

jects in the year before you sign up for coverage" only applies to our furry friends.)[12]

The market for divorce insurance collapsed. The market for pet insurance survived, just in a very limited and expensive form. Why does one market survive and another perish?

As we've already observed, part of the answer is how much one side knows *relative to the other*. If newlyweds and insurers are completely in the dark about a marriage's prospects, that's okay. It's also just fine if both look into the same (slightly imperfect) crystal ball and can tell with a reasonable degree of certainty whether the marriage will hold up — insurance rates can then be tailored to a couple's particular circumstances.*

It's even okay if buyers know just a little more than sellers. Then there'll be a correspondingly little bit of selection — prices are higher than they'd be if both sides were on an equal (informational) footing, but they don't rise so much that they set off a death spiral. Trade is sustained because, despite selection, insurance is valuable peace of mind. And so, despite the higher prices, many people keep their coverage.

You can think of an insurance market's survival as a struggle between the forces of a buyer's private information, which will drive it to destruction, and customer value, which can help it soldier on despite the selection problems that private information creates. As

---

* The market can work just fine if the informational advantage tips in favor of the insurer. It's possible, in fact, that an insurer might know more about the couple's ten-year divorce probability than the couple itself does. That may not have been true two hundred years ago, but the Age of Information and the development of machine learning has allowed lots of companies to find out more about their customers and make better guesses about everything from whether they'll click on a Google search ad to — more relevant for the matter at hand — whether their marriage is destined to last.

the first of these gets ratcheted up, prices are more apt to rise, and the market edges closer to total collapse; greater customer value, on the other hand, can keep even some of the "good customers" (those with lower costs) from dropping out and help the market survive.

In cases in which the market falls apart or fails to materialize in the first place – like divorce coverage or insurance for elderly dachshunds – the weight of buyer knowledge is such that no amount of customer value can keep the market alive.

In situations where the market can survive – like pet insurance for younger pups – selection still leaves its mark. It drives up prices and drives down the quality of coverage. As we've just seen, pet insurance provides, well, a lot less insurance than it otherwise might. It's riddled with exceptions and exclusions, not to mention tight caps on how much insurers are willing to pay out. These shortcomings are – no surprise – entirely by design, a result of the necessary limitations that insurers insert into policies that make them less useful but at least keep the market from unraveling. The fact that selection doesn't kill the insurance market most certainly does not – the usual saying notwithstanding – make it stronger.

What Does Not Kill Insurance Markets . . .

If you've given any thought to dental insurance, you may have wondered why its coverage is so meager. Ray sure has, in large part because he is someone who could benefit a great deal from a comprehensive dental plan. His teeth are in such bad shape that he hasn't bitten into an apple for decades. Fifteen or so years ago, his dentist recommended that half his bottom teeth be pulled out and replaced with implants – fake teeth that would allow him, in theory, to go back to eating apples, peanut brittle, and anything else he wanted. The longer Ray put it off, his dentist warned, the more the bone holding his teeth in place would erode. And the more the bone eroded, the more complicated and expensive the implant operation would become. (Not that it wasn't complicated and expensive enough already—instead of implants, Ray could've bought a BMW, albeit a low-end one.)

Ray had never had dental insurance before that grim prognosis. Upon receiving it, however, he became interested—very interested, in fact—in the particulars of his employer's dental plan. He had always imagined that dental insurance worked a lot like health insurance: you buy coverage during the annual open-enrollment period, and all doctor-advised procedures are paid for in the next year. So he figured he'd put off the operation by just a few months, purchase whatever insurance would cover medically recommended implant operations, and maybe buy a gold Rolex or sports car with all the money he'd save.

But Ray's little scheme had one big problem: insurers don't cover dental implants, nor do they cover most other expensive dental procedures that one might wish to buy insurance to protect against. At the time, Ray was teaching at Columbia University, and a quick review of the school's policy made clear that implants—which always run into the thousands of dollars—were not covered. In fact, it wouldn't even be right to describe Columbia's dental plan as "insurance": the annual cap on benefits was only about $1,000, so the cost of truly serious dental work of any kind would mostly be borne by individual policyholders.

If you're wondering why, it's precisely because of people like Ray, who try to game the insurance market to get more out of the system than they put in. Ray's less-than-honorable (if perhaps understandable) scheme to sign up for coverage in anticipation of massive dental work is exactly the type of behavior that's to blame for the limited nature of dental coverage at Columbia and elsewhere. If the market for dental insurance is to survive, insurers need to set payout limits to prevent the "bad types" like Ray from enrolling ahead of much-needed (but potentially delayable) procedures.

We can observe this kind of dental insurance gaming clearly thanks to the work of the economist Marika Cabral. She obtained dental data from all employees at the once-mighty aluminum producer Alcoa.[13] The particulars of Alcoa's dental plan were a dream come true for a data-minded health economist like Cabral. All employees were automatically enrolled in a minimalist plan that has an annual maximum benefit of $1,000. But workers who wanted more extensive coverage could pay a premium to raise the cap to $2,000, while leaving all other features of the plan unchanged. That allowed Cabral to assess the extent of selection problems by looking at the dental care of workers who upgrade to the higher-coverage plan during the once-a-year opportunity they have to change plans. Did they then go straight to the dentist for higher-cost procedures? The answer was a clear yes — in the month following an upgrade, total dental spending of employees who switched into the higher-cap plan was, on average, about 60 percent higher and remained elevated for half a year.

The type and timing of employees' high-cost procedures was also telling. Those who came close to or went over the annual cap toward the end of the calendar year also saw their claims nearly double in January, when coverage reset and a new annual cap kicked in. The beginning-of-year jump in spending came entirely from claims for procedures that weren't time-sensitive — crowns and partial dentures, for example — while urgent treatments (like root canals) showed no jump early in the year.

—

It turns out that it isn't just Ray. When contracts allow it, lots of other people also think to upgrade their dental coverage when costly treatments are in their near future. And given that everyone's doing it (or would if they could), insurers have for the most part decided that it just isn't worth it to offer "real" insurance. This leaves us all worse off relative to a world in which we could find a way around selection problems — people who are unlucky enough to have bad teeth bear the cost of financially ruinous dental expenses on their own, and insurers miss out on making money from managing this "bad teeth" risk on their customers' behalf.

Love Story: Harvard Edition — from Anecdote to Evidence

Cabral's research isn't just important for reassuring Ray that he's not alone in trying to game the dental insurance market. She provides direct evidence that selection — not mismanagement or price gouging — is what drives up prices and limits product offerings for dental insurance. By contrast, with products like Wedlock, Income-Assure, and Paycheck Guardian, we could only speculate about the reasons for their demise. There are, of course, many reasons why businesses fail, and while we argued that selection is a likely candidate, we can't be sure. Divorce insurance, for example, is unpalatable for obvious reasons that have nothing to do with private information; newlyweds — like everyone else — are sure they're above average and assume that only *other* people's marriages will end in failure. And it is rather awkward to talk about how to deal with a divorce before you're even married (though let it be said that prenuptial agreements suggest at least some limits to this argument).

In the rest of the chapter, we'll draw on research that pins the blame on selection with greater certainty. In our next example, we will be able to closely follow the consequences of selection around the loop of higher prices and higher-cost customers and yet higher prices still. The victim wasn't some inexperienced rube looking for easy money in the insurance start-up space. It was that most venerable of institutions, Harvard University.

Harvard's missteps warrant retelling because they can help us appreciate exactly how a market can be thoroughly undone by one side's informational advantage. And because it's, well, Harvard, the moral of the story may also be that sometimes even people who should be smart enough to know better don't really appreciate the pernicious effects of selection. Finally, it's also a win for the theory of adverse selection: in the Berkeley economist George Akerlof's famous 1970 "Lemons" paper that launched the study of selection markets, he warns of the possibility of an adverse-selection "death spiral." This turned out to be an apt description of what happened to Harvard and one of the health plans it offered to its employees.

The details of Harvard's misadventures in insurance design come to us courtesy of Sarah Reber, who was a Harvard undergraduate in the 1990s, the time our story takes place. She was looking for a senior thesis project just as her school came up with what must have seemed at the time like an easy way to save some money. She ended up with a courtside seat to Harvard's death spiral and a killer thesis (which she later turned into a published paper coauthored with her thesis adviser, Harvard professor David Cutler).[14]

During Reber's Harvard days, the university was running a deficit in its budget for employee benefits. This deficit threatened to take a tiny bite out of its ever-expanding multibillion-dollar endowment. The main culprit behind the shortfall was the rising costs of its employee health insurance program, where the university was paying out more in claims each year than it was taking in in premiums.

What's a natural response to finding that costs are unexpectedly exceeding revenues? Raise prices, of course (duh!). Which is precisely what Harvard did, without apparently fully grasping the consequences of selection.

To better appreciate both why Harvard made the changes it did and how it came to be blindsided by selection, you first need a bit more background on how the university had been pricing its employee benefits in the first place. Harvard, like many other employers, offered its employees a choice of different health insurance plans. What we'll call the "more generous" plan imposed fewer restrictions on which doctors or hospitals a patient could go to. Naturally, it also had higher annual premiums than the "less generous" plan.

Like many other employers, Harvard also covered a substantial share of its employees' health insurance premiums, leaving only a small portion of the total to be paid by the employee. But to reduce its costs and close its deficit, Harvard changed its approach, requiring employees to pay more themselves in order to be covered by the more generous policy.

Up until then, even though total annual claims for an individual were about $800 higher for the more generous plan, the employee only had to pay an extra $280. Harvard paid the rest.

Under the new system, put in place in 1995, Harvard instead contributed a fixed dollar amount toward an employee's insurance, regardless of which plan they chose. As a result, an employee who wanted the more generous plan for themselves now had to pay the entire $800 difference in costs, almost tripling the $280 extra payment that was required earlier.

It's easy to see why this policy might have seemed both better economics and fairer than the previous system. Why not let employees who want more generous coverage pay for it themselves? Nothing comes for free — if Harvard is picking up part of the tab for employees' health coverage, it's using money that could have gone toward higher salaries. Why not just pay employees more and let those who want less-than-gold-plated insurance spend the extra money on nicer TVs or vacations or whatever? Why favor workers who happen to prefer more generous health insurance? Well, the economics look a lot worse once one accounts for selection.

When Harvard raised the price employees had to pay for the more generous plan, fewer people bought it. That's just what basic economics would predict. (Yes, what they teach in intro economics really is true: when prices go up, demand goes down. You didn't hear it here first.) And just as the economics of selection predicts, the employees who dropped out of the plan were different from the ones who chose to maintain their more generous coverage at the higher price. Employees who switched to the less generous alternative were those who tended to use the least amount of health care, while the ones who stayed in the more generous plan even at the much higher price tended to use *a lot* of health care. For example, the employees who stuck with the generous plan had higher claims in previous years than the ones who left. They were also older — four years older on average — so that they could reasonably expect higher health costs going forward, regardless of how much they spent in prior years.

By now, you can hopefully guess how the story goes. Although the price employees had to pay for the more generous plan went up, so too did its (per-enrollee) costs. As a result, Harvard found itself back in the same bind the following year. It was déjà vu all over again.

—

Harvard raised prices further the next year, with the same consequences. And round and round they went, as Harvard chose to play out the death spiral to its bitter conclusion: higher prices scared off the healthiest, lowest cost of the remaining enrollees, requiring yet more price hikes in an effort to keep its benefits out of the red. Eventually, Harvard cut its losses and ceased to offer the more generous plan. That may have been one way to save money, but it surely wasn't part of the original plan.

Harvard's actions triggered the sort of death spiral that George Akerlof had theorized and warned about. But lest we come across as overly condescending toward Harvard's esteemed administrators, we should note that Harvard wasn't the only university to make this mistake. Around the same time, for example, the University of California system tried similar cost-saving measures and triggered a death spiral in some of its health insurance plans.[15] Even though it was the system's own UC Berkeley economist, George Akerlof, who had originally warned of this very problem! (In a case of life imitating art, Akerlof himself contributed to the UC death spiral. When the price of his family's high-end plan shot up in the late 1990s, the relatively healthy Akerlof clan switched to a plan with less coverage. Before too long, the higher-coverage option was dropped from the university's insurance offerings.)

The reason that employers like Harvard and Berkeley and many others inadvertently ended up in a death spiral was probably the combination of two factors. First, there was actually the kernel of a good idea behind the policy change, which tried to make the employer's subsidy for health insurance benefits more equal (and fair?). But second, they didn't seem to have thought hard enough about how selection would repeatedly make a mess of their good intentions.

I Know Something You Don't Know:
Life Insurance Edition

In both dental and health insurance, we see how customers can "outsmart" insurance companies. Dental care often involves procedures that can be delayed for at least a few months or even a few years. Harvard's health plans couldn't set prices based on health status (a topic we'll return to in much greater detail in chapter 7), so when it came to any efforts at screening out "bad" customers from more generous plans, their hands were tied. Yet even in a case in which, we would argue, the informational odds are plausibly stacked in the insurer's favor, we still see that there's something that customers know that insurers don't.

That case would be life insurance. Insurers are largely free to pick and choose whom they cover and how much to charge in premiums. They can kick the tires on a customer, so to speak, putting them through a physical exam, documenting any dangerous pastimes, and taking a family medical history. You might think that, with all of this information, an insurance company could outpredict its policyholders on when they might be expected to die – which for many prospective customers is decades in the future. You might think so, but you'd be wrong.

The story of life insurance – from its sixteenth-century origins to the present – is instructive in how far the industry has come in slowly but surely learning from its mistakes. Yet it has never fully gained the upper hand on its customers' informational advantage.

Let's start with Life Insurance 101. Just as Sky Masterson wisely avoided the Mindy's cheesecake bet, if someone asks you to sell them a life insurance policy that covers the next twelve months, don't accept. They're the type of customer you don't want. This nugget of wisdom was unknown to the very earliest life insurance brokers, who were fleeced by their short-lived customers as a result.

The deal that launched the life insurance business was more of a gamble on the Grim Reaper's appearance than what life insurance is today, insurance against a loss of a breadwinner's income. In the late 1500s, a man by the name of Richard Martin paid £30 2/3 for a policy that would pay him £383 1/3 if one William Gibbons expired within twelve months.* The contract, which was underwritten by a consortium of sixteen investors who pledged £25 to £50 apiece to cover the possible payout, went into effect on June 18, 1583. Mr. Gibbons died on May 29 of the following year — with less than three weeks left on the contract. Mr. Martin made a 1,250 percent return on his bet.[16]

Perhaps Mr. Martin had some inside information on the state of Gibbons's health or the nature of his activities, or perhaps he, let us say, helped the process along when the contract neared its expiration.† Either way, Mr. Martin would appear to have been the bad

---

* The particular wording of the contract refers to earlier life insurance policies, suggesting that there were others that came before, but no direct evidence of these earlier cases exist. Burial societies — first cousin to life insurance — date back at least to 100 BC, when the Roman general Caius Marius created an arrangement among his troops whereby if one died unexpectedly (not uncommon among Roman legions), his comrades would cover the funeral expenses. Charles Kelley Knight, *The History of Life Insurance in the United States to 1870* (Philadelphia: University of Pennsylvania, 1920); Thomas C. Wilson, *Value and Capital Management: A Handbook for the Finance and Risk Functions of Financial Institutions* (Chichester, U.K.: Wiley, 2015).

† The life insurance murder plot has played out so many times in both real life and fiction that it is now something of a well-worn cliché. In case you're curious, there are webpages that catalog the many instances, both made up and real. Fact and fiction intersected in the case of the Menendez brothers of Beverly Hills, who staged a murder of their parents in 1989 to get to a $14 million inheritance, which included a $650,000 life insurance policy. Younger brother Erik had made the B-league mistake of writing a screenplay that describes on

type of customer from the underwriters' perspective. (In a lawyerly twist to the story that will sound painfully familiar to anyone who has ever filed an insurance claim for damage or losses, the underwriters argued that, since Mr. Gibbons had survived twelve successive twenty-eight-day periods and since twenty-eight days constitute, by some definition, a month, he had in fact lived — by some definition — a full year following June 18, 1583. The court sided with Mr. Martin and ordered that the insurers pay up.)

The first documented instance of an individual insuring against their own death for the benefit of their heirs came a few decades later. It is described in a 1622 tome on commercial law that details the story of a ninety-year-old "Master of the Mint" who paid £75 for a one-year £300 policy. Once again, things didn't work out well for the insurers; "the ancient Knight did die within the year, and the said Assurors did pay the Money." The "ancient Knight" happened to be a fellow by the name of Richard Martin, who, one historian speculates, may have been the very same Richard Martin who profited from William Gibbons's death some decades before.[17]

Fast-forward a few more decades, and the London bookseller John Hartley launched what would go on to become the first life insurance company, when the Amicable Society for a Perpetual Assurance Office received its corporate charter in 1706. From each of its approximately two thousand members, the Amicable Society collected annual premiums of £6, 4 shillings, for each share owned (a member could buy up to three shares). Upon one's death, the share-

---

page 61 how a teenage boy murders his parents for their money. The police, who had initially suspected a gangland slaying, took a serious interest in the manuscript. Elena Nicolaou, "Here's How Much the Menendez Brothers Spent on Their Spree," *Refinery29*, September 26, 2017, https://www.refinery29 .com/en-us/2017/09/174002/menendez-brothers-money-spent-shopping -law-and-order.

holder's beneficiaries would get a payout from the Amicable, expected to be about £150. (The historian Geoffrey Clark observes that the Amicable's membership list included many who purchased their shares to take care of a family in case of the death of a breadwinner and thus reflected what we now see as the primary function of life insurance.)[18]

By then, people like Hartley had evidently learned a few basic lessons about how to run an insurance company without going broke. Ninety-year-old men need not apply. Only those aged twelve through fifty-five could join. And the society's directors themselves would inspect any prospective member in person to ensure that they weren't taking on the sick or infirm (for those who lived some distance from London, reference letters from appropriate authorities attesting to an individual's health and sobriety were deemed sufficient). But whether Amicable's directors were any better at detecting ill health than Richard Martin's Assurors were, we can't easily discern from the historical record.[19]

Today, it seems more than plausible that life insurance companies and their contracts can outguess their customers, both because of better contract design and because they collect much, much, much better information. Most policies have a two-year waiting period or a two-year contestability period, so that short-term predictions of the sort that gave Richard Martin's heirs their windfall are no longer possible. (That may be where Logan got his idea of a waiting period for divorce insurance, although, as we saw, he upped the wait to four years.) To outwit a life insurer today requires you to be able to predict the more distant future.

What do you think your chances are of surviving at least another two years but not another five? What about ten years in the future? Or twenty? An incalculable number of contingencies might need to be taken into account. It's hard to do the math in your head, or on paper for that matter, even if you know the probabilities of various mishaps and maladies.

And it's not simply a question of what *you* know — rather, what matters is whether, on balance, you know more than the insurer does. Perhaps you have high blood pressure. Or your mother died relatively young from lung cancer and your father from heart disease. But your life insurance company knows that as well, because it now requires a physical exam and an extensive questionnaire before it will offer you a policy.[20]

Not only that, but your insurer is armed with reams and reams of information on how long people with your family and medical history have tended to live, as well as how mortality varies with factors like your income, your home address, your credit score — things you might never have thought would be relevant to whether you'll be alive ten years hence. To top it all off, while you're left contemplating your own mortality with only pen and paper, your insurer has legions of PhD statisticians who work full-time figuring out how best to predict who will die when.

What we're getting at is that, in the battle for better information, you might know something about your own life and death that an insurer doesn't, while the insurer, with its armies of actuaries, may figure out something about you that you are not even aware of yourself. For selection to cause problems, when the dust on the battlefield clears (if you'll pardon our stretching of the wartime metaphor), the buyer needs to have some secrets left.

Which is why it's so surprising — certainly to us — that life insurance customers today *still* know more about how long they'll live than the companies that provide their coverage do. We know this is true thanks to some research by the economist Daifeng He.[21] She showed that, even today, customers outwit the best predictions that the life insurance industry can buy. Here's how she did it: she found a group of life insurance customers and also a group of noncustomers — people who didn't buy life insurance. Then she followed both groups over time to see who died when.

Dr. He's analysis is based on the following insight. Suppose customers have private information about their chances of, say, living to see at least another dozen birthdays. If those who know these prospects aren't so great are also the ones who are more inclined to buy life insurance, then when Dr. He follows people over time, she should see that purchasers of life insurance will *actually* end up dying sooner than people who don't purchase life insurance — their private information reveals itself through early death. In other words, life insurers attract customers who are *adversely selected*, in the sense that they die younger (and hence are more expensive to insure) than do the ones who chose not to get insurance.

In any insurance market, it's pretty easy to figure out how much it ended up costing to insure a customer — just look at how much insurers have to pay out in claims. The challenge is that in most cases, it's hard to figure out how much the noncustomer *would have cost* if they had been a customer. (How much wood could a woodchuck chuck if a woodchuck could chuck wood?)

Dr. He's insight was to realize that, for life insurance, what makes customers expensive or cheap is simply a function of whether they live a long time or die shortly after buying the policy. The long-lived ones are cheap because they pay lots of premiums before they expire. The short-lived are the ones insurers want to avoid — they're all payout and not enough premiums. And death — unlike, say, automobile accidents or house fires — turns out to be something that is well recorded for both those with and those without insurance.

In Dr. He's case, she used a survey that has been following individuals aged fifty and older for decades. Every couple of years, the surveyors go back and ask more questions about respondents' lives — about their jobs, their kids, their marriage, their health, their eating and exercise habits, and yes even what kind of insurance they have. If the surveyor can't collect information on someone because they've died, they record that too. Dr. He looked at the respondents who didn't have life insurance at the start of the survey and compared people who subsequently bought life insurance to those who remained uninsured. She compared these buyers and nonbuyers who were similar on *every dimension* that insurance companies ask about — for example, whether they smoked, whether they have diabetes, and whether their own parents were alive (or if not, when they died). In other words, she was able to put herself in the position of the insurer and consider how buyers and nonbuyers fared after accounting for everything the insurer would know about its customers.

What He found was startling to us, given our faith in the power of number-crunching insurance actuaries. Over a period of twelve years during which she tracked mortality, those who died were nearly 20 percent more likely to have bought life insurance relative to people who remained alive during the period and looked similar on the many characteristics that insurers ask about. To put it a different way, they're 20 percent less likely to continue with their premium payments into the far distant future. That is, the bad customers (from the insurer's perspective) bought insurance, and the good customers (the healthier, longer-lived ones) stayed away.

How is this happening? How are insurers' experts failing to outguess their customers? Your first reaction might be that people just make stuff up to get the best rates they can: maybe we all tell insurance companies that we are gym-going, almond-munching, nonsmoking teetotalers with centenarian grandmothers.*

It might seem tempting to lie. After all, the insurance company doesn't even bother vetting applicants' details. However, that's only because they have a better, more profitable way of dealing with deceit: the not-so-fine print of the application will inform you that the policy will be invalidated if any information provided proves to be false or misleading. The insurance company sends out the fact-checkers only when they need to make a payout. From beyond the grave, you better hope you were truthful.[22]

If outright lying is off the table, what sorts of truly secret secrets can the high-risk life insurance customers manage to withhold? Maybe it's a fondness for scuba diving, bungee jumping, or hang gliding? Nope — insurers have thought of that one and ask about it on the application. Do work or vacation plans take you to destinations with civil unrest or violent crime? Insurers ask about international travel as well. A tendency to drive a bit too fast on the interstate? They'll check whether you've had any speeding tickets (or refuse coverage outright if you have a drunk-driving record in recent years).[23]

---

* If you're an economist, another natural reaction might be that life insurance makes people behave more recklessly — take up skydiving, for instance, since you know your family won't be left without a breadwinner if your chute doesn't open. In other words, maybe people *become* higher-risk customers precisely because insurance cushions the blow if something bad happens. As this particular example suggests, while it's possible that insurance turns people into risk-takers, in practice, in many (if not most) of the examples we look at in the book, insurance-driven risk-taking is at most a secondary concern. And because economists are entirely aware of this issue, the research we describe generally accounts for it. If you're desperate to know more about how this kind of risk-taking affects the insurance business, you'll need to wait for *Risky Behavior*, one of the many sequels we have planned.

Honestly, we're not exactly sure *what* people are able to keep to themselves that is both relevant to their survival prospects *and* isn't on the application. It's the thoroughness of information collection that has allowed the life insurance market to survive and indeed thrive, despite the Richard Martin types who surely are still around today. But it also does leave us baffled as to what exactly this private information is that leads to at least some adverse selection in the life insurance market. In the final example we'll discuss, we *are* able to pinpoint some of the secrets that people have, thanks to clever work by creative researchers.

Woody Guthrie, Genetic Testing, and Insurance Research: An American Folktale

Huntington's disease is a genetic brain disorder. Its inexorable progression is excruciating for those who suffer from it and extremely expensive for any insurers that cover the related costs. In particular, when (not if) a Huntington victim requires home health care or needs to move into a nursing home, long-term-care insurance picks up the tab. That tab can easily run to six figures, since the decline, while steady and unrelenting, can take decades to run its full course.[24]

Huntington's affects movement, behavior, and cognition. It arises from an abnormal expression of a single defective gene on chromosome 4. This gene carries information for a protein, previously known as IT15; ever since it became associated with Huntington's disease in 1993, it has been known as the huntingtin protein.[25] (No, that's not a misspelling. "Huntingtin" refers to a protein that may or may not function normally. "Huntington" refers to the *disease* that results from abnormal expression of the huntingtin protein, whose normal function is not yet understood.)

—

The gene that carries the huntingtin protein is dominant. That means if the person has the gene on either of its two copies of chromosome 4, they will be afflicted by Huntington's disease. It also means that if a parent has the gene, their child has a fifty-fifty chance of falling prey to it as well, since they will get one of the parent's two copies of chromosome 4. However, because Huntington's is also a late-onset disease — typically first appearing in middle age and then becoming progressively worse over the ensuing decades — parents may pass it on to their children before even realizing that they have the disease themselves. (This is also why, despite the incapacitating nature of the disease, it has not been weeded out by natural selection. Onset typically occurs after reproduction.)

The disease is named for George Huntington, a physician who observed that, among his patients in East Hampton in the 1870s, dementia and involuntary movement disorders often seemed to run in families. In earlier, less scientifically minded eras, those who were afflicted with Huntington's were sometimes seen as possessed by the devil — it's been conjectured that the poor souls burned at the stake at Salem's infamous witch trials in the late 1600s may have been suffering from the disease. (The *Mayflower* is thought to have carried the Huntington's gene to the Americas.)[26]

It was another one hundred years after Huntington's initial identification of the symptoms before modern medicine came to better understand and diagnose the disease. The American folksinger Woody Guthrie, for example, suffered from Huntington's but went undiagnosed for years. He was treated for, among other maladies, alcoholism and paranoid schizophrenia, before eventually being arrested and hospitalized for vagrancy in 1954, at which point his Huntington's was finally diagnosed. He was committed to Greystone Psychiatric Hospital, where the disease continued to progress, as it inevitably does. He had so lost control of basic movements that, according to his daughter, Nora, "when he picked up his food, he couldn't control his fingers, and he lost half of it" in getting it from plate to mouth. His cognitive and physical decline went on for more than a decade after he was committed to Greystone, where he died in 1967.[27]

Scientists have also learned a great deal about the underlying biology of Huntington's since Woody's death. We now know that it's a genetic disease (no one thought much of the fact that Guthrie's mother had grown clumsy and forgetful before she herself was in-stitutionalized decades before her son). Those with a parent who developed Huntington's know they have a fifty-fifty chance of hav-ing inherited the disease, and if they do, there is no doubt that they will end up as the high-cost "type" — Huntington symptoms appear in early to middle adulthood, but the neurological degeneration it causes is gradual. Patients live for decades and generally require extensive — and expensive — assistance, such as placement in a nurs-ing home or the hiring of in-home caregivers. Long-term-care in-surance to pay for home care and nursing-home care in the event that it is needed serves as a hedge against exactly these types of expenses.[28]

From the perspective of studying selection, the insidiously ran-dom nature of Huntington's is a feature, not a bug. The theory of adverse selection predicts that individuals whose parents had Hun-tington's (and who therefore have a fifty-fifty chance themselves of inheriting the disease) should choose to get long-term-care insur-ance at vastly higher rates than typical individuals in the population: They know they are more likely than average to end up needing long-term care. This is a case in which we know exactly what a key source of private information could be.

—

And it's a case that has been studied by the economist Emily Oster, who collaborated with a team of physicians to follow a population of approximately one thousand individuals whose parents had had Huntington's and therefore were at risk for it.[29] The subjects in the study were surveyed periodically by medical researchers, who aimed to better understand the lives and decisions of people at risk for Huntington's. One survey question asked respondents whether they had long-term-care insurance.

Oster and her coauthors calculated the fraction of this at-risk group for Huntington's that had long-term-care insurance. They compared it to the coverage rate for a group of individuals surveyed as part of a random survey of the U.S. population, who were similar in all other observable respects (e.g., similar age, income, and marital status). Exactly as the selection model predicts, the at-risk sample chose to get long-term coverage at far-higher rates than that of a sample of random Americans (27 percent versus about 10 percent).

The researchers then looked for a further layer of selection *within* the set of at-risk Huntington's patients. Since 1993, it has been possible — via genetic testing — to determine with certainty whether someone will develop Huntington's. Not everyone who is at risk gets tested. Woody's son, Arlo — who went on to have his own illustrious folk-singing career — chose not to get tested, as do many offspring of Huntington's sufferers. For some, it's better not to have to think about such a dark future. Also, as Oster has shown in other work, not getting tested makes it possible for at-risk individuals to trick themselves into thinking they're part of the lucky 50 percent that doesn't inherit the disease.[30]

Among those who did get tested, the researchers compared long-term-care insurance purchases for those who tested positive and those who tested negative. These two groups of individuals were otherwise, on average, the same: they all had a parent with Huntington's and therefore a fifty-fifty chance of inheriting the disease. All decided to get tested. But some won the genetic lottery and tested negative for the gene, while others lost the same genetic lottery and tested positive. Among Huntington-positive individuals, they found that the reported rate of long-term-care insurance was more than double the rate of those who tested negative and five times the national average.

The Huntington's study is fascinating for any number of reasons. For our purposes, it provides an example of the type of private information that individuals may have – and use in deciding whether to buy long-term-care insurance – that can affect insurer costs. The differences in enrollment rates for individuals at risk of Huntington's compared to the general population, as well as the different enrollment rates between those at risk who have positive as opposed to negative test results, translate into vast cost differences for insurers between their typical customer and the general population.

At the same time, the diagnostic technology that enabled the study's design raises a number of thorny ethical and legal issues, around what insurers and their customers can and should know and when they can know it. We'll return to the legal questions when we talk about government policies that affect selection markets in chapter 7. For now, we'll just say that providers of long-term-care insurance are, in many states, legally permitted to include genetic-testing information in their coverage and pricing decisions but choose not to.[31]

That leads to the seemingly obvious question: Given that a simple and dispositive test for Huntington's disease has been available for decades, why didn't insurance companies simply ask applicants whether they suffered from Huntington's disease and either jack up their prices or screen them out completely? As Oster and coauthors report, long-term insurance providers *did* ask applicants whether they'd been diagnosed with Huntington's, along with a host of other preexisting conditions (and warned that affirmative responses would probably make them uninsurable). But, at least when the researchers were looking into this over a decade ago, insurers didn't ask about *risk* or family medical history. They either didn't or couldn't probe into such matters — some states prohibited long-term-care insurers from asking about genetic risks, and while others imposed no such constraints, it appears that insurers nonetheless refrained from asking.[32] (If you find the insurers' don't-ask-don't-tell approach to prospective customers' genetic risks puzzling, you're not alone; in chapter 4, we'll tackle the puzzle of why insurers may choose not to use every informational advantage available to them.)

Personalized genetic information is but one example of the type of secrets customers may hold, which insurers could uncover if only they asked. And it isn't limited to Huntington's — one can test for genes associated with breast cancer, colon cancer, Parkinson's disease, and Alzheimer's disease, among others. Genetic testing surely isn't the only source of customers' information advantage. It's just one that is really, really easy for us — and them — to see.

The proof of the pudding is in the eating, as the saying goes — we may not always know exactly what they know, but, as we've seen in this chapter, the evidence from multiple different insurance markets (or nonmarkets) is clear. Insurance customers know things that their would-be insurers do not.

———

In the course of a single chapter, we've offered up an assortment of evidence — ranging from anecdotal to up-to-date academic research — that selection is indeed a problem that continues to afflict insurance markets. Before moving on to examine how businesses and government policy makers try to manage or regulate their way around the selection problems that we've now (we hope) convinced you are widespread and worthy of your attention, we'll first take a step back and take in several millennia worth of history for one particular insurance market. (If insurance salesman isn't the world's oldest profession, it turns out it's pretty close.) This will give us a chance to revisit many of the ideas and insights we've developed so far and along the way discover how these insights eluded some of history's greatest minds — creating not only market mayhem but, sometimes, even all-out government collapse.

Chapter 3

THE TWO-THOUSAND-YEAR-OLD MARKET

People always live forever when there is an annuity to be paid to them.
— Fanny Dashwood, in Jane Austen's *Sense and Sensibility,* 1811

When Jeanne Calment died on August 4, 1997, in Arles, France, she had lived for 122 years and 164 days, the longest verified life span of any human in history. Near the end of her life, she reminisced about meeting Vincent Van Gogh as a teenager (she wasn't impressed — he was apparently ugly and drank too much). She outlived her husband — who died of cherry poisoning at the age of seventy-three — by more than half a century.[1]

In 1965, Mme. Calment — then already ninety years old — signed a contract on her Provençal apartment with a local notary by the name of Andre-Francois Raffray. Calment would get a monthly stipend of twenty-five hundred francs (about US$500 at the time) for life. She could continue to live in her apartment till she died, at which point ownership would be transferred to Raffray.

While it is hard to ascribe intentions to the notary, it's also not hard to imagine that he thought he was putting one over on a poor, unsuspecting old woman. We can't ask him — he died in 1995, two years before Calment, having paid her twice the apartment's value and gotten nothing in return. As Calment wryly put it at the time, "in life, sometimes one makes bad deals."[2]

—

One might add that in life, when you're dealt a bad hand, sometimes it's the result of bad luck, and sometimes it's because you didn't follow the advice of Sky Masterson's father (whom we met at the start of chapter 2). Someone offered you a bad bet. And you took it.

Maybe Raffray *was* unlucky. After all, as he surely intuited, actuarial tables worked in his favor—an average ninety-year-old could expect to live only a few more years.[3]

Or maybe Calment knew she wasn't average. In one of the many interviews she gave in later life (long, long after signing her agreement with Raffray), she claimed that since the age of twenty, she'd never had so much as a common cold. When she signed the deal at age ninety, she was still riding her bike around Arles and continued to do so past her hundredth birthday.[4] In short, to a degree that the conniving notary was probably unaware, she was the healthy "type" to the extreme.

That is, maybe Raffray made a bad decision—he didn't heed the "seller beware" problem of doing business in a selection market. (We hope that if Raffray had read chapter 2 and been schooled in the basics of information economics, he would have had second thoughts about entering into a contract in which the cost was so dependent on his counterparty's continued survival.)

But is the curious anecdote of the world's oldest woman and a conniving notary just that—the story of a truly exceptional case that departs from the more general rule of market function, the exception that proves the rule? We'll own up to cherry-picking this example. In fact, by definition, it's selected on the basis of a uniquely unfortunate (at least from the seller's perspective) outcome. After all, only one insurer can have the misfortune of betting against the survival of a customer who turns out to be the longest-lived person in history.

—

Perhaps others in France or elsewhere (perhaps even Raffray himself?) wrote similar contracts for elderly individuals who promptly died, and most of his apartment deals made money. (Although in the many, many accounts of the Raffray-Calment story, we've been unable to find any reference to Raffray having ever made comparable arrangements with other senior citizens.) Or maybe Raffray was hoodwinked, but only because he was an amateur in the world of insurance contracts.* Surely a for-profit company that tried what Raffray did would do well enough overall to stay in business.

Not so. It turns out that the example of Calment and Raffray goes beyond a simple anecdote. That's why we selected it.

The type of selection that Raffray experienced also works against for-profit corporations, which we'd expect to be more sophisticated than a French country notary. The result is a far smaller market—with much-higher prices—for a potentially very valuable insurance product.

---

* It's even possible that he was hoodwinked by something much more prosaic than selection concerns: downright fraud. Doubts about Calment's age have surfaced occasionally over the years, most prominently in 2018 with the posting of an article titled "Jeanne Calment: The Secret of Longevity" by an amateur gerontologist in Moscow by the name of Nikolay Zak. Possibly a genius (he holds a PhD in mathematics from Moscow State University) and probably a crackpot, Zak claimed that Jeanne had died of tuberculosis in 1934 and that the woman claiming to be the world's oldest human was actually her daughter, Yvonne, who, according to medical records, was the one who died in the 1930s. Zak revisited various inconsistencies in the recollections of the elderly Jeanne/Yvonne, though few scientists accept his arguments as at all convincing. For our purposes, it would make for an even better story if the Jeanne-Yvonne body switch had taken place—if so, "Jeanne" would still most certainly have used private information to her advantage, hoodwinking not just Raffray but the entire world as well. Nikolay Zak, "Jeanne Calment: The Secret of Longevity" (unpublished paper, December 19, 2018), https://doi.org/10.13140/RG.2.2.29345.04964.

In the remainder of this chapter, we'll recount the story of this insurance market. It dates back millennia — at least as far back as the Roman Empire. It was plagued by selection back then, and it still is today. Along the way, we'll describe how this selection problem has bankrupted individuals, companies, and governments, with no solution in sight.

We'll give you a whistle-stop tour of the history of the annuity — which is what the type of contract Calment and Raffray signed is known as. Raffray received a fixed payment (in the form of an apartment) in exchange for providing a stipend to Calment as long as she lived. More typically in annuity contracts, people fork over money (not houses) in return for a lifetime stipend, and they pay the lump sum up front (rather than when they die). Whether they're handing over money or housing, the basic idea is the same. An individual — most commonly a retiree — gives an insurance company some of their savings and in return is promised a fixed monthly amount as long as they remain alive. The retiree naturally hopes to enjoy a long life, filled with golf, grandchildren, and guaranteed payments from their insurer for as long as they live. These payments give them the security of not having to worry that they will run out of savings, so that they really *can* enjoy their retirement. That's the value proposition that annuities provide.

The insurance company, on the other hand, hopes that the payments will soon come to an end. Just as Calment's remarkably long life — an extra thirty-two years as compared to the average ninety-year-old's survival rate of just over four years[5] — meant that she was a "bad" customer for Raffray, long-lived annuitants are bad customers for insurers. And as the quotation from Jane Austen at the opening of the chapter suggests, that's just the sort of customer that annuity sellers tend to attract.

If it seems obvious at this point that annuity contracts would attract long-lived (and thus expensive) customers, the extent of this problem was sufficiently nonobvious to have cost fortunes and bankrupted governments that aimed to refill their coffers and finance their wars by issuing annuities. In modern times, selection hasn't caused the annuity market to completely disappear. However, it has made annuities a nonviable option for average (as opposed to exceptionally well-preserved) retirees who would like to ensure that they don't fall into destitution if they're lucky enough to live longer than they expected.

I'm Gonna Live Forever

Annuities have been around for just about as long as there has been insurance, which is to say a very long time. As early as the Roman Empire, history's first annuity salesman, Domitius Ulpianus, calculated "death tables" that showed, for example, that a Roman citizen who had already made it to the age of, say, thirty-five, could expect to live another twenty years.[6] These precursors to modern-day actuarial models were rather coarse, providing life expectancies for only five- or ten-year intervals. They also failed to account for differences in life expectancy between annuity buyers and everyone else, a mistake that persisted for literally well over a thousand years.

Annuities outlived the Romans, surviving into the Middle Ages, when they served primarily as an end run around the Catholic Church's disapproval and eventual prohibition of usury. The annuity loophole worked as follows: Instead of taking out a loan in exchange for a stream of repayments plus interest (i.e., a standard loan), someone in need of immediate cash could sell an annuity. The seller got a lump-sum payment in exchange for a stream of payments to the annuity buyer until death. They're quite similar, except one ends when the loan is repaid and the other when the "lender" (that is, the annuity buyer) is dead.* Annuities also afforded lenders a way of charging above interest rate caps, which existed (and still exist) to protect borrowers from "usurious" rates. England, for example, outlawed interest on loans above 5 percent in 1714, which led to an explosion of alternative financial instruments that served as thinly veiled substitutes for traditional loans.[7] In the case of annuities, it was precisely their uncertain endpoint that allowed for this loophole: Who was to say whether the interest rate on an annuity contract was 5 or 20 percent? It all depended on how long the annuitant lived. As Lord Hardwicke, an eighteenth-century English judge, put it, "I really believe in my conscience, that ninety-nine in a hundred of [annuities] are nothing but loans turned into this shape to avoid the statutes of usury."[8]

---

* To paraphrase theologians' arguments to the point of caricature, charging interest was a violation of natural moral law, which held that money's worth was reflected in its face value and that to pay more than that amount for its *use* via a loan (hence the term "usury") entailed double charging for it. In the writings of Thomas Aquinas, an analogy is drawn to selling ownership and use of any commodity: "if a man wanted to sell wine separately from the use of the wine, he would be selling the same thing twice." Putting aside whether there is any sensible economic (or philosophical) merit to Aquinas's arguments, they were highly influential over the years. Annuities – and insurance contracts in general – were not without their theological controversies. If your house burned down or ship sank, it was God's will. Who are mere mortals to intercede in such matters? More economically minded (and perhaps ethically malleable) theologians had come up with a range of counterarguments by the sixteenth century, which allowed modern trade and production to proceed without exposing merchants to undue risk. Ray D. Murphy, *Sale of Annuities by Governments* (New York: Association of Life Insurance Presidents, 1939); Thomas Aquinas, *Summa Theologiae* (1485); James Poterba, "Annuities in Early Modern Europe," in *The Origins of Value: The Financial Innovations That Created Modern Capital Markets*, ed. William N. Goetzmann and Geert Rouwenhorst (Oxford: Oxford University Press, 2005), 207–24.

Governments also used annuities as a fund-raising mechanism, serving the function that government-issued bonds do today. Cities paid for stone and brick to fortify their defenses (and for municipal infrastructure more generally) by selling annuities, and nations did so as a shortsighted way of financing their military campaigns, as well as the extravagances of their monarchs. The Dutch issued annuities to wage war on France in 1554. England did the same, via its Million Act, to finance its own wars with France, nearly one hundred years later. France sold annuities in the late 1600s to launch *its* war on the Dutch and a coalition of other European nations in the Nine Years' War. And King Louis XIV went on an annuity-financed spending binge, racking up obligations that some historians claim led to the French Revolution (and Marie Antoinette's decapitation).[9]

King Louis wasn't alone in bankrupting his government via annuity-driven debts. The city of Ghent, in Flanders, did so in the 1300s with similarly dismal results. The situation was so dire — and afflicted so many local governments — that in the late 1400s, Philip the Handsome, Duke of Burgundy, suspended annuity payments for all Dutch municipalities, to try to avoid widespread municipal defaults. But cities like Amsterdam and Haarlem were undeterred, and within a few decades, well over half of their collective revenues were again committed to annuity payments.[10]

Some of the debt problems have nothing to do with selection problems: greedy rulers with iffy credit ratings and eager for spending money need to price their bonds attractively enough to interest buyers, so some annuities may have had high payouts because that was the only way anyone was willing to buy government debt. In France, Louis and his financial advisers concocted a variety of schemes to attract investors, whatever the future costs (very possibly borne at a future date, when Louis himself was no longer around to bear the consequences).*

There's ample evidence, however, that some government shortfalls resulted from annuity pricing that assumed there was no selection at all. And the historical record indicates that annuity buyers had little trouble intuiting how to take advantage of governments' annuity offerings.

The selection problems in these earlier years were surely much aggravated by the fact that, unlike today, one could purchase an annuity whose payout was dependent on any annuitant one might like — referred to as the "head," or nominee — whose survival determined whether payment continued. You could appoint your granddaughter or your grandmother as the head. Or your neighbor's grandmother. Or some stranger living a tranquil, stress-free life in a quiet French village who, in your estimation, had a good shot at living to a ripe old age. The earliest annuities didn't even account for

---

* For example, a loan of 2.4 million livres in 1777 (near the beginning of France's borrowing spree — it only went downhill from there) was divided into 20,000 lots of 1,200 livres apiece (one livre at the time was roughly a laborer's daily wage). Each of the 20,000 were essentially sold as lottery tickets, in which a select set of lucky buyers got a big payday via annuities with high yearly payouts. Fifteen thousand of the "tickets" paid off as straightforward loans, which earned 4 percent interest per year, payable when the loan matured. This was at the low end of interest rates offered on the private market at the time. The government — already neck deep in debt and its credit rating and reputation in tatters — needed to sweeten the deal to attract lenders. So the remaining 5,000 tickets were sold as annuities that paid anything from 150 to 50,000 livres per year, as long as the person specified by the annuity holder remained alive. The terms on the 5,000 annuity notes were so attractive (at the high end, representing interest of well over 4,000 percent per year) that the entire 20,000 subscription sold out in less than a day. George V. Taylor, "The Paris Bourse on the Eve of the Revolution, 1781–1789," *American Historical Review* 67, no. 4 (1962): 951–77.

—

age – the annual payout was the same, whether the head was a grand-father or an infant.[11]

Shrewd investors responded to these offers exactly as an economics textbook would predict – they scoured the countryside for healthy young specimens, then invested in maintaining their health. When Amsterdam raised funds via annuities in the late 1500s, more than half of the nominees were under ten years old, and 80 percent were younger than twenty. Two centuries later, the French issued age-independent *rentes viageres* (life annuities), and the nominees were primarily girls between ages of five and ten with very healthy parents. The selected girls had also all already survived smallpox – a wildcard for even those who were blessed with the best of genetic endowments. Swiss investors, who purchased some of these *rentes viageres*, whisked the girls off to Geneva, where the air was "salubrious" and the bankers whose fortunes were riding on their survival could keep a close watch on them.* It was a highly profitable operation. As the historian George Taylor put it, "these *rentes viageres* enriched the speculators and ruined the state."[12]

By the time the Amsterdam government got up the courage to sell another round of annuities in 1672, it had learned from past mistakes. It now offered lower annuity payouts for younger nominees. As expected, the result was that far-fewer annuity buyers named

---

* These payouts from surviving "Demoiselles of Geneva" were bundled into securitized assets in groups of thirty girls, and the income stream from the thirty-girl bundle was then sold off to investors. The idea was that you could buy a share in the thirty-girl payout, which would allow investors to avoid exposure to the risk of buying an annuity on an individual who was unfortunate enough to contract, say, measles. You can think of these as the Renaissance-era predecessor to the collateralized mortgage obligations that led to the financial crisis. François R Velde and David R. Weir, "The Financial Market and Government Debt Policy in France, 1746–1793," *Journal of Economic History* 52, no. 1 (1992): 1–39.

—

heads that were under the age of ten.[13] Indeed, by the late 1700s, many (but not all) governments had learned to offer lower payouts for younger nominees and also for women, who already had higher life expectancies than men.

Varying the annuity payouts with the head's age and gender did away with the most obvious ways of gaming the annuity market through careful selection of heads. But savvy investment syndicates were still able to find profitable selection angles. When the payouts tilted in favor of elderly males in England's 1829 issuance of annuities, investors searched for healthy old men. If their nominee survived just two years, investors would earn back their initial stake plus 34 percent; if the nominee could make it even three years, investors would double their money. Scotland was thought to be full of vigorous octogenarians, and so speculators went to the bonnie, bonnie banks of Loch Lomond in search of the most promising candidates for their annuity wagers.* As with the young heads of France,

* Incidentally, savvy selection of Scotsmen wasn't the only problem the hapless British government faced in its annuity offering. Another issue is that when it tried to estimate the life expectancy for elderly annuitants—in order to figure out how to price annuities—it did so by looking backward and asking: How long did young people who bought an annuity a century earlier end up living? In doing so, they made two mistakes. First, someone buying an annuity at ninety is likely to live longer than someone buying it at thirty (the ninety-year-old has already survived until ninety after all!). Second, life expectancy was already on the rise in the 1700s, so using life spans of an earlier generation also proved to be problematic. Sadly, U.K. annuity companies were still making this second mistake in the twentieth century, forcing the British government to bail out the Equitable Life Assurance Society, which didn't anticipate the increase in life expectancy from public health and modern medicine in the twentieth century. As we noted in chapter 1, selection is, after all, just one of many issues that can plague markets. Phelim Boyle and Mary Hardy, "Guaranteed Annuity Options," *ASTIN Bulletin: The Journal of the IAA* 33, no. 2 (November 2003): 125–52, https://doi.org/10.1017/S0515036100013404; James Poterba, "Annuities in Early Modern Europe," in *The Origins of Value: The Financial Innovations That Created Modern Capital Markets*, ed. William N. Goetzmann

—

the chosen country folk were then given a royal treatment. As one chronicler of nineteenth-century life insurance observed, when the annuity investors arrived, "the inhabitants of [some] rural districts . . . were surprised by the sudden and extraordinary attention paid to many of their aged members. If they were sick, the surgeon attended them at the cost of some good genius; and if they were poor the comforts of life were granted them." The same historian noted that one investor even put a physician on retainer to tend to his nominee, paying the doctor "twenty-five golden guineas a year, so long as he kept his ancient patient alive."[14]

These many deficiencies in annuity contracts persisted despite some of the best scientific minds of the era applying themselves to the seemingly mundane question of how to price annuities.[15] In fact, no less a scholar than the astronomer Edmond Halley (of Halley's Comet fame) devoted himself to the matter.*

Halley was responsible for the first systematic annuity pricing calculations. He based these figures on painstakingly collected birth and death tables from the German city of Breslau and published them in 1693 in a book chapter titled "An Estimate of the Degrees of Mortality of Mankind." Halley's approach, however sound, unfortunately required extensive calculations for insurers that, in those

---

and Geert Rouwenhorst (Oxford: Oxford University Press, 2005), 207–24; Ray D. Murphy, *Sale of Annuities by Governments* (New York: Association of Life Insurance Presidents, 1939).

    * This work of Halley's has largely been forgotten to history by everyone except actuaries, who seem to take some offense at this lack of recognition. To wit, following the publication of a Royal Astronomical Society article commemorating Halley's many contributions to astronomy, an actuary by the name of Geoffrey Heywood, MBE, wrote to express his disappointment at the lack of reference to Halley's "activities in the field of actuarial science." Geoffrey Heywood, "Edmond Halley – Actuary," *Quarterly Journal of the Royal Astronomical Society* 35, no. 1 (1994): 151.

days, lacked even rudimentary calculating machines.[16] So it was of much practical use when the great mathematician Abraham de Moivre also turned his attention to annuities and developed a way of approximating annuity prices via an algebraic formula.*

Unfortunately, while Halley and de Moivre were great scientists, they weren't great social scientists. They didn't realize — as George Akerlof would some centuries later — that their calculations would bankrupt any insurer that deployed them because they failed to account for selection. In fairness, even if they had understood this, it might not have done any good. Then, as now, the experts were often ignored. In the seventeenth century, Jan de Witt, a Dutch scholar and statesman, told his government that it was selling annuities too cheaply to finance its war with England. But his fellow lawmakers paid him no mind.[17]

Even when mathematicians realized the need to make payments dependent on nominees' ages, the calculations were often coarse. Jan de Witt, for example, lumped everyone under the age of fifty-four into the same category, because doing otherwise would have entailed overly burdensome calculations. It was very common to pool annuitants by decade, so a forty- and forty-nine-year-old were offered the same contracts. Today, as you might expect, companies set annuity payments differently for every age of a potential buyer.[18]

These days, it is also no longer possible to buy annuities on

---

* De Moivre had a knack for approximation — he also showed that the binomial distribution could be approximated by the bell-shaped normal distribution. This fact, along with much of the work in de Moivre's *The Doctrines of Chance*, was of great utility to statisticians and gamblers alike in the centuries that followed. Abraham de Moivre, *Annuities upon Lives; or, The Valuation of Annuities upon Any Number of Lives* (London, 1725); de Moivre, *The Doctrine of Chances; or, A Method of Calculating the Probability of Events in Play* (London, 1718).

others' heads. This has helped to eliminate some of the more extreme selection concerns: the bankers of Geneva, the most sophisticated investors of their day, were quite efficient in gaming whatever payout rules were set by annuity sellers in the 1700s, whether they favored French schoolgirls or Scottish octagenarians.[19] The prohibition against betting on the lives of others also turned annuities into something more like insurance against the high cost of living into one's nineties, rather than a lottery-like gamble on a five-year-old's continued health.

If the nature of annuities has changed, it is partly because insurance, like just about any other business, has become vastly more sophisticated over the past few centuries. And our interest here is not the folly of King Louis's famously shortsighted borrowing or the obvious errors and omissions of eighteenth-century annuity contracts. Rather, we'd like to know how big a role selection plays in twenty-first-century markets for annuities.

When annuities today are offered by cold, calculating, and sophisticated insurance companies, do they suffer from the same problems as Renaissance-era financial products?

Spoiler alert: they do. And really, this should not be a surprise. We already saw how selection plagues modern life insurance markets. Why should the situation be any different for annuities? One is a bet on a long life, the other on early death — really just opposite sides of the same circle-of-life gamble.

Back to the Present

Today, the annuity market is surprisingly small — surprising because annuities offer what should be an attractive way of solving a dilemma faced by many retirees. Take, for example, a woman who's worked hard for forty years and managed to put away some savings for retirement. How quickly (or slowly) should she spend her nest egg now that she's retired? Should she heed the advice to "eat, drink, and be merry, for tomorrow we die," or should she follow that other worn-out cliché and save for a rainy day instead?

Suppose she exercises caution and keeps substantial amounts of her savings aside for the future, just in case she lives as long as Jeanne Calment and has to support herself out of her savings for a very long time. She risks dying early, thus leaving money in the bank that she might have used to take luxury cruises, shower her grandchildren with presents, and otherwise live it up in retirement. But if she lives only for the moment, she runs the "risk" that she ends up outliving her savings. That may sound silly — a long life is a good thing! — except it's less so if she ends up with little to spend on eating or drinking tomorrow.

Annuities offer a way out of this rock-and-hard-place dilemma and can allow our retiree to enjoy a higher standard of living in retirement than she would otherwise be able to. They accomplish this by removing the element of chance — exactly what insurance is supposed to do. An annuity guarantees her a constant monthly stream of income as long as she is alive. No need to hold back in case she lives "too long" — the annuity will keep providing for her needs. At least among economists, it is a no-brainer that just about everyone should put most of their retirement savings into annuities. (The arguments we've sketched out here have been made in excruciating and thoroughly convincing detail in a number of research papers.)[20]

And yet, who listens to economists? Precious few, it seems. Almost no one buys annuities if they can help it. Indeed, many other economics papers have been written trying to explain the so-called annuity puzzle: Why don't more people behave the way economic theory says they should and annuitize their savings?[21] If nothing else, annuities have kept economists busy creating and then trying to solve their own puzzle.

There are many possible explanations for why annuities are so unpopular, including but not limited to the selection concerns that will be our main focus. If you ask your parents (or if you're of a certain age, engage in a little introspection), you'll find that many people hate the idea that they would tie up all their savings in an annuity, then die "too soon" and not leave anything to their kids. It's also easy to imagine that any product that tends to target the elderly — widows and retirees, with minimal financial sophistication — might be fertile ground for financial confidence men. Indeed, the FBI has a webpage exclusively devoted to fraud against the elderly, which enumerates the various reasons that seniors are commonly targeted by scammers.[22]

Another reason why few people buy privately sold annuities is that they already have annuities, whether they like it (or even know it) or not. If your employer offers a defined-benefit pension plan, it means that, once you retire, you'll receive a fixed amount of money each year till you die. That is, you've effectively been given an annuity.[23] Every American — no matter who their employer is — has an annuity provided by the government. Social Security — which, as we noted in chapter 1, is the federal government's single biggest program — provides everyone with an annuity, even if it isn't usually described in those terms. Look at your last pay stub. There's almost definitely an entry for "Social Security Tax." That's what you paid this month for your government-provided annuity. In return, once you get old enough, the government will send you a check every month, from the time you retire and file for benefits until you die.

As we said, it's an annuity. For anyone who's put away additional retirement savings, however, it's a highly incomplete one.

You might think that private annuities are rare because they're already provided in part by employers and the government. Or it might be the reverse: employers and the government have stepped in to provide annuities because the private annuity market just doesn't work very well. And why doesn't the private market work as it should? Precisely because, as we'll show next, selection leads to annuity prices that are so high that average retirees aren't interested in buying them.

Yes, Virginia, There *Is* Selection

Think back to how, as described in chapter 2, Daifeng He detected selection in life insurance: she looked to see if people who bought life insurance died sooner than otherwise-similar-looking people who didn't. We can do the same for annuities, except remember, here it's in reverse. Life insurance companies want to avoid customers on the brink of death, while annuity sellers want to avoid customers who are brimming with health and longevity. All we need is to observe survival rates for the population as a whole and for the small subset of the population who buy annuities.

Once upon a time, this was hard to do. Edmond Halley had to build his Enlightenment-era mortality tables by hand and could do so only for one German town that had been meticulous in recording and storing its life tables.[24]

Today, the U.S. government provides meticulously recorded and stored life tables for the entire country, available to anyone with an internet connection. Curious how long the average seventy-five-year-old can expect to survive? Or the chances that seventy-five-year-old will live to see his or her seventy-sixth birthday? (The answer is quite different depending on whether it's a him or a her.) It's in the Social Security Administration's annual report.[25]

The Social Security Administration has a lot at stake in making sure it gets these forecasts right: recall that the government is providing *everyone* with an annuity through the Social Security system. And just as an annuity company's costs depend on how long customers survive, federal expenditures depend in large part on how long the population is likely to live and therefore how much will be paid out via Social Security, which eats up an ever-larger share of the budget (almost one-quarter of the total $4.4 trillion federal budget in 2019).[26]

So the government tables detail the mortality prospects of the whole population — separately by age and gender. We can think of this collection of figures as roughly the same as the mortality prospects of the nonbuyers of annuities, since such a small share of the U.S. population actually buys them. For the few who do, the Society of Actuaries helpfully provides the other figure we need: among people who buy annuities, what do *their* mortality prospects look like (again by age and gender)?[27] It does this to help insurers set annuity prices. The data would have blown Halley's seventeenth-century mind.

A comparison of mortality rates between people who buy annuities and everyone else shows exactly what we'd expect if the annuity market suffered from adverse selection. Annuitants are less likely to die in any given year than the general public is. In other words, those who choose to buy annuities are the ones who are more expensive for insurance companies to cover. These differences are consistently large.

—

According to calculations from the economists Jim Poterba and Adam Solomon, a sixty-five-year-old male annuitant had a one-year mortality rate that is half that of the sixty-five-year-old male population at large.[28] Even for individuals as old as ninety-five, these differences between annuitant and nonannuitant mortality rates persist, although they are somewhat more modest; a ninety-five-year-old male with an annuity has a one-year mortality rate that is about one-quarter less than that of the general ninety-five-year-old male population.

When you think about it, it's rather amazing. There are so many ways that the end can come for centenarians, with the end arriving quickly and unpredictably in a way that modern medicine cannot intercede. Yet even the very old clearly have some idea of when the end is near. Whatever the reason, the higher survival rates of annuitants at any age translate directly into higher costs to insurance companies for covering their customers compared to what it would have cost to cover noncustomers.*

As a result, insurance companies need to price annuities assuming that only the fittest will apply. That's why selection drives up the prices of insurance. It also means that annuities tend to be a bad deal for the average retiree. Calculating just how bad a deal it is becomes a bit more of a complicated exercise than comparing survival rates for annuitants and nonannuitants. It's true that the longer a person survives, the more the insurance company will need to shell out in

---

* If relatively infirm applicants could readily identify themselves to annuity providers, you'd think they could get a better deal. Ray's uncle had his first heart attack in his thirties. His grandfather died from coronary disease in his sixties. So he should get a better deal than his wife, whose Grandma Lil survived to her nineties. But with few exceptions, annuity payouts are determined by age and gender alone. Why insurers don't ask for more information when selling annuities is a puzzle we'll discuss further in chapter 4.

—

annuity payments and thus the higher its costs of covering that individual. But the cost of a customer also depends on interest rates.*

Poterba and Solomon have done the hard work of calculating how much annuities cost to provide, relative to the price insurers charge for them. Their estimates suggest that in 2020, insurers made about an 8 percent profit on their annuity customers — reasonable given the costs they incur calculating, selling, and administering insurance products. But if an average person in the population (as opposed to the average annuity buyer, who is much healthier) were to buy an annuity, the profit rate would be over twice as much — about 20 percent, because the average person's expected life span is so much shorter.

Which all goes back to help explain why our parents (and most people their age) don't buy annuities: they're a bad deal for the buyer and a great deal for the insurance company, unless you're quite a bit healthier than average (and know it).

————

Thus far, we've mostly taken businesses as somewhat passive and clueless bystanders in the marketplace, hoodwinked by their shrewder customers. But the lure of profits and the threat of red ink can serve as powerful motivators to figure out better ways around

---

* Interest rates matter because there's always the option to not buy an annuity and just put your money in the bank instead and live off the interest. Intuitively, an annuity should pay out somewhat more than this market interest rate: if you put money in the bank, your original deposit (the principal) remains intact, whereas the insurance company keeps whatever you pay up front for an annuity. The higher the interest rate, the more that an insurance company can cover its future costs just by putting an annuitant's up-front payment in the bank. Interest rates don't vary, though, whether the insurance company is holding onto sick or healthy annuitants' cash. So while they matter for prices and profits, interest rates aren't important for our selection story.

the problem of customers' private information. And that's just what businesses have done. In chapters 4 and 5, we'll explore some of these many strategies. We'll describe insurers' attempts to find out more about the likely costs of prospective customers — using everything from coffeehouse gossip to Big Data — as well as the myriad and often creative ways they design their contracts to try to get their customers to (perhaps unwittingly) reveal their own secrets.

It's not only up to businesses to manage selection problems. Where markets are failing, there may also be room for governments to step in to save them. In the final part of the book, we'll see what policy makers have come up with and, crucially, what that means for businesses and customers who are forced to play by the rules that governments devise.

PART II

MUCH ADO ABOUT SELECTION

Chapter 4

THE PRICE ISN'T RIGHT

The unhappy distinction as the first reported traffic fatality in history goes to Bridget Driscoll. She was run down and killed in August 1896 by a Roger-Benz car giving demonstration rides at London's Crystal Palace. According to one witness, the car was moving at "a reckless pace, in fact, like a fire engine." In fact, the car had a maximum speed of eight miles per hour, which had further been reduced to four and a half miles per hour because of safety modifications.[1]

The first car insurance contract followed shortly thereafter, appearing just three months after Ms. Driscoll's untimely demise.*

* Vehicle insurance predated the automobile by a number of decades — after all, horse-drawn carriages themselves posed significant risks to both riders and pedestrians. The first horse-carriage indemnity insurance appeared in Paris in the 1820s and spread rapidly from there to the rest of France, as the Napoleonic Code held carriage owners liable for damage done to others. You can still to this day buy insurance on horse carriages — which are far more dangerous than modern automobiles. Robert M. Merkin and Jeremy Stuart-Smith, *The Law of Motor Insurance* (London: Sweet and Maxwell, 2004); American Exchange and Review, *Insurance and Its Collateral Sciences* (Philadelphia: Review Publishing, 1901).

—

Even the earliest automobiles were as safe as horse-drawn carriages, per mile traveled. But cars traveled so much farther and began to appear with such ubiquity that vehicle-related fatalities increased at a rapid clip during the early part of the twentieth century. There were thirty-six motor-vehicle deaths in the United States in 1900. In 1920, there were more than twelve thousand.[2] Those who were injured or killed were often bystanders rather than motorists, and victims' only recourse was to sue the guilty party for pain, suffering, and loss of livelihood. Drivers needed insurance to cover their own unanticipated expenses and also to compensate other aggrieved parties.

The first contract in the United States was issued in 1897 by Traveler's Property Casualty to Gilbert Loomis of Westfield, Massachusetts, for a car he built himself. Loomis's premium was $7.50 for $1,000 in liability coverage should his driving cause injury, death, or damage to others' property. When Traveler's started issuing auto policies on a larger scale, premiums were set based on the car's horsepower alone.[3]

In contrast to life insurance and annuities, there is little research on the history of auto insurance. So while we can't say for sure, we'd conjecture that what followed is the now-familiar story line. The worst drivers would buy the most generous coverage, which led to high insurance payouts, then higher prices to cover those losses, followed by yet higher payouts and higher prices. Loomis himself may have been a part of this unraveling from the very beginning—his car was made by the eponymous Loomis Automobile Company, which Andrew Carnegie had reportedly passed on investing in because the cars it built were too dangerous.[4]

The business of insuring drivers is much more complicated these days. Try getting a quote on any major insurer's website, and you'll see what we mean.[5] First, a driver has a lot of latitude to tailor their coverage to their particular tolerance for different types of risks. Drivers who are worried about costly litigation may choose to pay extra to pay the victims' costs beyond the required coverage, which is generally far less than the expenses generated by a serious accident. There's also a range of options for how much of the driver's own medical bills the insurer will cover in an accident, regardless of who is at fault, and a choice as to the deductibles (the amount that you must pay out of pocket in case of accident before the insurance company will pay anything) for both vehicle damage and personal injuries.

More choice is good! It is what responsive, profit-maximizing businesses offer to customers with different preferences to make them happy, lest they start shopping around for other options. Why should everyone have to buy the same cookie-cutter insurance regardless of how they feel about risk or the financial resources they have for managing that risk?

All true, but where there is choice, there are opportunities for selection. While all drivers are required to get at least some "third party" coverage to provide at least some money to compensate victims or their loved ones, that still leaves the customer a range of choices about how much (if any) coverage to get to cover personal injury or damage to the policyholder's car.[6] In our previous examples, the problem was that "bad" (i.e., expensive) customers would buy, say, life insurance or annuities, and "good" customers would not. For auto, the problem is that bad customers — reckless and inattentive drivers, in this case — will buy more generous coverage, while the careful ones and people who hardly ever drive at all will be more apt to get the barebones third-party coverage.

What's an insurer to do? We'll try to answer that question in the course of the next two chapters. The upshot is that they can try to do a better job of setting the "right" prices, or they can rewrite their contracts to try to appeal more to "good" customers and less to "bad" ones.

In this chapter, we'll focus on whether insurers are able to get the price "right." If only insurers had some way of recognizing which customers are likely to have more accidents than others. Then they could set their insurance rates accordingly, and everyone could buy the insurance they want, at prices that reflect their chances of getting into an accident.

The road to market salvation, then, might run through better information: more information lets insurers set better prices, which leads to a market that works better for everyone.

This brings us to the second battery of questions that you'll encounter on an auto insurance application: questions not about the contract you want but about you. Insurers go through great pains to collect as many relevant details before offering you a contract (for example, as we mentioned earlier, requesting the right to pull your credit history), precisely so they can charge higher prices to costlier customers and offer comprehensive insurance at lower prices to less expensive ones.

We'll explore what this means in practice — the kinds of information insurance companies collect and how this can help reduce selection. But at the same time, we'll see the limitations to this approach: some types of information are very hard to collect, and sometimes insurers decide that it'd be bad business to use all the information they have at their disposal in forecasting customers' costs, even if it means that their prices aren't quite right as a result.

To be clear, it doesn't matter to us whether the insurance business is good or bad for its executives and shareholders — they can end up as billionaires or paupers for all we care. We're interested in their ability to keep their businesses in the black only insofar as it enables their millions of customers to keep purchasing peace of mind via insurance coverage. To see how they've done so over the years, we can again go back to the early days of the insurance business. We'll start by looking at how maritime insurers managed to find enough information to keep their industry afloat, despite the very substantial problem of selection. For who most wanted to buy policies on seventeenth-century ocean voyages? Those who owned ships with rotting timbers, captained by drunkards.

Saving Insurance Markets with Better Information

The search for better information on potential insurance customers is much older than the automobile. It is probably as old as the insurance business itself. We can date it at least as far back as the late seventeenth century. That was when London's famed Lloyd's Coffee House opened on Tower Street, where it quickly came to function as a meeting place for insurers to exchange gossip about the goings-on in global shipping.

As many readers might guess, Lloyd's Coffee House is where the insurance giant Lloyd's of London got its start. Fewer may realize that Lloyd's isn't actually a single insurance company. Rather, it's a platform where multiple insurers band together to offer insurance for risks that don't fit neatly within any standard policies offered by, say, Allstate or Progressive. Many of the requests for coverage involve such vast and hard-to-quantify uncertainties that no single insurer wants to shoulder it on its own. Lloyd's syndicates insured pinup idol Betty Grable's legs back in the 1930s; in the 1970s, they wrote a $1 million policy on KISS lead singer Gene Simmons's remarkably elongated tongue and a $5 million policy on Tom Jones's highly marketable chest hair. Lloyd's started covering space satellites in 1965, years before Neil Armstrong took his giant step for mankind, with an $8.5 million policy on Intelsat I, the world's first commercial communications satellite.*

In the seventeenth century, the patrons of Lloyd's looked not to the skies but to the seas. In its early days, the coffeehouse was simply a venue for merchants, sailors, and ship owners, who came to buy and sell marine insurance. Some of the risks were straightforward to observe and evaluate: if a ship sailed through the West Indies in August, the chances of getting hit by a hurricane were higher than if the trip were taken a few months earlier or if the captain charted its path farther north.[7] So insurance contracts specified the particular timing and route that a ship was to take. However, the chances of a ship surviving a storm — or other hazards like war and pirates — and safely delivering its cargo depended on a host of other factors that were harder to observe.

As the economic historian Christopher Kingston explains in

---

* It was actually a pair of policies: $3.5 million for damage to the satellite prior to liftoff and $5 million to cover any liability resulting from harm to bystanders during the launch. Claire Suddath, "Top 10 Oddly Insured Body Parts," *Time,* September 1, 2010, http://content.time.com/time/specials/packages /article/0,28804,2015171_2015172_2014872,00.html; Jay MacDonald, "8 of the Weirdest Insurance Policies," *Fox Business,* January 12, 2016, https:// www.foxbusiness.com/features/8-of-the-weirdest-insurance-policies; "Report: Tom Jones Has Chest Hair Insured," *New York Daily News,* February 5, 2008, https://www.nydailynews.com/entertainment/gossip/report-tom-jones -chest-hair-insured-article-1.308721; Piotr Manikowski and Mary A. Weiss, "The Satellite Insurance Market and Underwriting Cycles," *Geneva Risk and Insurance Review* 38, no. 2 (September 1, 2013): 148–82, https://doi.org/10 .1057/grir.2013.2.

his account of the development of modern marine insurance, "A poorly manned or fitted out ship, or one with rotten timbers or an inexperienced crew, would be less likely to survive a storm." As with the automobile several centuries later, the skill—and sobriety—of the person behind the wheel was another key risk factor. "[A ship] with an incompetent or alcoholic captain would be more likely to run aground or miss its intended landfall," Kingston notes, while "one that could sail close to the wind would have a better chance of outrunning enemy privateers." A captain's drinking habits, the degree of rot, and the quality of a crew were all hard for would-be insurers to assess. But they might very reasonably be better known to the vessel's owner. Kingston explains, "merchants often knew more about some aspects of the risk, and had incentives to conceal negative private information in order to try to keep the premium low."[8]

The genius of the coffeehouse entrepreneur Edward Lloyd was to foster the active exchange of such information among the sea merchants and insurers who frequented his establishment (who were often one and the same—who better to evaluate shipping risk than sea merchants themselves?). Much of the information about which captain was a drunkard and where pirates lurked on the open ocean most likely came from the customers themselves. Among the coffeehouse patrons, it was possible to find someone with relevant expertise to kick the tires, so to speak, of any potential voyage. Mr. Lloyd made his particular coffeehouse indispensable by gathering information himself; he employed runners who went along the docks picking up all the latest shipping news and developed a network of paid informants who sent him gossip from other ports. As information came in, it was announced from a pulpit that Lloyd had installed at one end of the coffeehouse.[9]

From Coffeehouses to Computers

The insurance industry has come a long way since it relied on coffeehouse gossip to write insurance contracts, but the same basic principle is at play: the more information an insurer can gather on the applicant, the more it can try to overcome the customer's informational advantage and reduce the chance that it insures a high-risk customer without realizing it (and charging appropriately).

Auto insurance offers a case study in how businesses have tried, in the modern era, to solve their own selection problems through better data and thus better pricing. In 1897, insurance depended only on horsepower, not the driver. In 1908, Rhode Island became the first state to make sure car owners could drive before letting them out on the road, issuing licenses only to those who passed a driving test.[10] Soon, licenses were also a requirement for insurance. In the 1950s, as the automobile became a teenage obsession, it just as quickly became clear that car-obsessed youths were not the best of drivers. A 1959 article described the automobile as "a weapon of juvenile transgression," and according to statistics reported that same year, one in eight fatal crashes involved at least one teen. Insurance rates were thus set commensurately higher for, say, teenage boys as compared to middle-aged women (though teens could reduce their premiums by 15 percent if they took one of the driver's-ed classes that were just becoming popular at the time).[11] Today, online insurance applications require responses to pages and pages of detailed questions before you can get a quote.

Auto insurers can now estimate drivers' risk with great precision, thanks to the information that they require applicants to provide. Even before the age of Big Data arrived, a 2005 *Businessweek* article described the shift at Allstate from only three pricing tiers

—

based on a handful of applicant attributes to as many as fifteen hundred different pricing levels based on a wide array of customer characteristics.[12] Naturally, many of these attributes related very directly to whether a customer's history suggested they were careful or inattentive, safety minded or reckless—like whether they'd racked up speeding tickets or a history of fender benders. Others had a less obvious link to driver quality, such as an applicant's creditworthiness. Even allowing for some journalistic hyperbole, Allstate and its competitors have clearly become far more sophisticated in how to tailor prices to individual customers' characteristics and behaviors than when Traveler's was basing auto insurance premiums on a car's horsepower alone at the dawn of the twentieth century.

For fun, we tried applying for automobile insurance in a bunch of different states (yes, we have a strange idea of fun). We fully expected that there would be a longish list of queries but were taken aback by the applications' length and intrusiveness.

Questions that seem a natural way to assess how likely we are to have accidents seemed like fair game. So we weren't surprised that they asked our age, gender, how long we'd had a driver's license, and lots of questions about our car and what we use it for and who in the household might use it. Nor were we surprised that the applications contained very detailed questions about all motor-vehicle accidents or violations (going back five to ten years depending on the state we tried). Often the past is the best predictor of the future: drivers with lots of speeding tickets or fender benders in the past few years are more likely to have accidents in the years ahead.

Some of the questions, though, seemed less immediately linked to accident risk—like the highest level of education of someone in the household (sadly, PhDs didn't seem to get a better deal), our grades, whether we owned or rented our home, or our marital status. And some of the questions seemed a bit creepy: it's obvious why State Farm wants to know whether we'd been in a car accident recently before giving an auto insurance quote, but why does it want our GPA and Social Security number as well?[13]

It's because companies love any information that might be related to how costly you're going to be to insure. Whatever they might glean from your driving history, car make, and mileage, there is still a lot of uncertainty about what you're likely to cost them in claims. And it turns out that knowledge of things that are seemingly unrelated to driving — such as financial problems like a home fore-closure or bankruptcy, your criminal record, and even your grades — can help reduce that uncertainty. Honor-roll students, for example, tend to be more careful and future-looking than slackers, which is why there can be a "good student discount" for current students with a B average or better.*

Since the mid-1990s, automobile insurers have been using information on individuals' credit scores to set prices for their cus-tomers (at least in states where they are allowed to do so — more on this later). At first, this seemed strange, even sinister, prompting newspaper stories like the one about a Texas woman whom auto-mobile insurers would only cover at above-standard rates despite a clean driving record.[14] The reason? She'd filed for bankruptcy eight years before (due to "a little real estate trouble"). The article even

---

* Apparently, in the 1950s, better students didn't really want cars any-way. A *New York Times Magazine* story reported that, of straight-A students surveyed, zero owned an automobile, whereas 71 percent of D students had one. As one student who was probably from the latter group put it, "If I had three wishes the first would be to be 16 and drive a cattlelike." *Grease* was roughly accurate in its portrayal of at least this aspect of high school life at the time. Dorothy Barclay, "A Boy, a Car: A Problem," *New York Times*, November 22, 1959, https://www.nytimes.com/1959/11/22/archives/a-boy-a-car-a -problem.html.

noted that she'd never actually declared bankruptcy — she managed to pay off her bills before the bankruptcy court ruled — but this almost decades-old "smudge" on her credit report was enough to prompt higher automobile insurance premiums. Why? Because insurance companies had discovered that people with a history of financial problems also tend to have more automobile insurance claims. So despite the lack of any direct connection to driver aptitude, a bad credit history can raise your auto insurance premiums.

So Does It Work?

You might imagine that by the time the auto insurer has sleuthed out all these details about your past and fed the relevant information into its proprietary algorithm, the company may have as good an idea of your likely auto insurance claims as you yourself do, maybe even better. Yay for Big Data and the end of selection-driven failures in insurance markets?

Not so fast. Researchers have found ample evidence of adverse selection in automobile insurance markets, despite the pages of data entry and background checks. For example, one study in Israel found a much higher rate of automobile accidents among experienced drivers who purchased more automobile insurance coverage compared to otherwise-similar drivers *who faced the same price for their insurance* but who chose less generous coverage. The same basic patterns have been documented in other countries as well.[15]

If you engage in a bit of introspection, perhaps it's not surprising that adverse selection in auto insurance is particularly extreme for experienced drivers. Beginners are all bad, and more importantly, they haven't had time to learn whether they're *especially* inept when compared against other new drivers.

—

That's certainly not to say that the pages and pages of data are useless. Indeed, the study of the Israeli automobile insurance market found that, while average claims were about a third higher among experienced drivers who chose more generous coverage than those who chose less generous, that gap narrowed by about 90 percent once the researchers adjusted for all of the information about the driver and their car that the insurer collected and then used in determining the driver's insurance premium. That is, by some measure, the detailed data and advanced pricing algorithms get rid of most selection. Yet some selection remains — even for people with identical past driving records, reckless drivers who know they were just lucky not to have had even a minor accident buy more coverage, and careful drivers who know they were unlucky buy less.

That is, whatever advantage data science confers on insurers, it turns out that there are still skeletons ferreted away in applicants' closets, so to speak. Amy, for example, had more than ten years with a spotless driving record when she was in graduate school. She was therefore rated as an excellent driver and offered the very lowest price for auto insurance when she bought her first car in her late twenties. However, by her own admission, she was a terrible driver (a view shared by everyone who knew her). What did Amy know that insurers couldn't? That as a seventeen-year-old Manhattanite, she had only gotten her license to satisfy her mother's demands that she get one as an "invaluable form of ID," learning just enough about parallel parking and turn signals to pass the test; that after she got that license at her mother's behest, she didn't drive again for nearly a decade, leaving her with only the vaguest recollection of the difference between parallel parking and angle parking, let alone how to do one or the other or to actually . . . well, drive safely.

Amy's was a case of being a worse risk than her hapless insurer thought. But private information can also cut the other way. Liran has complained vociferously that when his oldest son, Shiley, went to college at Stanford — about a ten-minute drive from where Liran lives — the family's automobile insurance premium didn't go down. Liran swore that Shiley was no longer going to be driving one of their cars — its exclusive use had been promised to his younger brother, Yahli, in a great intrafamily negotiation. But the insurer had a hard and fast policy that college kids living within one hundred miles of their parents still "counted" against their insurance. If Liran wanted to keep the car, he was going to have to pay a premium that reflected the theory that not just one but *two* teenage boys would be driving the car, even though in fact only one would ever do so.

Amy's and Liran's stories may both sound a bit, well, idiosyncratic. But then we all have our idiosyncrasies, don't we? It's hard for insurers to collect data on some aspects of a driver's history. Let's go back to Amy and her "spotless driving record." There's no online registry listing miles driven, and companies don't even bother to ask how many miles you've gone in the past decade (Who can remember? And who — besides a few eccentric New Yorkers — gets a license and doesn't use it?).

There *are* public accident records, so that if you try to get a fresh start on auto insurance rates by, say, switching from Allstate to Progressive, it won't work. Progressive can check the accident registry database to make sure you're telling the truth. We know these public records can be important, thanks to the work of the economist Alma Cohen, who looked at the behavior of auto insurance customers in Israel before it had a national accident database. Whether intentional or due to selective recall, insurance applicants lowballed their past accidents to the tune of 75 percent. Since the current insurer *did* know its customers' accident history, this gave accident-prone drivers an incentive to start with a clean slate at a new company. And that's exactly what happened: Cohen found that customers who switched insurers tended to have worse claims histories (which were invisible to the new insurer) than those who stuck with their existing policies. In other words, drivers who had had an accident would "flee their record" by switching to coverage from another provider.[16]

But even with public accident records—such as we have in the United States—there remain customer characteristics related to driving risk that may be too difficult or expensive to obtain, which is why, while insurers can squeeze 90 percent of accident risk out of the data, there's still going to be scope for customer selection based on customers' private information.

Uninsurable at Any Price

Perhaps the most striking illustration of the failure of insurance companies to collect enough information on their customers to eliminate adverse selection comes from the widespread practice of insurance rejections: many people who apply (or might apply) for insurance are turned down by all insurance companies for coverage. In other words, not everyone can buy insurance; a lot of people are (to misquote Ralph Nader) "uninsurable at any price."[17]

You might think it would be straightforward to calculate how many people can't get insurance because they have a rejection-worthy condition. But it isn't—you can't look at the fraction of applicants rejected, because applicants who know they don't have a chance of getting approved for coverage don't bother even trying.

The economist Nathan Hendren found a clever way around

this problem in his PhD dissertation.[18] He got his hands on several insurers' guidelines that list the conditions that are used by their agents to decide whether to reject (or at least discourage) applicants for life, disability, and long-term-care insurance. A past stroke, for example, triggers automatic rejection for both life and long-term-care coverage. Anyone who'd previously been a resident in a nursing home also gets rejected for long-term care. For many conditions, coverage depends on the particulars of the disease. Esophageal cancer was okay, as long as the last date of treatment was at least four years prior. There were also some criteria that left at least some discretion in the hands of doctors or insurance agents. For esophageal cancer, for example, ongoing weight loss is listed as grounds for rejection, without specifying precisely what that constitutes in terms of, say, pounds lost in the past month or year.

Hendren then matched these rejection criteria to data from a survey composed of thousands of older (fifty-five years old and older) Americans, which included detailed information on their health conditions. By combining these two data sets, Hendren could determine what would happen if a given individual were to apply for insurance — whether they'd be a sure rejection, a near-certain acceptance, or somewhere in between. In the end, Hendren concluded that a very substantial fraction of people who might want insurance couldn't get it if they tried: nearly 30 percent of his sample was ineligible for long-term-care coverage, and nearly 20 percent couldn't get life insurance. The proportions that would be sure to be able to buy coverage were similar — 30 percent for long-term care and 20 percent for life. The remainder — which included an awful lot of people — were in the gray intermediate category of maybe, maybe not.

Rejection, then, isn't a rare or even unusual occurrence — for

—

people over fifty-five, it's entirely common. It's also not limited to humans. Although Hendren didn't include it in his academic study, we've already seen how dogs that are sufficiently long in the tooth (to mix metaphors with bunnies) or have certain health conditions also can't be insured.

Your first reaction might be, "That makes perfect sense! Why insure someone who's already sick?" We'll respond to this question with a question of our own: Why not instead offer coverage at a very high price that reflects those customers' expected future costs? After all, even among past stroke sufferers, there are those who will have assistance-free lives and those who will ultimately spend years in a nursing home. Why not let this high-risk group pool their risks and pay commensurately high premiums to insure against potentially financially ruinous nursing-home expenses?

Instead, they can't buy insurance at all. At any price.

That's puzzling, because it really shouldn't be so hard to calculate the future medical expenses of cancer patients and stroke victims and set their insurance premiums accordingly.

Why can't Big Data solve this problem, to the benefit of both people with preexisting conditions and the companies that could then profitably sell them insurance? It turns out that this thorniest of selection problems would require a view into a prospective customer's soul, not simply a copy of their hospital records. If that sounds a bit obscure, let us give you a more detailed version of Hendren's explanation.

Hendren provides an answer to this question. He argues that despite all the information that life insurers collect, people suffering from certain health conditions know something about their future costs that insurers simply can never discern from medical histories or physical exams. As a result, not only are they a lot more expensive to care for, but they also know a lot more about what their cost of care is likely to be in the future. And it's this inside information that makes the market for covering preexisting conditions break down.

To understand Hendren's theory, it's useful to think about an extreme case. Consider the agonizing decision of whether or not to treat terminal cancer with costly and painful chemotherapy, which often provides only a small chance of remission. If you ask us what one of us would do, we have no idea. As healthy fifty-something-year-olds, we've never had to think much about such situations and have no real basis for weighing the costs and benefits. How painful would treatment actually be? And how might we face an end-of-life decision?

Someone who already has cancer, by comparison, has a much greater appreciation for the treatment options available and presumably has a much clearer sense of how far they're willing to go for a chance at survival. Different people will have reached different decisions after going through this difficult calculus, and the outcome has significant financial implications for any insurance company that's agreed to provide coverage. (This is very similar to the selection problem – discussed in chapter 2 – that afflicts pet insurance. One pet owner might be at peace with their dog's demise; another will rush their pet to the doggy ICU to see whether dear Rover can be saved, whatever the cost – whether measured in vet bills or canine suffering. The insurer can't tell the two customers apart.)

So now let's consider the problem facing an insurance company that wants to offer coverage to cancer patients with similar diagnoses. While they may look similar to the company's statisticians, different patients may choose very different courses of treatment. Some may decide to pursue aggressive options. Others may opt out of what's expected to be a long and painful fight. The patients' medical expenses will be drastically different, despite their similar prognoses.

This is essentially a description of the standard selection model, in which cost differences depend on an applicant's willingness to pursue aggressive treatment — something that's impossible for the insurer to observe — rather than overall health. As a result, the market is prone to exactly the same unraveling we described in chapter 2: patients who expect to follow aggressive treatment buy coverage; patients who expect to opt out of treatment don't; insurer expenses are higher than what might be expected, and if they raise prices to try to compensate, it only makes things worse.

There are two critical ingredients to Hendren's argument. First, as he puts it, there's only one way to be healthy but many different ways to be sick. As a result, there's wide variability in the costs that someone with cancer, heart disease, and other uninsurable conditions will impose on an insurer. With a bit of luck, a heart-attack victim who takes their medicine, watches their diet, and exercises regularly can stay healthy and out of the hospital for a long time. Less diligent survivors are more likely to be in and out of the hospital and end up in the operating room for multiple bypass surgeries, running up a tab of hundreds of thousands of dollars in expenses. Similarly, a cancer sufferer who opts out of aggressive treatment won't cost much to an insurer, while the monthly cost of many chemotherapy drugs runs into the tens of thousands of dollars.

Second, and equally important to Hendren's argument, is the idea that sufferers of heart disease and cancer have greater self-knowledge than healthy people do with regard to what their likely medical care costs will be. The market for insurance unravels, in Hendren's model, when patients have a clear view of their future health-care costs and people who anticipate lower-cost futures self-select out of insurance coverage. While Blue Cross can easily uncover whether you've had cancer in the past, it's a lot harder – perhaps impossible – for it to figure out whether you are inclined toward hospice care or intensive chemo treatment.

Hendren didn't just *propose* his theory of rejections in his PhD dissertation. He also *tested* the theory in a clever way. The survey he used to construct information on people's existing medical conditions also asked a battery of questions about the respondents' futures, including what they thought their chances were of surviving for at least another ten years.

Hendren found that survey respondents with uninsurable pre-existing maladies (i.e., those who had medical conditions that would lead to rejection) could predict their subsequent demise very well; in fact, they could outpredict the model that actuaries use by a significant margin. Until insurance companies can hire mind readers to supplement their statisticians, there will still be private information that makes it unprofitable to insure people with preexisting conditions like prior strokes or cancer.

At this point, you may wonder why some people end up totally uninsurable – at any price – while others merely pay "too high" a price because insurers know that they are offering coverage to a set of (from their perspective) bad customers. As with the general problem of selection, it's a horse race between how much value customers put on insurance and what an insurer can expect to pay out. For some conditions, like leukemia, private information dominates, and insurers won't cover its victims. For others, like esophageal cancer, the value proposition of offloading risk onto an insurer is such that it overcomes whatever self-knowledge a prospective customer might have.

Keep It to Yourself

There are secrets that Big Data will never uncover. And then there are the secrets that are just too expensive to unearth, the promises of techno-optimists notwithstanding. As with many other realms, they may have overplayed their claims that information would become free — or at least dirt cheap — with bigger, better computers and algorithms. And sometimes, their predictions come true, but the new technology is appealing only to the techno-optimists — the rest of us find them to be off-putting or downright intrusive and would pay a little more for insurance, thank you very much, for the privilege of keeping their noses out of our business.

Let's go back to Amy's "secret" that she's a bad driver but doesn't get in accidents because she doesn't drive much at all. It's fine for the insurance company to keep charging her low premiums as long as she sticks to her practice of getting chauffeured by her ever-accommodating husband or riding her bicycle instead — her past accident rate will be a good indication of her accident rate in the future. Suppose, however, that she starts commuting to work by car. As far as the insurer is concerned, Amy's still a model driver, as evidenced by her spotless driving record. But Amy knows that her expected costs have increased by an order of magnitude and may adjust her insurance coverage accordingly.

A seemingly obvious solution to this problem of misclassifying Amy's risk would be to charge for auto insurance by the mile driven. It's an idea that's been around for a while: the economist William Vickrey, who won a Nobel Prize for his work on auction design, enumerated the advantages of per-mile automobile insurance back in 1968.[19] At the time, it was a mere intellectual exercise. For in that bygone era, by-the-mile insurance might have been impractical, requiring, at a minimum, periodic check-ins with a company representative to take an odometer reading. It's too expensive and too much of a hassle. The same might be said of monthly check-ins to track health status: it would provide more detailed information, but it's again not worth it—too much expense and hassle.

Today, we can't so easily explain away the lack of per-mile insurance. It's now feasible to install an onboard tracker that plugs into your car's computer and can capture not just how far you've traveled but also when and where and how carefully you drive. Do you exceed the speed limit? Do you slam on the brakes very often? Do you drive at rush hour (when there are lots of other cars to collide with), at midday, or at 2:00 a.m., when no cars are around but you're at risk of dozing off?* (The onboard trackers presumably help both by improving selection—higher prices for frequent drivers and ones that have to commute during rush hour—and by disciplining bad behavior: The same driver may choose to go slower or travel at a different time of day to bring down their rates.)†

Onboard tracking seems like an appealing way to reduce, if not

---

* These data could easily be pulled off your smartphone, which captures the same "telematics" features as onboard trackers, in addition to your phone usage while driving, another fantastic predictor of accidents. Of course, it would be easy enough to outsmart the insurer by just getting a cheap phone and leaving it at home. Alicja Grzadkowska, "Harnessing the Power of Telematics through Smartphone Sensors," *Insurance Business America*, March 21, 2018, https://www.insurancebusinessmag.com/us/news/technology/harnessing -the-power-of-telematics-through-smartphone-sensors-95514.aspx.

† No incentive system is perfect. It's been observed that onboard trackers might, for example, make drivers push down on the brakes more gently even if a hard stop would be the best way of avoiding an accident. Yuanjing Yao, "Evolution of Insurance: A Telematics-Based Personal Auto Insurance Study" (Honors Scholar Program, University of Connecticut, 2018), https://open commons.uconn.edu/cgi/viewcontent.cgi?article=1563&context=srhonors _theses.

eliminate, customers' private information about their likely auto accident risk. Not surprisingly, therefore, insurance companies have advertised heavily to convince existing customers as well as new ones to use onboard trackers. Progressive offered its Snapshot program as far back as 1998. Every major insurer soon followed suit, with products that promised lower rates in exchange for customers' data. Tech start-ups like Metromile and Cuvva popped up with promises to "disrupt" auto coverage with by-the-day, by-the-mile, and safety-adjusted rates.[20]

We're still waiting for the great disruption. As of 2018, usage-based insurance (which describes policies that incorporate distance driven, driving quality, or both) had a 5 percent share of the U.S. market — much higher than the near-zero share it had just a decade or so before but well short of dominating the marketplace.[21]

Online commentary suggests that part of the reason may be that — insurance companies' promises notwithstanding — this type of insurance can lead to higher rates even if you're not that bad a driver. If the rate-setting algorithm ends up raising rates for better drivers — or even if people simply believe this is a possibility — some good drivers might stay away. That is, maybe Big Data isn't as smart as we thought it was. (One of the more colorful Reddit comments on the topic: "Roommate used the Progressive one and his rate ballooned like crazy. He's also not sensitive with his brakes, so he'd slam them and the thing would beep. I'd always joke and say 'insurance just went up' and we'd laugh about it. Then the bill came and it was no longer funny lol.")[22]

A deeper problem — one entirely unrelated to selection — may be the reluctance of most customers to install onboard tracking devices in their cars because it feels creepy — in a Big Brother sort of way — for insurers or anyone else to know so much about you. That would help to explain why, in a study of onboard-tracker use at one major U.S. insurer, a pair of economists found that only 20 percent of drivers opted into the program, despite their estimates that (the wisdom of Reddit commenters notwithstanding) it allowed customers to reduce their premiums by 7 percent. This lines up with the results of a Pew Research Center survey in 2016, which found that 45 percent of Americans would refuse an insurer's offer of a discount if it required an onboard tracker (the flip side is that 37 percent — much more than the current 5 percent — said that they *would* take the deal). While some noted that, at least for them, the discount wouldn't last ("because I drive like a crazy lady"), for most, it felt too intrusive in a 1984 sort of way.[23]

Maybe more drivers will become accustomed to life in the surveillance economy — after all, Google, Apple, and others can already track our movements based on cell-phone data, so why does it matter, really, if Allstate knows our whereabouts as well? But at least for now, fears of Big Brotherly insurance companies keeping tabs on your driving has kept auto insurers from solving selection problems via better information.

If customers "don't like" business practices, these practices may not be good for business — witness the failure of usage-based insurance to take off. And if something isn't good for business, companies won't do it even if it is good for fixing selection problems.

This means that even if insurers don't face any legal restrictions, they may appear to be leaving money on the table by not fully using everything they learn about their customers. Sometimes "pricing on everything" can seem intrusive or simply unfair. In such cases, insurers may allow selection problems to persist because they decide that the public-relations costs of doing otherwise outweighs the selection benefits of better information. So private information sometimes persists in the insurance marketplace not because insurers *can't* learn everything but because "don't be creepy" can be good business, even if it means that selection problems remain.

Choosing Not to Use the Information You Have

If Amy doesn't give Allstate access to her car's computer, the company can never know how far she drives or how often she slams on the brakes. But there are cases in which insurers don't even use data that *are* legal for them to use and readily available to anyone – including ourselves – who might choose to go looking for it.

Amy has studied one of these instances with her colleague Jim Poterba. They looked at annuity data from the United Kingdom.[24] Recall from chapter 3 that a sixty-five-year-old man with an annuity is 50 percent less likely to die in the year ahead than a sixty-five-year-old man without one. To state the obvious, there's a lot that one might learn about someone beyond age and gender that would help refine predictions about the chances someone expires in the year ahead. Have they had cancer? Do they smoke? Do they have a family history of heart disease?

Here's the example Jim and Amy found in the data. It's well known that richer and better-educated people live longer and that neighborhoods differ in how wealthy and educated their residents are. So it is perhaps not surprising that they found that the education level in an annuitant's neighborhood is a useful predictor of when they are likely to die, above and beyond what the insurance company could already predict based on the annuitant's age and gender. For example, a sixty-five-year-old man who came from a ward in which fewer people had the equivalent of a good high school degree would have a higher chance of dying in the following year than if he had come from a ward with more educated inhabitants. Amy and Jim showed that offering a discount on the annuity to those who come from lower-education wards could generate millions of additional pounds in profits. Importantly, the annuitant's neighborhood is *already something the annuity company knows:* it had to collect the customer's address, after all, in order to mail them the check. (Of course, the customer's own education is surely a better predictor of their life expectancy than the average education of their neighbors. But that is something that the insurer would have to make an effort to collect and verify, which is why Amy and Jim focused on the possibility of pricing based on publicly available data on characteristics of the neighborhood.)

Everything that Amy and Jim used to generate their mortality tables is freely available to the public. There were no laws against using information on an applicant's ward (or even data from narrower geographies that might allow for even more refined predictions) in setting annuity prices. Amy and Jim's work showed that insurers could increase profits by revising annuity contracts on the basis of this readily available and entirely legal-to-use data.

Why, then, were insurers effectively leaving money on the table?

Back in the 1700s, it was much easier to make the case that the failure to incorporate appropriate risk factors in pricing annuities and other selection-market products was because there were so many unknowns — actuarial science was still in its infancy. Indeed, it was only with the publication of Edmund Halley's death tables in 1693 that estimates of death rates for different age groups came into better resolution.[25] Amy and Jim's work emphasizes that there are data that we can all access on the internet that insurers can straightforwardly incorporate into contract pricing and make more money.

Economists assume that businesses maximize profits, a not-

—

unrealistic presumption. So what gives? Part of the issue, we suspect, has to do with basic notions of what is "fair" to price on. But, as we'll see, even if we could overcome these ethical concerns, it's not obvious that we (as economists, not ethicists!) would want insurers to price on everything they could—not because of "fairness" per se but because it destroys people's ability to buy insurance against being (or becoming) a bad risk, such as being born with a genetic disease or coming from a family of people who tend to die prematurely of heart attacks. If those conditions were priced, how could we buy insurance against being born unhealthy? The information is known at the time we are born (or even before, in the case of family history).

It's Not Fair! Pricing Edition

For centuries, people have grappled with the question of what constitutes a fair price for a seller to charge for their wares. At the risk of caricaturing a debate that goes back to Roman times, there are, roughly speaking, two views. There's the libertarian school of fairness, which says that if a seller is willing to sell and buyer willing to pay, by definition the price is fair—both parties to the transaction enter into it willingly. This roughly describes the view that most economists have about most markets.

Then there's the "just price" view, which sees an intrinsic value in a particular good or service and injustice in charging a higher price, even if there's a willing buyer on the other side of the transaction. As the thirteenth-century philosopher and theologian Thomas Aquinas put it, "to sell a thing for more than its worth, or to buy it for less than its worth, is in itself unjust and unlawful."[26]

Aquinas's argument raises the near-intractable question of what determines this fundamental value, if not customers' demands. And

—

if a good or service has an intrinsic or underlying value, how can it be that you paid $10 for your snow shovel in the summer and a neighbor paid $50 for the same type of snow shovel the day after a blizzard in February?

We're not going to come to any deep conclusion about who is right and what is and isn't fair—not because we think the question is uninteresting or unimportant; rather, it's a matter of what we in economics call *comparative advantage:* we leave questions of ethics and justice to moral philosophers, who are trained and more devoted to such questions.

But what is important for our purposes is that—whatever we or you believe is fair—people simply *hate* the idea that businesses charge different prices for exactly the same thing. Amazon, for example, once—and only once—tried to charge different prices on the same DVD titles back in 2000. Customers noticed and were sufficiently outraged that the experiment was abandoned within three days. CEO Jeff Bezos later called the company's foray into personalized pricing "a mistake," and Amazon—a famously data-obsessed company that knows a lot about you and your buying history—has pledged never to personalize the prices that online shoppers see on the site.[27]

It's indicative, we suspect, of why we see less personalized pricing—insurance or otherwise—than you might expect, given the ever more intimate details of our habits and preferences that companies glean from web-browsing behavior, cell-phone tracking, and data we often freely provide to any online vendor that asks. (Certainly some amount of personalized pricing is out there, as you'll know if you've ever discussed with your seatmate how much each of you paid for what is effectively the same product—say, a flight from Boston to L.A. You'll also know, if you have ever had that conversation, that

—

whoever paid more is not happy about it. We aren't saying that personalized pricing is nonexistent but, rather, that there's less than there "could" be given how much money is to be made from it.)

A now-classic study by Daniel Kahneman, Jack Knetsch, and Richard Thaler can help shed light on why.[28] Via a telephone survey, the authors presented several hundred respondents with hypothetical pricing decisions and asked whether a business had acted fairly. Their conclusion about what most people think about fair pricing isn't so far from Aquinas's thirteenth-century intuitions: a company's practices are seen as unfair if they exceed some "reference" price. Where does this reference price come from? Roughly speaking, it's what allows businesses to earn a reasonable (reference) level of profits.

If personalized pricing of DVDs raises tricky questions of fairness (and we assure you it does), a far thornier set of issues arises when you start to think about the various attributes that go into insurers' algorithms. Should Arlo Guthrie (whom we met in chapter 2) be penalized financially when he goes to buy life or health insurance because his dad had Huntington's disease and therefore there's a fifty-fifty chance he will too?[29] If someone is living on the wrong side of the tracks, should they be penalized with higher auto insurance rates than those offered to others with identical driving histories who live in nicer parts of town?

It's not that insurance companies want to stick it to the sick or the poor — it's simply more expensive to provide automobile insurance to a lower-income individual because odds are they live in a higher-crime neighborhood where there's a greater chance their car will be vandalized or stolen.[30] The explanation, while entirely logical, doesn't help to alleviate the sense of injustice when insurance rates are higher for people who are already struggling to make ends meet.

—

116

The same visceral "that's not fair" reactions seem to occur in the insurance-company setting as with Amazon's DVD debacle. Let's go back to the apparent mystery of why annuity contracts in the United Kingdom didn't account for neighborhood characteristics in pricing annuities, despite the fact that the data were available, legal to use, and relevant for pricing. It turns out that the answer is that, as with Amazon and its brief foray into personalized pricing, one British insurer did, in 2003, start to consider offering different contracts to applicants as a function of their postal codes. It created a furor! Amid newspaper headlines such as "Postcode Prejudice" in the *Sunday Times* and complaints about customers getting "ripped off" and "penalized" for looking after their health or living in wealthier neighborhoods, the insurer felt compelled to publicly disavow the rumors and to back off its plans.[31] (At least for a little bit. A few years later, several large insurers started pricing annuities by postal code. Evidently, they concluded that the extra profits were worth the public-relations headaches.)

What's even more striking about the "fairness" reaction to insurers' pricing on certain characteristics as compared to Amazon pricing DVDs based on a customer's browsing history is that survey evidence suggests that people *do* think it's okay for businesses to raise prices if their costs are higher. (This also fits with Aquinas's thirteenth-century notion of fairness.) For example, in Kahneman and his coauthors' classic study, survey respondents were presented with the following scenario: "Suppose that, due to a transportation mix-up, there is a local shortage of lettuce and the wholesale price has increased. A local grocer has bought the usual quantity of lettuce at a price that is 30 cents per head higher than normal. The grocer raises the price of lettuce to customers by 30 cents per head." Is the price increase fair? In this case, 79 percent of respondents think it is.[32]

—

We would have thought that the same reasoning that led to acceptance of the price hike on lettuce would also make it acceptable to charge accident-prone drivers more for their auto insurance – the higher prices are needed to let the company earn "fair" profits. It seems (to us) a bit of a puzzle that this doesn't seem to be the case.

What's in the Black Box Matters

Part of the answer may be that even if the public believes higher prices can be justified by higher costs, the public may have good reason to wonder whether that's what's really going on behind some insurer pricing decisions. One recent example illustrates why such skepticism may be warranted.

Pricing algorithms are often a black box – you type in your personal information and driving history, and out pops a set of prices for your automobile insurance. But in some states, these algorithms need government approval, which gives the public a glimpse inside the box. In 2013, Allstate planned to roll out a new automobile insurance rate-setting algorithm across the country.[33] In the state of Maryland, it had to file for permission to do so. The state requires that auto rates be "cost-based" – that is, it's fine to set higher prices for riskier drivers but not okay to charge more for other reasons. And when the state of Maryland reviewed Allstate's proposal, it found that Allstate didn't abide by those rules. Its algorithm, for example, would have given higher-than-warranted price increases to middle-aged customers than to the very young and very old – not because they were worse drivers but presumably because they were less price sensitive; that is, Allstate knew they were less apt to switch to another insurer even if their premiums went up.

An assessment by *Consumer Reports* and the public-interest

news organization The Markup described the proposal as a way for Allstate to generate "a suckers list of Maryland customers who were big spenders [to] squeeze more money out of them than others." While the state rejected Allstate's proposed pricing scheme, The Markup observed that the company used similar algorithms in at least ten other states. Often, regulators don't look inside the black box at all — New Mexico approved Allstate's algorithm without review — so it's hard to know how much a higher price results from a driver's riskiness and how much because the company's flagged them as a sucker.[34] Allstate's shenanigans make it clear that customers may have good reason to wonder whether insurers are also using their data to figure out whether they're suckers or spendthrifts in deciding how much to charge for a policy.

From Behind the Veil of Ignorance

As we already alluded to, there is another reason why we (as a society) might not want to allow insurance companies to price on certain customer attributes, even if they do reflect higher costs (and we can be confident that that's the reason for the higher price). It applies even if you (like us) are sympathetic to the economic logic that insurers need to charge higher prices for higher-cost customers in order to fight back against adverse selection and enable the market to work its wonders of efficiency.

It relates to a question that comes from the classic thought experiment set forth by the philosopher John Rawls in his famous 1971 treatise *A Theory of Justice*.[35] The thought experiment asks us to imagine stepping behind what Rawls calls "the veil of ignorance," which would obscure any idea we might have of our place in society — rich or poor; college educated or grade-school dropout;

family history of Huntington's or not. What principle of fairness would you adopt in the absence of any knowledge of who you are or your place in the world?

While philosophers consider this a question of fairness, some economists (and we plead guilty to this) have managed to think of it instead as a question about the efficient operation of insurance markets! Here, we're thinking about preserving the ability to buy insurance against being a high-risk type: for example, being born with a congenital disease or into a family with a history of health problems.

In a sense, you can think about the "veil of ignorance" exercise as embodying the ultimate insurance policy: Before you know anything about your future self or its circumstances, how much cushion do you want to have against the risk of being born unlucky? It's effectively asking how much insurance we should offer to every member of society from the day they're born and indeed even before. (In part because you can't buy insurance before you're born — at which point something is known about future risks — governments often provide what's called *social insurance,* which gives every member of society protection against financial hardships resulting from sickness, disability, unemployment, and other misfortunes.)

But if we allow insurers to constantly update their prices on the basis of a customer's current health status or circumstances, it means that, for example, a twenty-year-old can't insure against, say, the vulnerability to cancer that a future fifty-year-old self may uncover via a later-life colonoscopy. In other words, letting insurers price on *everything* they know about their customers can destroy the market for insurance against becoming a bad risk sometime in the future. That's one reason why it's not obvious to us as economists whether legal restrictions on pricing in insurance — such as limits on

—

requiring genetic testing to apply for health insurance — are bad policy, even if (as we will discuss in chapter 7) they make the insurance market at a snapshot in time work less well. In our example, customers with clear colonoscopy results will opt for less insurance, and those with concerning ones will keep their more generous coverage and drive up its price.

———

At the end of the day, whether because of technological limitations, fear of consumer backlash, or legal restrictions, our brief tour through insurance companies' attempts to collect information on their customers reveals that while it can help, it's not enough. In many cases — including automobile insurance for experienced drivers, life insurance, and annuities — customers end up with private information and use it in buying insurance. Adverse selection lives on.

Since insurance companies can't rely on better data to "solve" the problem of private information, there's money to be made by trying to find other ways of removing adverse selection from the marketplace. Businesses are well motivated to find them. If they can't — or won't — extract the last bit of private information from their customers, they'll try to trick their customers into revealing it themselves. Chapter 5 will show you how they do it.

Chapter 5

OPENING THE CHAMBER OF SECRETS

In Sir Arthur Conan Doyle's "A Scandal in Bohemia," the great nineteenth-century detective Sherlock Holmes is called upon by Wilhelm Gottsreich Sigismond von Ormstein, Grand Duke of Cassel-Felstein and King of Bohemia, to retrieve a scandalous photo in the possession of the "well-known adventuress" Irene Adler. The picture — of Wilhelm and Irene (scandalously) together — was taken during a brief fling between the King (then merely the Crown Prince) and Adler, at the time a singer with the Imperial Opera of Warsaw. The King, now engaged to a young Nordic princess who comes from a most proper family, fears that if his past indiscretion comes to light, the wedding will be called off. He has tried both the carrot and the stick, offering to pay for the photo and also sending his agents to try to retrieve it by other means. But Adler is resolute in her determination to hold onto the photograph and is too smart for the King's men. ("Twice burglars in my pay ransacked her house. Once we diverted her luggage when she travelled. Twice she has been waylaid. There has been no result.")[1]

The King comes to Holmes as a desperate, last resort (a com-

—

mon opening to many Sherlock Holmes stories). And how, in this case, does the brilliant detective triumph where others have failed? Holmes explains his simple strategy in advance to his faithful assistant and chronicler, Dr. Watson: "I will get her to show me." How on earth will he do that? wonders dear, faithful Watson, along with the reader, at this juncture in the story.[2]

The answer: he gets her to reveal her secret unwittingly, which is why we find ourselves recounting this particular Sherlock Holmes ruse in a book on insurance design. Much as Holmes "tricked" Adler into revealing her secret, getting potential customers to unwittingly reveal their private information about whether they're cheap or costly to serve is an essential tool in the insurer's tool kit and is the focus of this chapter.

Up until now, we've focused on what insurers can do to try to set prices based on their best guess of a prospective customer's cost — using what they can observe from, say, past traffic violations or a medical exam or what they can get their customer to tell them (such as family medical history). But as we've seen, this approach is limited by customers' willingness to truthfully supply the requested information and by insurers' ability (and sometimes also their willingness) to compel them to do so. It's the insurance equivalent of Holmes asking Adler where she hid the photo, which we already know she'll refuse to say. What's a real-world insurance company or a fictional sleuth to do to get someone to truthfully disclose information they have no desire to reveal?

In Holmes's case, the answer is stage a fake fire. He explains his thinking thus: "When a woman thinks that her house is on fire, her instinct is to at once rush to the thing which she values most. . . . Now it was clear to me that our lady of today had nothing in the house more precious to her than what we are in quest of. She would

—

rush to secure it." And indeed, Holmes doesn't miss his mark—that's exactly what happens. Adler, fearful that her home is soon to be engulfed in flames, rushes for the item she holds most dear, the photograph, which Holmes (trailing her) observes is ensconced "in a recess behind a sliding panel just above the right bell-pull."[3] Success! The scheme has its desired effect—Holmes has located the elusive photo.*

This chapter is about some of the ways that insurance companies can get customers to reveal their secrets, once they've collected all the information about the customer that they can. As we emphasized in chapter 4, getting better information isn't a panacea—even after insurance companies have found out all that they possibly (and legally) can, they often still can't fully distinguish the sick from the healthy and the careful from the reckless in picking their customers or setting their prices. In such cases, they need to get customers to sort *themselves*. No, they don't fake fires, but they do have the selection-market equivalent: designing insurance policies to appeal to the customers they want (i.e., the secretly low-cost customers) and to repel the ones they don't (the secretly high-cost ones).

---

* How exactly Holmes does this is naturally more involved, as he needs both to convince Adler that there's a real fire *and* to be present when she reacts in panic. To pull off the scheme, Holmes dresses up as an elderly clergyman (what could be less threatening?) and enters into the melee of young men fighting for the privilege of opening Miss Adler's carriage door (which apparently happens every single time the beautiful Miss Adler arrives on her street). Pretending to be struck in the scuffle and bleeding profusely from the head, Holmes is invited into Adler's home, where he asks to lie down in her sitting room and have the window opened for more air. The window opening is the cue for Watson to execute stage 2 of the plan, in which he throws a "smoke-rocket" into Adler's apartment and cries "fire!" with others on the street following his lead. There's also a surprise twist to the whole story, which we'll come back to in chapter 8. For those of you who can't wait—and even those of you who can—we recommend reading the original story.

These design tricks get the customers to reveal their secret—their cost type—in much the same way that Holmes got Adler to reveal her hiding place: with a cunning scheme that the customer may not even realize is exposing what they'd hoped to hide.

There are a lot of common insurance practices that you may have seen but not realized that this is why they exist. The minutiae of insurance contracts contain all sorts of restrictions and stipulations that can appear designed simply to save insurers from having to pay out a nickel more than what's necessary in claims, if indeed you can make any sense of the rules at all. But often these rules and regulations can be understood as businesses' attempts to mitigate selection problems by having customers effectively reveal who they are.

The reasons behind many of these tricks of the insurance trade are not always obvious (or only become so if you stop and think about them, which we rarely do). For example, dental insurance doesn't cover procedures that can be delayed or timed, to prevent enrollment just ahead of expensive operations. Waiting periods, as are required before roadside assistance kicks in, serves a similar purpose (though, as we saw in chapter 2, even a forty-eight-month wait before a new couple can claim a divorce payout wasn't enough to save that market). Then there are the offers of free gym memberships that come with some health insurance products and the "fine print" exclusions of certain risks from coverage under the policy.[4] Ever wondered why you can only buy health insurance in November? That'll be explained here too. Understanding the motivation behind these business practices is also essential to understanding what kinds of constraints governments can or should place on businesses in their efforts to make selection markets work better, a topic we'll turn to in part 3 of the book.

—

Getting Customers to Reveal
Who They Really Are

An urban legend that is famous among insurance aficionados (and surely no one else) is that of the health insurance company that deliberately chooses to place its sales office on the fifth floor of a walk-up building (i.e., a building with no elevator). The first (and, as far as we can tell, only) written record of the fabled walk-up insurance office is the 2001 Nobel Prize address by the economist Joseph Stiglitz, who won that prize — along with George Akerlof, whom we've met already in chapter 1 (and Michael Spence, whom we haven't) — in large part for his work on adverse selection in insurance markets.

As Stiglitz explained it in his Nobel lecture, the five flights of stairs would be a good way for insurers to deter the really sick from becoming their customers. While presumably most people would prefer not to trudge up the stairs to apply for insurance or to discuss a claim, it would be particularly unappealing to prospective customers who were sick or lazy. (Remember, this was 2001, back in the day before much could be done online.) Stiglitz observed that a wily insurance executive would "realize that by locating [the office] on the fifth floor of a walk-up building, only those with a strong heart would apply."[5] The company might even be willing to pay extra for the privilege of renting this inconvenient locale precisely because of its benefit in screening out undesirable customers. (Stiglitz also noted that a truly astute insurance CEO would recognize the trade-off between locating high enough to keep away undesirables but not so high as to discourage too many others. The second floor probably wouldn't be enough, but the tenth would surely be overkill.)

Stiglitz's example is surely apocryphal — not to mention now ineffective in the world of online insurance purchases. But something

—

that closely approximates this made-up example does exist and is in fact quite common in the real world of health insurance offerings. Think of stair climbing and insurance as offered as a bundle – you're buying insurance, but it comes with a free side of stair climbing. Why not, instead, offer insurance that's bundled with something that customers see as a free benefit rather than an extra cost to be endured? One that might be appreciated by all but particularly by the low-cost customer you're trying to attract?

This is why some health insurers offer to throw in free (or subsidized) gym membership along with your health insurance policy. Of course, insurers typically describe the offer as a way to make it easier for their customers to stay fit and thus out of the doctor's office. There may be some truth to that (then again, as we'll see shortly, there may not be). But what *is* clear is that these types of benefits can be a way for an insurer to attract and retain the good customers.

This evidence comes from a type of health insurance plans known as "Medicare Advantage" plans. We'll encounter them in more detail in chapter 7. But for now, it's enough to know that, under Medicare Advantage, private insurers get a payment for each customer that varies based on some characteristics of the customer that can be observed and that are predictive of health costs – like their age and their medical history.[6] At this point of the book, it should come as no surprise that would-be customers are still left with a lot of private information about their likely future health-care costs. Private insurers offering Advantage plans would like to attract the ones who – among those of a given age with a given health history – are the healthiest.

So one thing these private insurers often do is include – and heavily advertise – free gym memberships as part of their plans. Why? Because they hope that by offering free gym access, they'll attract

—

healthy customers; sicker ones presumably find a gym membership less of a perk.

Their approach seems to work as intended, according to a small-scale but convincing study by two public-health researchers, Alicia Cooper and Amal Trivedi.[7] They looked at how the customer base changed in a few Medicare Advantage plans that added fitness-club memberships to their list of benefits. Specifically, they examined the self-reported health of a random sample of each plan's members, based on a survey that the government administers each year. Cooper and Trivedi's headline finding was that the share of seniors enrolled in these plans who reported themselves to be in very good or excellent health — as opposed to good, fair, or poor health — rose substantially between 2004 (before the free membership was thrown in) and 2005 (after the plans started offering free membership). This suggested that once the gym membership was added, the plan attracted members who were healthier (or who at least thought they were healthier), exactly as intended.

Of course, you might worry that maybe there was just a general improvement in the health of senior citizens around 2005, and that's all Cooper and Trivedi were picking up. Fortunately, Cooper and Trivedi thought of that: they compared changes in self-reported health among enrollees in the health plans that added free gym memberships between 2004 and 2005 to changes in self-reported health in similar, "control" plans that had no fitness benefit in either 2004 or 2005. For control plans that didn't add fitness memberships, the share of enrollees reporting very good or excellent health increased by just 1.5 percentage points, significantly less than the 6 percentage-point increase they found for the plans that added fitness memberships. Other results were even more striking: the fraction of enrollees who reported having difficulty walking dropped from

33 to 25 percent in plans that added fitness benefits; for control plans, the fraction was virtually unchanged, at around 32 percent.

If you're wondering why there were plans to serve as controls, given the apparent improvements in enrollee selection that came with free fitness memberships, Cooper and Trivedi suggest an explanation: the control plans may not have initially gotten the memo, but eventually they did. Cooper and Trivedi find that among all 101 Medicare Advantage plans that were offered continuously from 2002 to 2008, the number offering free fitness memberships more than quadrupled over those six years, from 14 in 2002 to 58 in 2008. And the numbers have kept climbing: By 2020, the fraction of Medicare Advantage enrollees with fitness benefits was up to 74 percent.[8]

One potential issue that Cooper and Trivedi didn't think of — or at least didn't have a way to deal with — is that they could only measure plan participants' healthiness *after* they had enrolled in their plans. It's possible, therefore, that the free gym access worked wonders on seniors' wellness, getting them off their couches and also feeling better about themselves (and thus more likely to say that they were healthy in their survey responses). In other words, maybe the plans offering fitness benefits didn't *attract* healthier enrollees but *created* healthier enrollees by getting them to work out at the gym.

Maybe . . . but if gym-going New Year's resolutions are any indication, it seems a stretch to imagine that gym subsidies turn couch potatoes into fitness enthusiasts. If you're looking for more concrete evidence that gym memberships attract the healthy rather than making them healthier, we can offer that as well, based on the work of economists Damon Jones, David Molitor, and Julian Reif.[9] The team created a new workplace wellness program for employees at the University of Illinois at Urbana-Champaign (where both

—

Molitor and Reif work), to analyze who enrolls and what effect enrollment had on the university's workers. The so-called iThrive program offered eligible employees a range of health-related services including on-site health screenings, online health risk assessments, and a variety of wellness activities, such as smoking-cessation programs, in-person classes about chronic disease management and weight management, and recreational athletic classes. The researchers recruited almost five thousand employees and randomly assigned them either to a control group, which didn't have access to iThrive, or a treatment group that did. They tracked the participants for the next two years in the university's employment records and through biometric health screenings and surveys.

The study made quite a splash with its headline nonresult: employees who were randomly invited to participate in iThrive did not show any improvement in health behaviors, health, or work attendance, relative to the randomly selected control employees who were not given the option. But the researchers also found evidence that, despite not improving employees' health, employers might want to offer wellness programs anyway, as a way to attract healthier employees. Specifically, they found that among the employees offered the workplace wellness program, the ones who chose to participate were *already* healthier—with lower health-care costs and healthier behaviors when the study began—than those who chose not to enroll.

A free gym membership may be a less prominent perk for a new job, relative to a health insurance plan. But the authors' results do raise the possibility that employers might design various inducements to attract healthier employees rather than to help their employees to be their healthiest selves. It certainly suggests another angle to the fabled on-site massages and Kombucha-on-tap that

—

deep-pocketed Silicon Valley firms use to attract coddled millennial software engineers (with healthy lifestyles); they seem designed to appeal most to employees who will take the fewest sick days and have the lowest chance of needing medical care that would be charged to their (also gold-plated) insurance plans.[10]

Making a Product That Customers Hate

Free gym memberships – whatever their ultimate purpose – are a nice perk. Many of the ways insurance companies try to make sure they get the "right" customers are less appealing. Indeed, Stiglitz's apocryphal health insurance company, strategically located on the fifth floor of a walk-up building, captures a crucial feature of many of the real-life examples we discuss in the rest of this chapter: in order to keep away high-cost or riskier customers, an insurance company often has to make its offerings worse for everyone – not only for the high-cost people it is trying to avoid but also for the low-cost customers whom it would like to attract.

We emphasized in chapter 1 that one key problem with adverse selection is that low-cost individuals who would still benefit from having insurance are unable to buy it at a price that reflects their risk (and hence their cost to the insurer). Now we're going to highlight another critical way in which selection interferes with markets doing the job of providing customers with quality products at a decent price: those who *do* get insurance may be buying something that's twisted and distorted in all kinds of ways that make it less desirable. In the apocryphal fifth-floor-walk-up example, stair climbing is unappealing to almost everyone (after all, most people take the elevator or escalator to the gym, even if they're headed there to make use of its stair-climbing machines). But the insurer still finds it worthwhile to "damage" its product in this way because the stairs are particularly tough on people with chronic health problems.*

Indeed, insurers, for better or worse, have more of a reputation for never paying up, rather than sweetening their offerings with perks like gym passes. It can sometimes seem to undermine the whole point of insurance in the first place, what with all the deductibles, exclusions, and other fine print. Just ask one of literature's greatest losers, Willy Loman.

Arthur Miller's classic Pulitzer Prize–winning play *Death of a Salesman* is traditionally viewed as an exploration of loss of identity in a changing economic world. It centers on the failed life and early death of the traveling salesman Willy Loman. Willy clings to a vision

---

* Intentionally offering substandard products is a standard trick for separating "good" from "bad" customers. In a normal market, in which everyone costs the same to serve, good customers are the ones who are willing to pay a lot, and bad ones are the ones who are unable or unwilling to pay a steep price. The French economist and engineer Jules Dupuit explained that this could account for the hard benches and lack of roof in third-class train carriages, despite the very low cost of providing cushion and cover – the discomfort of third class was necessary to get better-off travelers to pay a premium for higher-class travel. As he observed in 1849, "It is not because of the several thousand francs which they would have to spend to cover the third class wagons or to upholster the benches that a particular railway has uncovered carriages and wooden benches; it would happily sacrifice this for the sake of its popularity. Its goal is to stop the traveler who can pay for the second-class trip from going third class. It hurts the poor not because it wants them to personally suffer, but to scare the rich. The proof is that if today the State were to say to this railroad: here are one hundred thousand francs to improve your carriages, this subsidy would be certainly refused. . . . Improving the third class carriages could reduce revenues by two million francs and ruin the company." Jules Dupuit, *De l'influence des péages sur l'utilité des voies de communication* (1849), quoted in Rakesh V. Vohra, *Prices and Quantities: Fundamentals of Microeconomics* (Cambridge: Cambridge University Press, 2020), 55.

—

of the American Dream in which being well liked (not just liked but *well* liked) brings success in business and family life. But nothing works out for him. He's a terrible salesman. His older son, Biff, despite some promise as a high school football star, drops out of college and drifts from job to job. He sees Willy as a loser, whose big talk is nothing but a delusion. (The audience is primed to see Willy that way too, starting from Miller's not-so-subtle naming choice, Low-Man.)

We, of course, remember this classic mostly for the plot device of Willy's life insurance contract. As the story progresses, the walls close in on Willy. He loses his job; he can't keep up with payments on his car, his refrigerator, or anything else. Near the play's end, Willy has an imagined conversation with his now-dead but far more successful older brother, Ben, about how to make things right. Willy explains, "A man can't go out the way he came in, Ben, a man has got to add up to something." He sees salvation in his life insurance policy, which he tells Ben is "a guaranteed twenty-thousand dollar proposition." By ending his own life, he can finally provide for the needs of his long-suffering wife and redeem himself in the eyes of his son. The imaginary Ben, while seeing the merits of Willy's proposition, cautions that the insurance company "might not honor the policy." Willy is indignant, telling his brother, "How can they dare refuse? Didn't I work like a coolie to meet every premium on the nose? And now they don't pay off? Impossible!"[11]

The play's "Requiem" takes place at Willy's funeral, which is attended by only his wife, sons, and next-door neighbor (rather than the hundreds he imagines in his reverie with Ben). His son Biff still disdains him. Although we never learn what happens with the insurance policy, there's a decent chance that the imagined Ben was

—

right to be skeptical that the $20,000 payout was guaranteed: Suicide exclusion clauses (or at least suicide waiting periods) are near ubiquitous in life insurance.*

The Lomans (and the audience) might well see this exclusion as yet another way in which The System crushes The Low-Man — here by the fine print that saves the insurer from having to pay up on the policy Willy paid into for all those years. And there's surely some truth to that. But these exclusions also serve another purpose: they are one of the ways that insurers try to keep away the wrong types of customers — like the ones who plan on ending their own lives — even if they can't identify these customers directly. Willy's policy probably had a murder exclusion, for similar reasons.

That is, one way to keep away "bad" customers is to refuse to pay for the things that make a customer expensive in the first place and that they might already be aware of when purchasing insurance. That might include suicide in life insurance or the high-priced medications or expensive roof repairs that an undesirable customer may know they're likely to have in the near future when buying health or homeowner's insurance. When you think of insurance contracts in these terms, you can start to see a lot of the fine print as designed to keep expensive customers from signing up in the first place, rather than just offering ways for insurance adjusters to stick it to their

---

* One way that fact departs from fiction, however, is that suicide exclusions only apply toward the beginning of a policy — to deter people who buy the policy at the same time that they're planning to kill themselves (or to murder the person for whom they are buying the policy). In the play, Willy tells us that he'd been paying his premiums for years, so perhaps he *was* covered after all. Gary Schuman, "Suicide and the Life Insurance Contract: Was the Insured Sane or Insane? That Is the Question — Or Is It?," *Tort and Insurance Law Journal* 28 (1993): 745–77.

customers who file claims. (It's likely that the fine print serves both purposes.)

One example is related to the exclusion we have already encountered of certain zip codes and occupations from health insurance coverage in the early 1980s at the start of the AIDS epidemic. By the late 1980s, pharmaceutical companies were finally coming up with ways of treating the disease, most notably with the introduction of the breakthrough drug AZT. But insurers often excluded it from coverage. This was not only because of its very high price tag — at $8,000 per year, it was then the most expensive prescription drug in history (although it has long since lost that title). Excluding AZT from coverage also kept away customers who might be at risk of getting HIV/AIDS, and thus of having much-higher medical claims, not only due to drug costs.[12]

Waiting for Insurance

There's a middle ground between offering insurance with so few restrictions that high-cost types bankrupt the company and having so many exclusions as to strip a policy of its insurance value. Instead of outright exclusions, waiting periods are a common way of making policies less attractive to those who know they have hard-to-observe expensive claims in the near future. Since few can see very far into their futures with any certainty, a wait of even a few months or years may be enough to keep selection at bay.

For those harder-to-discern risks, waiting periods are a common way of making policies less attractive to those who know they have hard-to-observe expensive claims in their near futures.

The suicide "waiting period" clause is a case in point. Since the

1950s, it's been part of any life insurance contract and is one of various contractual features that companies use to make sure the wrong types of people don't become their customers.* If you have a life insurance policy, go get it and read the fine print. If insurers find out you lied about your heart condition or family history, they can cancel the contract. If your hobbies include bungee jumping or skydiving and that leads to an early demise, your heirs won't get a penny unless you've disclosed these pastimes in your initial application (in which case your premiums will be way higher). If you die robbing a bank (or otherwise doing anything illegal), again, the company doesn't need to pay up.† And if you kill yourself soon after buying the policy, that's excludable too.

Suicides are typically excluded from coverage during an initial "contestable" period of a year or, more likely, two.[13] In fact, some life policies don't allow for any payout whatsoever in the first two years — a more general waiting period can deter anyone with foreknowledge of their imminent demise, whether by suicide or natural causes. (Recall, for example, Richard Martin from chapter 2, the first life insurance policyholder on record, who died within a year of signing his contract.)

---

* *Death of a Salesman* was first published in 1949; suicide exclusions were already common but became more standardized and regulated in the 1950s. Samuel Hsin-yu Tseng, "Three Essays on Empirical Applications of Contract Theory" (University of Chicago, 2006); Gary Schuman, "Suicide and the Life Insurance Contract: Was the Insured Sane or Insane? That Is the Question — Or Is It?," *Tort and Insurance Law Journal* 28 (1993): 745–77; Leland T. Waggoner, *The Life Insurance Policy Contract,* ed. Harry Krueger (Boston: Little, Brown, 1953).

† This can lead to some cases that one might think constitute a fair claim but are nonetheless contestable. Imagine that a homicidal maniac chases you down the street, and you smash a neighbor's window and jump inside to evade your pursuer. If you meet an early end on your neighbor's property, you were breaking and entering and hence ineligible to collect on a life policy.

Amy's husband, Ben, offers a more contemporary example on how waiting periods keep bad customers away. Living in Cambridge, Massachusetts, during graduate school, Ben knew that if his car ever broke down, he'd want coverage for a long-distance tow to get his car to his trusted family mechanic located in his childhood town about forty miles away. But he figured he would wait until he actually *needed* the tow before signing up for the more expensive coverage. Ben thus found himself one day calling his insurer from the side of the road to try to upgrade to a policy that would cover the tow truck he was about to call. Ben was a bad customer (although, Amy notes, a pretty good husband). And his insurer was ready with the auto insurance equivalent of the fifth-floor walk-up — a one-week waiting period before any changes to his roadside assistance plan kicked in.[14]

Waiting periods are common for many types of insurance. You may recall the hapless entrepreneurs we also met in chapter 2 whose business plans for divorce and unemployment insurance ended up succumbing to adverse selection — they had tried to stave it off by imposing waiting periods (four years in the case of divorce insurance, six months in the case of unemployment insurance). That was the right idea, but unfortunately in these cases, the forces of selection were too strong. In many other cases, though, they may be just what the doctor (or dentist) ordered for keeping the market alive.

Dental plans, for example, typically cover preventive care immediately but often have a three- to six-month waiting period for treating cavities and other basic procedures and an even longer waiting period (sometimes up to a year) for major dental work. The goal, of course, is to try to prevent people from waiting to buy dental insurance until they need a cavity filled. Pet health insurance often has similar waiting periods at the start of a policy.[15] For some conditions, such as injuries, the waiting period may only be a week or two, just to make sure that you don't wait till Rover gets hit by a car before signing up. In other cases, though, the waiting period can be as long as a year — such as for hip dysplasia for large dogs. That's because it can be a hereditary or congenital condition, and again, the insurer wants to discourage pet owners who discover that their pandemic puppy has hip problems from trying to immediately "insure" them.

For human health insurance, waiting periods take a slightly different form but one that you're probably familiar with: so-called open enrollment periods. During open enrollment (usually a few weeks in the fall), you're forced to pick the health plan that you'll need to stick with for the next year. This annual rite of health insurance selection is precisely to try to prevent you from waiting till you get a diagnosis of hepatitis C along with a prescription for Sovaldi (current price for a full treatment: $28,000) before signing up for gold-plated coverage. (Interestingly, health insurance for *pets* has the more traditional form of waiting periods: you can buy the insurance whenever you want, but coverage does not begin immediately.)

These "solutions" to selection are not without their shortcomings. Some risks that most of us would like to hedge against can't be insured — unanticipated deaths occur within two years of signing up for life insurance, along with anticipated ones. A life insurance policy with a two-year waiting period doesn't protect you from unanticipated demise, but is necessary to protect the insurer against the anticipated kind. Moreover, like pricing-based solutions, waiting periods may be helpful in dealing with selection, but they don't make the problem go away completely.

Some of the evidence on the limits to waiting periods as a solution to selection comes from work on the suicide exclusion periods in life insurance that we've already discussed. Samuel Hsin-yu Tseng's

PhD dissertation looked at causes of death for life insurance policy-holders in the early 1990s across the United States. He found that, sadly, suicides quadrupled among policyholders after the two-year exclusion expires. (A similar study in Japan—where life insurance policies tend to have a one-year suicide exclusion—found that the monthly suicide rate rose by 50 percent in the month immediately following the suicide exclusion period.)[16] So just like the fifth-floor walk-up, the suicide clause isn't foolproof—weak-hearted patients may struggle up the steps to secure a health plan that's cheap enough (because it's targeting healthy customers), and some profoundly depressed individuals may nonetheless patiently wait out the exclusion before acting on their intentions.

Tseng also suggests another means—also costly—of getting around the exclusion without waiting for years: in many cases, cause of death is ambiguous. High-speed car crashes, pedestrian fatalities, and drug overdoses might have been inadvertent or intentional—in the absence of a suicide note or other smoking gun, it's hard to say. A coroner who doesn't want to add to the anguish of a grieving family may record a questionable death as accidental, in which case the life policy gets paid out. While Tseng can't point to any individual case as a miscoded suicide, he observes that accidental deaths decline after suicide exclusions end, exactly when suicidal deaths jump up. He estimates that about a third of accidental-death claims were probably disguised suicides.

Amy can also provide a pointer, based on her own experience, on getting around waiting periods in health insurance. If you're planning on having kids, get pregnant in the early fall. Most insurers let customers switch plans once a year, generally in November or December, so a September pregnancy provides ample time to switch to a health plan that offers the best and most flexible options for child-

—

birth. When Amy found out in October that she was expecting a baby in July, she made sure to upgrade to an insurance plan that let her deliver at the hospital of her choice.

Locking In Good Customers

Amy's insurer could have prevented her from switching plans by locking her into a multiyear (or at least multi-nine-month) contract. In fact, if you think about Amy's little ruse, it seems like a longer-term commitment to a health insurance contract could have been good for her insurer — making sure she doesn't switch to a more generous health insurance plan when she learns she's about to be more expensive. And it could have been good for her too. A longer-term contract could help the customer, since it ties the hands of insurers that would want to ratchet up prices (or cut back benefits) once they learn that your health has taken a turn for the worse. You can think about a longer commitment on both sides as acting as insurance against an unfavorable turn of events. If we take this logic to its extreme, maybe the best insurance you can have is to sign a contract at birth (or even earlier) before anyone knows whether someone is careful or reckless, healthy or sickly — in short, cheap or costly to cover. That would protect the buyer from what is known as "reclassification risk" — the risk of getting reclassified as a bad (i.e., costly) customer and hence charged a higher rate.

Of course, newborns don't sign insurance contracts, and most twenty-year-olds we know don't think much about the health problems that their fifty-year-old selves might have. (And if they did, they'd probably be hopelessly overoptimistic. A classic study, aptly titled "Unrealistic Optimism about Future Life Events," found that

---

about two-thirds of college students thought they were more likely to live past eighty than their classmates were.)[17]

Besides, circumstances change for reasons unrelated to health: families move, jobs change, and so do preferences – how much risk one might stomach, for example, may be very different in middle age than in college. So consumers themselves probably wouldn't want to be locked into an immutable lifetime contract, and no law would enforce such an agreement in any event. Once we allow consumers to break their contracts, we're back to the world in which selection matters, because people who turn out to be particularly healthy will find that, by shopping around for other options, they're bound to find better deals.

There's a lot of room, though, between one-year contracts (which seem common enough) and lifetime commitments. As with all of the other "solutions" to selection, contract length might offer a partial fix. Just pick a point somewhere between day-to-day – in which customers sign up exactly when they need an expensive procedure – and forever, in which there's no selection at all. At some point in that continuum, selection presumably gets less and less severe. We know this is true not just in theory but also in practice, based on the analysis of dental insurance from Marika Cabral, whom we already met in chapter 2.[18]

Recall that Cabral studied the dental insurance policies of Alcoa employees and found that, when employees switched to more generous coverage (a $2,000 annual spending cap on their insurance claims rather than $1,000 cap), their claims were higher in the first part of the following year. In other words, when people realized they needed expensive but delayable procedures, they put them off until the following year, when they could enroll in the higher-coverage plan.

We revisit Cabral's work here because of another fortuitous (from a research perspective) feature of Alcoa's employee-compensation design: in 2005, conveniently in the middle of her data, the company shifted its dental-coverage options from a one-year to two-year coverage period. Cabral found that with the two-year contracts, there was less of the type of pernicious selection described earlier. You might be able to delay that root canal or implant by a couple of months to allow for more generous dental coverage to kick in. But it'd be ill advised if instead the wait were a couple of years.

Cabral argues that the contract length makes a big difference to the functioning of Alcoa's dental insurance "market" overall. She estimates that, if the company didn't subsidize dental coverage and contracts were annual, the market for more generous coverage would unravel almost completely, with prices so high that they would be attractive only to employees with awful dental problems, about 5 percent of them. But if the contract length increased to two years, there would be fewer problems of employees enrolling only when they already knew they needed dental work. As a result, costs, and therefore also premiums, would go down. By Cabral's calculations, the price drop would be enough to more than double enrollment. Extrapolating outward (well beyond the maximum contract period in her data), she predicts enrollment of nearly 40 percent if employees were locked into five-year plans.

So, longer contract periods do help. But even five-year contracts generate enrollment that is very, very far short of the theoretically possible 100 percent enrollment if we all signed on for a lifetime dental contract at birth, neither a contract that we can commit to nor one that can be enforced by law.

One way out of this box is to broaden our notion of "contracts" from legal contracts — what our readers probably think of first when

—

they hear the term "contract" – to social contracts: an implicit agreement within a society on the rights and obligations of its members. If we take this broader view of what might constitute an insurance contract, it's possible to conceive of tight-knit groups and extended families as insurance policies that last a lifetime and beyond – group or family members who are born unlucky or unhealthy are supported by the rest of the group. Ran Abramitzky, an economic historian, describes the intergenerational commitment of joining a kibbutz – the collectivist communities founded by Jewish settlers in what is now the State of Israel – in exactly these terms.[19]

Historically, kibbutzim have had very strong – and explicit – social contracts, which dictate that output is shared equally among their members. Abramitzky argues that this kind of extreme egalitarianism acts as a form of insurance – whether your kids are stupid or smart, lazy or productive, they'll be well taken care of by other members of the kibbutz. What about the good "types" – the smart and productive kids who are forced to support the less able? Just as healthier policyholders might opt out of medical coverage, what's to stop the high achievers from opting out of the social contract, perhaps moving to Tel Aviv to seek their individual fortunes?

To be clear, it does happen, so that a kibbutz can unravel in exactly the same way as an insurance market. Partly what holds it together is the strong ideological commitment that kibbutz members cultivate in their offspring, so that the fit and smart remain to contribute to the common good. But, Abramitzky argues, another important part of the "social glue" is that the kibbutz members had no private property – all their assets were locked up in the kibbutz, which made it pretty unappealing to strike out on their own, even if they were smart and productive. Indeed, he finds that when the value of their assets collapsed in the early 1980s as a result of a worsening

Israeli economy, suddenly many of the kibbutzim started to unravel, since there was nothing that kept more productive members financially tethered to their community.

Up-Front Commitment to Insurance

Short of running off to join a kibbutz, what are we to do? And short of setting up for-profit kibbutzim, what else might insurance companies offer that extracts something that approximates a longer-term commitment from its customers? It turns out that insurance companies and kibbutzim have more in common than you (or we) might have thought — insurers also try to get their members to fork over some of their assets, to decrease the temptation to renege on a long-term commitment. It's perhaps for this reason that *Wirecutter* advises pet owners to buy their pet health insurance when their pet is young, in order to lock in good rates before they find out that Fluffy has a bad back.[20]

Beyond advice from *Wirecutter*, a lot of what we know about the role of long-term commitment in trying to prevent selection in insurance comes from a study by the economists Igal Hendel and Alessandro Lizzeri.[21] Hendel and Lizzeri start with the observation we made earlier: it's not practical to write a very long-term insurance contract. For one thing, as they note, from a legal perspective, a company can be legally bound to insure its beneficiaries at an agreed-on price with agreed-on coverage into the indefinite future, but its customers can't be legally required to continue to uphold their end of the bargain — that is, to continue to pay premiums. Moreover, we would argue, even if it were legally enforceable, it would be difficult to execute in practice. Is it really practical for an insurance company to pursue a client who refuses to pay their premiums? How's the

—

company going to make the customer pay? (We'll revisit these types of issues in chapter 6, when we discuss the difficulties the government has enforcing insurance mandates.)

Since an insurer cannot force its customers to keep paying premiums year after year, the customer may switch companies if another company offers more favorable terms. In particular, if the customer learns that they're healthier than they thought, they'll go get a better deal from a new company, leaving the original provider stuck with only the "bad" — that is, sick — customers.

Hendel and Lizzeri suggest that this is why life insurance companies often try to front-load premiums — they have customers pay more in earlier years of the contract than the customer's mortality risk warrants and less in later years. Because once you've prepaid a bunch of your premiums, it's less tempting to switch to a new company.

To see this more concretely, consider two healthy forty-year-olds — let's call them Walter and Bart — who, as they start to worry about providing for their young families, each buy $100,000 life insurance policies with a $2,500 annual premium from the Pacific All Risk Insurance Company. The $2,500 premium reflects the *average* cost of covering both the unlucky policyholders — those who die earlier than expected and cost the company $100,000 after paying just a few premiums — and the healthier ones as well, who pay more than $100,000 in premiums by living beyond age eighty. (By paying $2,500 every year, living beyond eighty translates into more than forty premium payments, which exceeds the $100,000 life insurance payout.)

Let's now revisit Walter and Bart, five years down the road. Walter is as healthy as ever, while Bart finds, when he goes in for a checkup, that he has clogged arteries, diabetes, and a bum knee. If Pacific were able, it would drop Bart's coverage and hold onto Walter (and keep taking his $2,500 premiums). What actually happens is the opposite: Walter finds that if he shops around, he will find insurers willing to undercut Pacific's premiums for the same $100,000 payout. Pacific can either choose to meet their offers or lose Walter to a competitor. Pacific is stuck with Bart, however, who may expire long before making enough payments to cover the $100,000 check that Pacific will pay his descendants once he dies.

As Walter and Bart illustrate, the customers who stay with their contracts are exactly those who no one else wants because they've turned out to be a bad bet for Pacific. So Pacific doesn't want to commit to covering either of them in the first place. Absent some other fix, there will be no long-term contracts for life insurance, and we're back to the world of year-to-year contracts that don't provide much protection from life's misfortunes.

One solution is to front-load the coverage costs for the buyers — as a way of locking them into a relationship that they can, in theory, walk away from. In effect, it shifts a one-sided commitment into a relationship in which both sides are motivated to stay together, no matter what they learn about themselves or each other. You can think about this up-front payment itself as a form of insurance against future contingencies that affect whether the insurer wants to change the contract.

Again, this is all a bit abstract, so let's continue with the case of Bart, Walter, and Pacific All Risk Insurance. Let's say that Pacific offers Walter and Bart a contract in which, instead of constant annual payments, each pays $20,000 initially and $2,000 per year thereafter. Let's say both find this to be roughly as attractive as the contract that had a $2,500 annual premium, and both sign up.

Consider now the forty-five-year-old Walter and Bart, one

healthy and the other very unwell. Sickly Bart's still getting a great deal from Pacific, expecting to pay only a few more premiums before he goes off to meet his maker. What of healthy Walter? If the contract has been well designed, he'll also still be happy enough to stick to his contract. Any insurer now hoping to lure him away would have to offer Walter a $2,000 premium, rather than merely needing to undercut the $2,500 premium in the earlier case. If the up-front cost were high enough (and the stream of annual payments sufficiently low), even the healthiest customers can't get poached by competitors. Forty-five-year-old Walter may regret that his forty-year-old self paid $20,000 up front to Pacific back when he didn't know he was destined to live a longer life than his friend Bart—but that's the nature of insurance: you pay to protect against a downside risk, and if you're lucky, you never need to use it.

Like all the "solutions" we've discussed so far, this one isn't perfect either. In the extreme, customers would pay all their premiums up front and pay nothing thereafter. In practice, it's not hard to see why that doesn't happen. Ask yourself, for example, how responsive the insurer's customer-service line will be if there is exactly zero benefit to the company from keeping its customers happy. So once again, we find ourselves with a partway solution, asking people to pay some but not all premiums up front. This solves just some of the selection problem, but not all.

———

So where does this leave us? In a bit of a bind. On the one hand, there are lots of ways businesses can try to mitigate selection problems—even after having exhausted their ability to collect information on the customer to use in pricing. But these "solutions" come with their own problems: lack of coverage when you might legitimately need it for an expensive drug, suicide, and so forth. So selection problems remain, for a product that offers less insurance than customers might want. Can the guiding hand of government help? This is what we now turn to.

PART III
ENTER THE GOVERNMENT

Chapter 6

EAT YOUR BROCCOLI!

In March 2012, the Supreme Court passed judgment on whether one of the most contentious policies for selection markets in U.S. history was legal. The so-called individual mandate under the Affordable Care Act (ACA, or "Obamacare," as it became known) required that every American purchase at least basic health insurance coverage by 2014. Failure to do so carried a penalty of $285 per family or 1 percent of family income – whichever was higher – rising to over $2,000 or 2.5 percent of family income after the mandate had been in place for two years.[1]

The mandate's rationale was noted in the ACA's original text as a way of ensuring that the law would "minimize . . . adverse selection and broaden the health insurance risk pool to include healthy individuals, which will lower health insurance premiums."[2] It went on to note that the mandate was essential for sustaining health insurance markets, especially given that the law was going to require that insurers sell to everyone, regardless of preexisting conditions. That is, if the government wanted to ensure that all Americans could

—

get coverage, whatever their preexisting medical conditions, a mandate would be needed to short-circuit the adverse-selection death spiral. This was music to our professorial ears — someone must be listening! The analysis is exactly what we would teach in a course covering public policy for insurance markets threatened with adverse selection (as health insurance markets surely are; see chapter 2).

Rather than discussing adverse selection, however, the Supreme Court justices' debate focused on broccoli. Most famously, the arch-originalist Justice Antonin Scalia asked, essentially, what was next in the slippery slope of mandates: If the government could force Americans to buy health care, couldn't they also be forced to buy broccoli? The government's lawyer, Donald Verrilli, responded that health care was different from broccoli, for all the reasons we've discussed. (From the liberal wing of the court, Justice Stephen Breyer chimed in as well with all the weight of his judicial gravitas, urging his fellow justices not to get distracted by "a matter that . . . has nothing to do with this case: broccoli. Okay?")[3] But this argument didn't stick, and whatever the fate of the individual mandate, broccoli won the day: the decision written by Chief Justice John Roberts, along with the dissents from Scalia and his fellow conservatives (and also a partial dissent from the left flank by Ruth Bader Ginsberg) mentioned broccoli no less than a dozen times. Adverse selection is mentioned just once in passing.*

---

* In case you're wondering what all the broccoli fuss was about, the debate that consumed the court focused on the argument that, regardless of insurance status, we all need medical attention at some point. Those who choose to forgo health coverage will still receive care, which, odds are, the rest of us will pay for as hospitals ratchet up prices to cover the expense of treating the uninsured. Thus, supporters of the mandate argued, those who choose not to participate in the insurance market effectively pass their cost of care onto everyone else. But, Roberts countered, the same argument might apply to broc-

The emphasis on broccoli rather than information asymmetries surely owes itself to the evocative image of the nanny state literally forcing its citizens to eat its vegetables.* But it also may be because the ideas that we've aimed to convey in our book are subtle ones: while Scalia and his fellow justices surely grasped the fundamentals of asymmetric information and unraveling, they may not have fully appreciated their central relevance to the functioning of markets in which selection plays a crucial role.

The preceding chapters highlighted the various ways that businesses confront selection problems. One repeated refrain was that businesses could offer only partial solutions to the selection problem. This raises the question of whether the government, which gets to set the rules that determine how markets operate, can make insurance markets more equitable or efficient.

Forcing everyone to participate—like the Obamacare health insurance mandate or the requirement that all drivers have auto insurance—is the most straightforward way of stopping an adverse-selection death spiral before it ever gets started. But beyond the principled concerns of keep-the-government-out-of-my-business libertarians, this commonly proposed solution has its own problems. At the top of the list is the question of whether (or how) the mandate

---

coli, since those who don't eat their leafy green vegetables are also destined to burden society with the costs of caring for the vitamin-deficient and infirm.

*In a commentary on the ruling in the *New Yorker*, Adam Gopnik observed that the basic problem was that none of the justices knew how to cook broccoli properly. If they had, they would understand that the government need not force any American to eat broccoli. Rather, officials would simply need to explain that it must be roasted or pureed ("in the French style") rather than eaten steamed or raw, in which case the public would *demand* government-mandated broccoli. Adam Gopnik, "'The Broccoli Horrible': A Culinary-Legal Dissent," *New Yorker*, June 28, 2012, https://www.newyorker.com/news/news-desk/the-broccoli-horrible-a-culinary-legal-dissent.

is actually enforced; as any parent of a small child knows all too well, saying "Eat your broccoli!" at dinner doesn't necessarily make it so. And what exactly is to be mandated? Everyone may be forced to have health insurance, but what counts as health insurance? What has to be covered? If there are minimalist requirements, there may as well be no mandate at all: we get the insurance-market equivalent of a wily toddler eating the tiniest of broccoli morsels and then saying, "See, I ate it!" And different people might legitimately want different things. Insurance product options may be limited by government edicts on what constitutes adequate coverage (if you wish to stretch the toddler metaphor, a truly cunning response might be, "Why can't I get my vitamin K from brussels sprouts!").

The fact that it's complicated doesn't mean we should revert to eat-your-vegetables rhetorical flourishes. Rather, it requires that we do the harder work of understanding how government regulations impact adverse selection, as a first step in understanding how best to design the rules for insurance markets.

To do so, in this chapter, we'll look more closely at the motivations for and consequences of policies that aim to alleviate selection problems. We'll focus on the two main prescriptions. One is the mandate we've already mentioned. We'll also consider whether it makes sense for the government to subsidize part of the costs of coverage in order to entice people to get insured. In chapter 7, we'll consider government policies motivated by privacy or equity concerns, motivations that are entirely distinct from selection problems but that can nonetheless have unintended and sometimes devastating effects on the functioning of selection markets. That doesn't mean these policies are unwise; rather, we need to be aware of the trade-offs they invoke if we're to set policies wisely.

—

A Mandate for Mandates

In George Akerlof's classic 1970 "Lemons" study that launched the academic study of adverse selection and won him a Nobel Prize (and which we discussed in chapter 1), Akerlof focused on health insurance as one of his key examples.[4] Absent a requirement to be insured, he argued, sick customers (lemons) would flock to the market for health insurance, driving up prices for healthy individuals, who would then opt out of buying coverage. (Recall also from chapter 1 why this is so concerning: those healthy but uninsured customers really would benefit from insurance against unexpected medical costs, but they don't want it at a price that reflects the much higher health-care costs of the [sicker] lemons.) Akerlof gave a shout-out to Medicare — what was then a brand-new compulsory public health insurance program for the elderly. He argued that this type of mandate was exactly what the doctor ordered to fix the adverse-selection problem in health insurance.

It is this sort of reasoning that led most economists, including ourselves, to the intuition that mandates are the best and most straightforward solution to selection problems. From this perspective, the health insurance mandate in the 2010 Affordable Care Act offered *the* canonical approach to addressing selection. Indeed, it was one that was well anticipated by economists as much as a century before.

In 1916, the American Association for Labor Legislation, a Progressive-era organization of labor leaders and economists, published a brief urging state governments to adopt compulsory health insurance for wage earners. The brief explains that making health coverage compulsory was essential for including the young and healthy. Otherwise, an insurance program would "find itself burdened by the increasing claims of its members as they advance in age. It is then compelled to raise the contribution. This high rate, however, fails to attract young members, so that the society may eventually be forced into insolvency and fail to meet its obligations. Compulsory insurance, with a definite guarantee that each carrier will have its share of the young men and women just coming into insurance, presents a different situation."[5]

In other words, nearly a hundred years before the health insurance mandate in Obamacare and over fifty years before the Nobel Prize–winning academic work on the subject, proponents of a mandate already understood the basics of an insurance death spiral, as well as the role of compulsory insurance as a way to avoid it. The Progressives didn't get their way, however, and as even the most casual student of U.S. history knows, a requirement that everyone buy health insurance had to wait for quite a while.

When it finally arrived in the early twenty-first century, we learned two things. First, mandates work in exactly the way George Akerlof had predicted: they substantially reduce selection problems, a win for economic theory (and for combating adverse selection in an important market). Second, the world we live in turns out to be more complicated than our academic models anticipated: mandates aren't a panacea. This forced us to rethink what we mean by a mandate when abstract theory meets real-world policy.

Mass Mandates

The Obama administration wasn't the first government in the United States to mandate that everyone have health coverage. That distinction goes to President Obama's onetime political adversary Mitt Romney. Romney's 2006 health insurance reform when he was the Republican governor of Massachusetts served as the model for the subsequent 2010 Obamacare legislation.[6]

"Romneycare," as it was later termed, included a mandate that every Massachusetts resident have health insurance. What happened as a result of this mandate was exactly what Akerlof's model predicted: the mandate brought healthier individuals into the insurance market.

This was nicely illustrated in a 2011 analysis of the early days of Romneycare by a trio of Massachusetts-based health economists, Amitabh Chandra, Jonathan Gruber, and Robin McKnight.[7] The study looks at a program in Massachusetts (currently called Connector-Care), which offers subsidized health insurance for lower-income enrollees. ConnectorCare was set up in 2007 as part of the suite of health insurance reforms Romney undertook.

The particular way in which ConnectorCare was rolled out made it possible for the researchers to study the impact of the mandate, as distinct from other features of the new program. While Connector-Care opened for business in May 2007, the mandate didn't kick in until July, and the financial penalty for noncompliance with the mandate wasn't in place until December 2007. This made it possible to compare who signed up for health insurance when it wasn't mandated yet (May and June 2007) to who signed up once the mandate was fully in effect (the period after December 2007).

Luckily for us (and the researchers), the state government collected data on the health characteristics and subsequent insurance claims of all program enrollees. (This is why we're talking about Massachusetts rather than the United States overall—this type of data is not readily available for studying the nationwide mandate that came in with Obamacare.)

The data lined up nicely with the predictions of a simple selec-

—

tion model: the first wave of ConnectorCare enrollees, who signed up before they were required to have insurance, were the sickest. Enrollees in the pre-mandate period were forty-five years old on average, and about 36 percent had been diagnosed with a chronic illness requiring steady (and costly) treatment, like high blood pressure or arthritis. By contrast, once the mandate was fully in place, the average age of new enrollees dropped to forty-one years, and only 24 percent had a chronic illness diagnosis. There was a corresponding drop in the average monthly health-care spending and insurance claims of enrollees, from $518 per month in the pre-mandate enrollment period to $356 per month once the mandate was in place. This is a big deal from the perspective of selection and market unraveling: the mandate and its penalty brought customers into the ConnectorCare market whose medical expenses were more than 30 percent lower than those who chose to get insurance without a mandate.* As we said already, a win for Akerlof's theory!

"Stop! Or I'll . . . Say Stop Again"

The Massachusetts experience also illustrates, however, the challenges of defining what it means to have a mandate in the real world. We described a period from May 2007 through December 2007 when the mandate was "in effect" but without any penalty for noncompliance. You may not even have noticed (we slipped it in), but it turns out to be really important. For it raises the question: What

---

* As the authors of the study observe, it is possible that less healthy people, eager for insurance, jump at the opportunity to get coverage early on, so that as time passes, the people who overcome their inertia and sign up are healthier and healthier. However, one can see a very clear jump—particularly among those without chronic illness—at the exact date when the full mandate goes into effect, arguing against the "slow drift" hypothesis.

does it mean to require that people do something if you don't punish them at all if they don't?

Or there is the more general question: What does it mean to "mandate" that everyone has insurance? Again, the inevitable rejoinder to "Eat your broccoli" or any other parental directive is some version of "And what if I don't? You can't make me!" (and also, as we'll get to, the question from budding attorneys of exactly how much will fulfill their broccoli-eating obligations). Parents have lots of ways to try to make our kids do what we want: cajoling, threatening, and (maybe) punishing them. The government has similarly limited instruments at their disposal, which means that getting people to comply with an insurance mandate sometimes can feel about as successful as the average parent trying to get their toddler to eat their vegetables.

This point was driven home in the "broccoli" decision penned by Chief Justice Roberts.[8] He saved the crucial (from an adverse-selection standpoint) mandate in Obamacare by calling the requirement that every American get insurance a tax rather than a mandate. That is, he argued, the government has the constitutional right to levy taxes on people if they don't buy health insurance, even though it lacks the power of coercion — that is, it can't "mandate" insurance coverage. However, because the government can't use strong-arm tactics, the penalty (or should we say "tax") for failing to get insured can't be arbitrarily high. A billion-dollar-a-year tax on those who don't have health insurance wouldn't have cut it with the chief justice — a penalty that steep amounts in practice to coercion and is thus impermissible. Then again, if the penalty were arbitrarily low — a penny, for example — there would effectively be no mandate at all.

The legal mandate to get health insurance under Obamacare thus ended up a lot weaker than, say, the legal mandate not to drive at ninety miles an hour on the interstate. Sure, the first time you're caught speeding, an officer in a generous mood might "downcode" it to a $20 fine for failing to obey traffic signs. At that point, the speed limit does seem more like a tax than a mandate. After a few more run-ins with the highway patrol, the consequences will be elevated first to a $250 ticket—still a tax, albeit a steeper one—then a license suspension. If you don't stop speeding or indeed are caught driving at all, the fines just keep going up. The fines may be accompanied by jail time that, by your fifth offense, is as much as a year, which sounds pretty coercive to us, at least compared to a small financial penalty (tax) for not buying health insurance.[9]

The effectiveness of a mandate can depend on the stiffness of the penalty for flouting the mandate. Swiss citizens who fail to sign up for insurance coverage will, after a few reminders, be signed up for coverage and charged premiums both going forward and retro-actively. Thanks in large part to this ruthless enforcement, coverage is just about 100 percent, despite the absence of any public insur-ance option. By contrast, if there's a minimalist penalty (or meager enforcement of it), there may as well be no mandate at all. It's rem-iniscent of a classic Robin Williams line about the ineffectiveness of British police. Bobbies, as cops are called in England, do not carry guns. As a result, Williams deadpanned, the most intimidating threat an officer can make is yelling, "Stop! Or I'll . . . say stop again!"[10]

We can again turn to Massachusetts to see how the size of the penalty matters. In the Massachusetts mandate study we described earlier, the authors also looked at the "phase-in" period of July through November 2007, when there was a legal requirement to get insurance but no financial penalty if you didn't. They compared the enrollees from this "in-between" period to people who signed up before the mandate was in effect (May and June 2007) and after it was fully in effect in the sense that it was both required and there was a financial penalty for noncompliance (December 2007 and later). During the "phase-in" period, some relatively healthy people enrolled who hadn't done so in May and June, before the mandate phase-in began. For some people, evidently, it's enough for the government simply to tell them to do something, and they'll do it.

But a mandate without teeth didn't work for most people: the big jump in ConnectorCare sign-up didn't come until December 2007, when the penalty went into effect. Sign-ups nearly tripled relative to the previous month and brought in even healthier enrollees relative to the no-penalty phase-in period. (In case you think a "mandate with no financial penalty" was just a quirky and temporary blip during ConnectorCare's phase-in, think again. In 2019, the Trump administration removed all financial penalties for not complying with the Obamacare "mandate" for health insurance.[11] It's as if Britain's bobbies now threaten criminals by yelling, "Stop! Or I'll . . . do nothing.")

Even *with* a penalty (a fine of as much as $1,100 in 2010 for the highest earners), the Massachusetts mandate didn't get everyone to sign up for insurance. In 2010, Massachusetts did have the lowest rate of uninsured in the United States, with only 5 percent of residents lacking insurance – 5 percent uninsured is low, but it's not zero. And it's less impressive than it might sound once you realize that, even before Romneycare came into being, only 11 percent of state residents lacked health coverage, again the lowest rate in the United States. So while the mandate and penalty definitely moved the needle, it didn't drive the uninsured rate to zero. (If Romney had really wanted to get the rate of uninsured all the way down to zero, he might have taken a cue from Switzerland and upped the punishment, though we imagine that a Swiss-style penalty wouldn't fly in the United States.)[12]

And the Massachusetts mandate is one of the more successful ones. Other states have fared worse in implementing the federal mandate for health insurance that came subsequently in 2014 under Obamacare. Although the mandate was upheld by the Supreme Court, rates of uninsured are still extremely high in parts of the country. Intriguingly, the state with the highest premiums in 2018 was Wyoming, which also had nearly four times as many uninsured residents per capita as in Massachusetts that year. Massachusetts — with the lowest rate of uninsured — also had health insurance premiums that were, by some measure, the lowest.[13] This is exactly as we'd predict if the healthiest, cheapest-to-cover residents of Wyoming are the ones who are choosing to opt out of coverage. (Of course, there are many other differences between the two states and other factors that might contribute to differences in both premiums and rates of uninsured.) That is, states with weak incentives for everyone to get insured ended up with selection problems among those who did, which in turn resulted in high insurance premiums; in states that had stronger sign-up incentives, the vicious cycle of lower insurance enrollment and negative selection never got started.

One "solution" to enforcing a mandate is for the government to take over and provide insurance directly, financing it out of taxes it collects on businesses and individuals — including many of the very same people who benefit from insurance coverage. Then there's no issue of "enforcing" the mandate. This is exactly how the government provides universal hospital insurance to the elderly through Medicare.[14]

We said that the government providing insurance directly was only a "solution" to the problems with mandates. It too is not a panacea. While it deals with a mandate's enforcement problems, it still leaves open the question of exactly what coverage is mandated. (It also brings up other issues like the costs and benefits of the government getting into the insurance business, rather than individual insurance providers like Aetna and Blue Cross. But that, as they say, is a story for another day, or at least a question for another chapter. We'll return to this question a bit in chapter 8.)

The Goldilocks Problem of Insurance

Up to this point, we've described a mandate as a directive to purchase something we've generically labeled "insurance." Given that we spent a lot of time in chapter 5 describing the various contractual schemes that companies deploy in designing their insurance policies to address selection problems, you might already have realized that this is a bit too much of an abstraction when we start to think about what a policy maker must consider in practice.

In practice, when the government imposes an insurance mandate, it has the job of defining what it means to "have insurance" under this mandate. In other words, the government must decide what constitutes a minimally acceptable plan. "Minimally acceptable" under Obamacare, for example, was the ominous-sounding "catastrophic" coverage, which focused, as the name implies, on shielding enrollees from the financial catastrophe that comes with unexpected and costly illness. These plans cover preventive care like immunization vaccines, breast-cancer screenings, and a few checkups with your doctor—treatments that hopefully lead to better health and lower medical expenses in the long run. Other than that, the plan pays for nothing until you hit the rather substantial deductible, which in 2020 was $8,150.*

The law required that states provide up to five predefined levels of coverage, so available options went all the way from catastrophic coverage up to gold-plated (or, should we say, platinum-plated) "Platinum" coverage, which paid for 90 percent of any medical-eligible expense.

Obamacare *could* have mandated a minimum of Bronze coverage, the level just above catastrophic that at least paid for 60 percent of all medical costs. Or it might have had an even weaker mandate by offering, say, "cataclysmic" coverage that only paid for expenses after the patient had paid even more out of their own pocket than is required under catastrophic coverage (and which presumably could therefore be purchased at an appropriately discounted price). As we'll see, the choice of how minimal is minimal and the resulting gap between the least and most generous options matters a lot for whether government-mandated insurance helps at all with selection problems or makes them even worse.

As Daedalus warned his son, it is dangerous to fly either too close or too far from the sun. Or for readers whose tastes in literature don't run in the direction of Ovid's *Metamorphoses,* think of Goldi-

---

* We should note that the catastrophic plan is exactly what we, as economists, would say is closest to what insurance *should* be, at least for enrollees with reasonably high incomes. The point of insurance isn't to pay your doctor's bill every time you get a checkup but rather to provide protection from financial hardship when expensive and unexpected costs arise — say, an acute appendicitis that requires urgent removal at a cost of $25,000. A catastrophic plan that requires you to pay everything up to some level and covers everything above that provides exactly this protection. Centers for Medicare and Medicaid Services, "How to Buy a Catastrophic Health Insurance Plan," accessed November 2, 2020, https://www.healthcare.gov/choose-a-plan/catastrophic-health -plans/.

---

locks and the Three Bears: the little girl tastes one bowl of porridge that is too hot and one that is too cold, before finding one that is "just right."

This Insurance Coverage Is Too Little . . .

We can see the minimalist approach in Florida's auto insurance mandate. The state requires only that drivers get $10,000 in property-damage liability coverage to pay for repairs to someone else's car or other property caused by an at-fault driver and $10,000 in personal-injury protection to cover hospital bills for the policyholder and their passengers. It *doesn't* require that drivers have bodily-injury liability coverage, which would pay the medical costs of others who are injured if a driver is at fault in an accident;* Florida is the only state in the Union without this requirement. Nor does Florida require so-called underinsurance coverage — which would pay your own medical expenses if you're hit by a driver who lacks the aforementioned bodily-injury coverage.[15] If you go to any major insurers' websites, they'll nonetheless recommend that you buy both bodily-injury coverage and underinsurance coverage, even though they aren't mandated. Indeed, this is the default on their Florida insurance webpages; go to many Florida injury lawyers' websites, and you'll get strongly worded advice to do the same.

The problem with a minimalist mandate like Florida's is if the minimum requirement is set too low, it's as if there's no mandate at all. You can end up with selection problems for the optional add-ons

---

* If you have a drunk-driving conviction, Florida will then require you to have bodily-injury insurance going forward. That strikes us as a bit too little and a bit too late in terms of mandated coverage. Mark Fitzpatrick, "Cost of SR-22 & FR-44 Insurance in Florida and How Coverage Works," Value-Penguin, March 5, 2021, https://www.valuepenguin.com/car-insurance/sr22-fr44-florida.

that are purchased mainly by higher-cost enrollees. In other words, if the point of the mandate is to solve the adverse-selection problem but the mandate requirement is minimal, the proverbial can has just been kicked down the road — the selection problem is merely shifted to the market for meaningful (i.e., more than the mandated minimum) insurance.

This is exactly what we saw happen in the health insurance mandate in many states under Obamacare, given the gaping distance separating lowest- and highest-end coverage. It's easy to imagine that exactly the same people who wouldn't have wanted to buy insurance at all will enroll in the lowest-cost, least-coverage option required — the catastrophic plans or maybe the Bronze ones. The high-cost, sick enrollees will be the ones who are more likely to buy the more comprehensive coverage you get with Gold or Platinum plans, pushing up premiums and driving the healthy into the less generous options. (Remember why this is a problem: many of those healthy individuals might prefer the choice and peace of mind that comes with Gold or Platinum — and would be willing to pay more for this higher coverage — but only if "paying more" meant paying a modest premium above a healthy person's expected claims, rather than a modest premium above a sick person's expenses.)

You don't, in fact, need to use your imagination. You can see it in the health-care expenses of real-life Obamacare enrollees. Thanks to a study of California's insurance market in the economist Pietro Tebaldi's PhD dissertation, we have information on medical claims of participants in that state's health insurance exchange.[16] As you progress from catastrophic up to Platinum, the medical insurance claims of enrollees increase steadily. Most strikingly, Platinum-plan enrollees incur annual medical claims that are $9,000 on average, nearly double that of enrollees in the Gold plan, one level down. We wouldn't expect nearly so wide a gap if Platinum enrollees weren't sicker to begin with. As with everything in life, there are trade-offs – a range of plans gives Californians a range of insurance choices, so they can pick the one that best suits their preferences. But with choice, there is selection – and all the problems that go along with it.

This Insurance Coverage Is Too Much . . .

Let's now turn to the other extreme, of mandating too much coverage. We can see this also in auto insurance, if we travel up the Eastern Seaboard from Florida to Maine. Whereas Florida has no mandated bodily-injury auto insurance, Maine requires $50,000-per-person coverage, equaled only by Alaska's mandate and nearly 70 percent more than the next-highest states. Exactly the same is true for under-insurance coverage – Florida requires none, while Maine's minimum of $50,000 is at least $20,000 more than the minimum in every other state.[17]

Why do we care if Maine's regulators want the state's drivers to be insured to the hilt? Because it may be requiring more insurance than most Mainers need or want – in other words, more than they would buy in a world without adverse selection. One "tell" would be if every resident of Maine chose to get the minimum and nothing more – if that were the case, odds are that most drivers would opt for at least a little less insurance if given the chance.

We don't have access to Maine's insurance records to check. But we have our suspicions. We also have examples from other settings of the government mandating more insurance than many or even most of its citizens seem to want: up until 2015, the British government required that all of its subjects put at least 25 percent of their tax-preferred retirement savings into annuities.[18] This is equivalent to requiring that at least 25 percent of any retirement savings in an IRA or a 401(k) be annuitized upon retirement. (Recall that annuities—which we discussed in chapter 3—are the opposite of life insurance: they pay out every month until you die. So they insure against "living too long"—and running out of resources in retirement.)

It's a policy that should limit the problem of retirement annuities becoming dominated by long-lived Brits, who would thus start the inexorable cycle of higher prices and a shrinking pool of ever-healthier annuitants, a problem we documented in chapter 3. However, it also turned out to be more annuities than really anyone in the United Kingdom wanted—after annuitization was no longer compulsory in 2015, participation in the market dropped by about 75 percent.[19]

So What Is "Just Right"?

The "just right" mandate is a balancing act between too harsh and too lenient, too much and too little. If the mandate is for too little coverage, we risk ending up in a world that's a close approximation to the free market, with no mandate at all and the resulting selection problems. The problem of the uninsured is replaced by its close relative, the problem of the underinsured. Anything above the mandated coverage will suffer from the usual selection problems. As a result, lower-risk individuals—who could still greatly benefit from the security that a comprehensive insurance policy can provide—may instead opt only for the barebones, mandated coverage.

If the mandate is for too much, selection is no longer the concern. Now everyone gets plenty of coverage. The problem is that some may get too much coverage. Too much security may sound like an odd problem, like too much of a good thing. But that's only until you remember that although many of the best things in life may be free, insurance isn't one of them. (Here we find ourselves in unlikely agreement with Coco Chanel, who is reputed to have said, "The best things in life are free. The second-best things are very, very, expensive.")

Someone has to pay for the mandated insurance. It may be the customer — as in the case of mandatory automobile insurance. Which means they have less money to buy other things they'd like. Sure, they like insurance and the security it buys. But at some point, enough is enough; they'd rather save some money for a nicer car. And since people may want to strike that trade-off differently — they have different budgets and perhaps different views on what they want to do with that budget — a too-expansive mandate can force some (or possibly many) customers to buy more security than they would like. It may be the taxpayer who pays for the mandated insurance, as in the case of government-funded mandatory Medicare coverage. But that too comes at a cost — the cost of higher taxes or less government resources to devote to other things like, say, building roads or hiring more teachers. That's why "require everyone to have gold-plated, comprehensive insurance" isn't a panacea either.

So what is this elusive Goldilocks level of coverage? We'd love to end this little section with a magic formula that would spit out the exact penalty and minimum coverage that would offer the perfect, "Baby Bear" compromise. Of course, we can't. Getting porridge the right temperature for one little girl is a lot easier than figuring out the "right" amount of insurance to set as a mandate for health or auto coverage or anything else.

One reason why we rely on abstractions like Akerlof's classic lemons model is to strip the world to its simplest and most salient features, in this case to illustrate how a death spiral can occur and how, in the abstract, a mandate can straightforwardly fix the problem.

—

When we move from abstraction to practice, it's valuable for policy makers to appreciate the basic insights of the stripped-down model. It's just as important, however, to account for the details and complexities of the trade-offs that arise in implementing something as seemingly straightforward as a mandate. Regulators in Florida and Maine reached very different conclusions on how to set a mandate. Each presumably came to the question with different values and preconceived notions of how much interventions a market requires. We don't aim to sway them in one direction or the other—rather, we hope to highlight the trade-offs they've made and perhaps even some ways of diagnosing whether they've erred too much in either direction.

Helping Those Who Need It the Least

Pablo Escobar famously (or rather infamously) offered Colombian cops and government officials a choice between "plata o plomo"—silver or lead.[20] Most needed little or no persuading to select a suitcase crammed with hundred-dollar bills over the alternative of a bullet to the head.

Governments also give carrots and sticks to encourage or discourage all sorts of behaviors. Just as policy makers can pick and choose what types of medical care have to be covered to satisfy a mandate that everyone has health insurance coverage, they can pick and choose specific behaviors to penalize via fines or to reward via subsidies.

In encouraging desired behaviors, there's generally the possibility of a stick—in our case, the "sign up or else" threat of a mandate penalty—and also a carrot. For insurance sign-up, the carrot involves subsidies to make sign-up cheaper and thus more attractive. We'll

—

see that, like Escobar's ultimatum, in insurance policy, both carrots and sticks can be available to the same person at the same time in order to encourage them to make the "right" choices from society's perspective.

A subsidy, in its simplest form, isn't really any different from a penalty (or a "tax") for not complying with a mandate. One is a carrot and the other a stick, but both nudge everyone in the direction of wanting to buy insurance (just as Escobar's carrot and stick both nudged Colombian cops toward ignoring his smuggling operations). One reason why the Obamacare insurance exchanges have survived the disappearance of financial penalties is that government subsidies live on, so that even relatively healthy people still find it worthwhile to get insured.

We saw the selection effects of the stick when the Massachu-setts mandate penalty kicked in—more people enrolled to avoid the penalty, and they were healthier than earlier enrollees from the pre-penalty era. And we can also see that the carrot has similar conse-quences—in Massachusetts and in other states. When the govern-ment subsidizes health insurance, the people who sign up in response tend to be healthier.[21]

Moreover, there's no reason why the carrot (or, for that mat-ter, the stick) need be the same for everyone. Maybe we should give higher subsidies to people most in need, like the elderly and infirm, for whom health insurance is probably most expensive. Maybe. But sometimes the best of all feasible policies for helping the elderly and the sick is actually to subsidize the young and the healthy.

If that sounds confusing, it's because it is. It's a subtle and, yes, counterintuitive argument. So bear with us as we first explain why it *might* be a good idea in theory and then show you that there's evidence to suggest that subsidizing the young and healthy may

—

actually help the elderly and sick in practice. Fair warning: the material that comes next may be tough going. Those who want to can safely skip ahead to the last section of this chapter.

Why might it be a good idea to subsidize the youngest and fittest — who also tend to be better off financially than the elderly and infirm — even if your main objective is to help the least-well-off members of society? The basic idea is that a subsidy directed at healthier individuals may attract enough healthy, lower-cost individuals that the sick will benefit from lower premiums. If sufficient numbers of healthier individuals are enticed to sign up, that can reduce average insurance claims for the full set of market participants, which brings premiums down as a result. This may mean that the best way to help some of the sickest, neediest cases may be not to subsidize *their* insurance but to direct the subsidies at the healthy, to "bribe" them to participate in the market, and thus lower insurance costs overall.

We know . . . it sounds strange. Try telling people suffering from high-cost conditions like multiple sclerosis or diabetes that, rather than helping them pay for their own insurance, we're instead, "for their own good," going to give subsidies to their perfectly healthy neighbors. It's like the parental cliché of telling kids that they're getting punished for their own good. Parents keep saying it because they believe it's true. Those who are on the receiving end might be forgiven for feeling differently.

Hopefully, a relatively simple hypothetical example can help clarify. We're going to make some extreme assumptions, as theoretical economists are often wont to do in service of illustrating an idea. For those who don't like these kind of numerical abstractions (or theoretical economics more generally) and prefer to focus simply on the here and now, just skip ahead to the big reveal at the end of this section (helpfully foregrounded with a flashy "Ta da!"). We've al-

Table 1.

	Healthy	Sick
Expected expenses	$60	$100
Value to customer	$70	$150

ready given you the basic intuition, and you won't be any worse off for skipping the details if they're not your cup of tea.

Imagine that the world consists of equal numbers of two kinds of people: people who are healthy and people who are sick. Healthy people can expect about $60 of medical costs each month; sick people can expect about $100. However, this is just what they expect *on average*. Sometimes a healthy person gets the flu or trips and breaks a leg, racking up much-higher medical expenses as a result. Sometimes a sick person manages to go a whole month without needing any care, and sometimes they have a really, really bad month and end up with much higher than expected medical bills. That's why *both* individuals would like to buy insurance and are even willing to pay more than their expected monthly costs. As we discussed in chapter 1 when we gave the example of the accident-prone teenage driver and the never-even-got-a-speeding-ticket middle-aged mom, both are willing to pay more for insurance than they expect to get back in payouts.

We've summarized the numbers in table 1. Both healthy and sick are willing to pay more than their expected expenses for insurance – the healthy folks are willing to pay up to $70 (even though on average they have only $60 of expenses), and the sick are willing to pay up to $150 (even though their expected expenses are only $100).

In other words, everyone would want to buy insurance if they were charged the "right" price given their type: in each case, the value

—

173

of insurance to the customer is higher than the total cost of coverage. The sicker, higher-cost types anticipate monthly expenses of $100, whereas once you add in the certainty and peace of mind that insurance provides, they'd be happy to pay as much as $150. There's $50 in value to be created. There is a similar value-creation opportunity for healthy customers also, since they're willing to pay $10 more for policies than it will cost the insurer to provide coverage.

However, if an insurer can't discern which of its customers are healthy and which are sick, only the very sick will get insurance. Imagine, for example, that insurers charged a low-enough price to attract both types of customers, say, $65. They would attract both healthy and sick customers. Although they'd average $5 of profits on each healthy customer (since on average they only have $60 of medical expenses), they'd suffer average losses of $35 on each sick customer, who average $100 in costs. That's not a risky business; that's a bad business.

Suppose now that insurers *can* discern who is sick and who isn't, but the government forces insurers to charge a single price for all comers. (If we've been doing a good job so far, you probably think this sounds ill advised from the perspective of a selection market, and we certainly don't disagree. But, as we'll discuss in chapter 7, there are other good reasons that a government may want to have a one-price policy: most obviously, one price is fair, in the sense that no one is penalized for being born sick or disabled.) This is roughly what the Obamacare regulations impose on the plans offered via its exchanges. This rule makes the insurers' problem effectively no different from a world in which insurers can't see anything about their customers at all — in both cases, it's impossible to tailor prices to individuals' circumstances.

In this case, the insurer's only option (if it doesn't want to go broke) is to price insurance above $100 so as to attract only the sick types—who cost on average $100—and make some money. This is bad for the healthy individuals; they are priced out of the market and aren't able to get coverage even though they value insurance and are willing to pay more than the cost of covering them. It's the standard adverse-selection problem we've seen since the very opening pages, when we discussed American Airlines' introduction of the AAirpass and the residents of West Hollywood in the 1980s.

But since you've made it all the way to chapter 6, hold onto your seats while we show you what you'd learn in an Advanced Placement class on selection markets (if only there were one). In order to illustrate our counterintuitive result that the sick might be better off if the government subsidized health insurance for the healthy, we're going to throw in one further assumption, albeit one that plausibly reflects real-life circumstance: we'll assume that no one can afford monthly premiums above $80, regardless of the coverage that gets them, since at the end of the day, everyone needs to buy food and shelter and keep the heat on as well. (The sickest individuals tend to also be the poorest, so this assumption may be particularly plausible for this group.)

Now what do we expect to see? There's no point in offering any contract at a price above $80, since no one can afford it. And offering insurance at a price of just $80 will attract only the sick and lose money. Even setting the price at $70 won't solve the insurer's problem—it will now attract the healthy customers as well, but as we've already seen, the losses from the sick customers will more than offset any profits from healthy customers. In our (overly) stylized example, the combination of limited financial resources and selection problems makes the market dry up completely.

Here's where the rabbit comes out of the hat. Suppose the government, seeing that this market can't survive on its own, steps in to shore up the insurance exchange with subsidies. What will happen if it gives a subsidy of $10 to anyone who enrolls? It's now possible for insurers to offer a contract with an $80 premium: armed with a $10 subsidy, healthy customers will enroll (since the premium of $70 is something they're willing to pay), as will the very sick. And insurers are willing to offer this contract because the $20-per-customer losses from paying the medical bills for the very sick ($100) is offset by the $20-per-customer profits after paying the medical bills of the healthy ($60).

Notice, however, that the subsidy to the very sick is a giveaway — they would have enthusiastically signed on even without the $10 bonus. It puts more money in the pockets of the sick and frail, who might well need the extra cash. But it doesn't in any way affect the workings of the health insurance market.

And it's possible that a government might not have deep-enough pockets to subsidize everyone. If it can only afford a subsidy of $10 to one group, who should get it? (Remember, it's possible to observe who is sick and who is healthy, but, as in the Obamacare exchanges, customers must all be charged the same price by the insurer.) Your immediate reaction might be to give the money to people with the greatest need, that is, the very sick. But that wouldn't actually do much of anything: insurers would still need to drop their prices to $70 to attract healthy customers. At that price, the very sick also want to buy, thus making the business of selling insurance un-profitable. That is, the $10 subsidy to the sick does nothing at all, since no one offers insurance for sale, no one buys it, and no one gets a subsidy. What if the $10 subsidy is only available to the healthy customers? Now we're back to the case in which insurers can profitably offer coverage for $80, with healthy and sick customers each choosing to get insurance.

There's a feature of this example that's kind of amazing—the very sick benefit more from a subsidy to healthier customers than they do from a direct subsidy to themselves: the sick-person subsidy isn't enough to stem market unraveling, so they never even get to use their subsidy. Moreover, the $10 subsidy for the healthy customers doesn't actually help these healthier customers: their $10 subsidy translates into prices that are $70 for them—so they are paying exactly how much coverage is worth to them. Finally, the $10 subsidy for the sick also doesn't help the insurer, which earns just barely enough to stay afloat. The benefits all go to the sickest customers, who get an $80 insurance policy for $80, for which, if they were able to afford it, they'd be willing to pay $150.

Ta da! Now you see that the sick should *want* the government to subsidize not them but the healthy customers. Hmmm (we hear you mutter), we must have rigged the model to deliver the bizarre result that the best way to help the sick is to subsidize the healthy. Guilty as charged. We did indeed "imagine a world . . ." that delivered the result that we aimed to illustrate. But we did so in the hopes of making clear (or at least clear*er*) how this bizarre result could in fact be true in an imagined world built on assumptions that aren't entirely unreasonable.

Once again, though, you don't have to just imagine this possibility. There's evidence that this is going on in real life. One example comes from Tebaldi's dissertation on the California health insurance exchange, which we have already briefly encountered.[22] His analysis showed that the simple model we just sketched fits the data from California in two important ways. First, young people tend to have low insurance claims—no surprise there. Second, their insurance purchase decisions are very sensitive to price, more so, in fact, than those of older people. What that means is that a subsidy directed exclusively at young people brings in both customers who have lower costs and also ones who are attracted in relatively large numbers by even small discounts. When businesses can expand their sales by charging just a little less, it's worth it for them to cut prices— the higher sales volume more than offsets the lower profits they make off each customer. By making the insurance pool both lower cost *and* more sensitive to prices, a subsidy to the young would trigger price cuts from insurers that benefit all of their customers. Tebaldi shows that the young-person subsidy in fact benefits the elderly even more than an old-person subsidy would, in line with what we saw in the much-simplified description of an insurance market in our example.

Matthew Panhans conducted a similar analysis of the Colorado health insurance exchange in his PhD dissertation.[23] (Adverse selection in the Obamacare marketplaces was clearly a popular topic for budding health economists!) He studied a different state and took a somewhat different research approach but reached very similar conclusions. First, he found that cutting premiums was so effective in bringing in healthier customers that average medical expenses among enrollees dropped almost as fast as premiums: for every dollar in lower premiums, the average insurance claims of those who enrolled decreased by $0.85–$0.95. But Panhans also found that a blanket subsidy—one that gives the same discount to anyone who signs up on the exchange—isn't the best way of attracting participants. In fact, like Tebaldi, he found that the best way to help the sick was to subsidize the young (who are also healthier) and not the old. Indeed, his results suggest that every age group should be subsidized *except* the oldest. Of course, everyone likes a discount – sick and healthy alike. But if the goal is to get everyone covered at the lowest cost to the taxpayer (and that is often the goal), coverage can be accomplished at lower cost by giving discounts only to the young, which benefits even the elderly.

Giving Theory a Chance to Work Its Wonders – or Not

The upshot of everything we've gone through thus far is that well-designed and well-executed policies can help insurance markets combat adverse selection and work better. Mandates (or penalties or taxes or whatever the Supreme Court wants to call them) can bring the healthy into the market. We saw that clearly in the case of Massachusetts.

In theory, Obamacare's exchanges and its mandate of broccoli fame brought the same policies to the other forty-nine states. But residents of many other states saw much-higher prices on their exchanges – and enrolled in far lower numbers – than in Massachusetts, emphasizing that there can be a very wide gulf between what's possible in theory and how the theory plays out in practice. In this case, though, the problem isn't with the model – as we said, the Massachusetts experience is a big win for economic theory. There are, however, many ways that policy makers' choices can hijack real-life policies such that the theory never gets a fair chance to work its wonders.

Economics can help guide us to even more effective policies than the blunt instruments of the Obamacare penalty or uniform subsidies. The work of Tebaldi and Panhans highlights that, guided by economic reasoning and supported by data, we may be able to

—

design insurance markets that work better for everyone, at lower cost to the government.

But there's a catch: pity the policy maker who aspires to pick a set of rules that are not just economically sound but also politically feasible. Subsidizing the insurance costs of California's healthiest residents might turn out to make economic sense, even for those with costlier medical conditions, as our earlier example illustrates. Yet it's easy to imagine how "subsidize health care for those who need it the least!" might not play well in the court of public opinion. The old, the sick, and the needy may be as skeptical as the recalcitrant child when the parent-state assures them that really, it's for their own good. That may be why, to our knowledge, no government has taken up the idea of subsidizing insurance for the young and healthy.

Because unlike academic economists studying selection markets, government policy must operate in a world in which there may be other objectives than just saving markets from selection problems. Sometimes selection problems are surely the furthest thing from the policy maker's mind. Even policies that are enacted for reasons entirely unrelated to selection, however, may nonetheless have implications for how well selection markets work or whether they work at all.

Sometimes the results are fortuitous. To ensure that there will be money available to compensate people harmed by reckless (and bankrupt) drivers, auto liability insurance is mandated in all fifty states. And starting in the early 1970s, the federal government required flood insurance for government-backed loans on houses built in flood plains. It did so because it was sick of having to bail out uninsured, risk-loving homeowners who kept building flimsy houses on the Gulf Coast, but no politician could resist flying into a disaster area, walking around in a hard hat, and promising federal relief to

—

those without insurance.[24] Even though these mandates weren't motivated by selection problems, they surely help with them. Better drivers can't opt out of the auto insurance pool, and since the 1970s, homeowners with mortgages in flood plains can't selectively buy flood insurance on the basis of insider knowledge of their home's ability to withstand hurricane-force winds or their tenacity in pursuing claims against their insurer. These are "win-win" cases — a single policy accomplishes two objectives at once.*

Sometimes, though, the results are less than fortuitous. Many policies in insurance markets are designed to deal with concerns about privacy and fairness — entirely admirable objectives. As we'll see in chapter 7, however, efforts to protect privacy and improve equity can be at odds with selection concerns, creating adverse selection where none need exist. And this sets up important tensions in making policy. There are no right or wrong answers, only trade-offs.

---

* Auto insurance is actually an interesting example of a market where the government created two sets of dueling regulations — each created for reasons entirely unrelated to adverse selection — that can influence the extent of selection problems in different directions. First, to ensure equal access at comparable rates, most states limit what customer attributes can go into insurers' pricing algorithms. As a result, companies can't charge more for their customers who they *know* will get into more accidents — when rules outlaw the use of relevant data in price setting, it's as if the companies don't have access to the data at all. These pricing restrictions can exacerbate selection problems. On the other hand, mandates that drivers have auto insurance — which are put in place to protect victims from being unable to get compensation for damages wrought by reckless, uninsured drivers — have the opposite effect. They can combat selection problems: since all car owners must get coverage, the cycle of lower-risk, lower-cost drivers opting out of ever-costlier auto insurance can't get started — no one's allowed to opt out in the first place.

—

Chapter 7

YOU CAN'T DO THAT!

Sometime in the last week, you almost surely checked a box that signed over your right to some kind of personal data. Odds are you did it more than once. A lot more. Every time you install an app, some company starts tracking you. Every now and then, alarmist stories appear that grab our attention for a moment: "Your App Knows You Got Your Period. Guess Who It Told?" "There are Spying Eyes Everywhere — and Now They Share a Brain."[1]

The irony in writing a book about customers' private information in the Information Age hasn't been lost on us. We live in a world in which Target can allegedly figure out a teenager is pregnant before her parents do, and Apple and Google are, in a very literal sense, tracking your every action. It's a world in which the data that these companies collect are used to send ads or coupons that at times are so well targeted that it really does feel like they're eavesdropping on your conversations (which maybe they are) or reading your mind (which as far as we know they aren't).

The data stockpiled in Amazon servers may end up with insurers that may similarly use it to direct their ads at some prospective

—

customers – the good ones, of course, who won't get in accidents or get sick too often. Insurers may also deploy this information to provide you with personalized prices or to decide whether they're even willing to have you as a customer at all. The data from your health apps, driving apps, and shopping apps may provide hints as to how healthy or careful you would be as a customer and thus how much you'd cost to insure. It would help insurance markets work efficiently if they could spy on us nonstop, although it's also dystopian and decidedly creepy.

It can seem puzzling that in such a world, customers can still keep secrets from insurers. It's puzzling enough that we spent some time in chapter 2 illustrating what some of these secrets might be (and speculating about others we couldn't see).

It turns out, though, that many customer "secrets" aren't things insurance companies *can't* find out. Rather, they are things that insurance companies aren't *allowed* to find out or to make any use of even if they know them. To protect customer privacy – or to promote equity – the government often restricts the information that insurers are allowed to collect or use in offering policies to their customers.

From the perspective of selection markets, this seems completely backward. In chapter 6, we described the considerable policy effort and attention the government devotes to trying to *combat* adverse selection through mandates and subsides. Then it just turns around and with the other hand *creates* private information by legislating secrets into existence! What gives?

This is certainly not just another cliché about government incompetence. Rather, it's an illustration of an important set of tensions that almost inevitably arise in designing policy that affects insurance markets. If insurers are allowed to use any and all information available and set prices as they choose, the problem of selection will disappear (or at least come closer to disappearing), allowing markets to work their wonders of efficiency.

And therein lies the rub: On the one hand, laws that aim to promote equal access in the name of fairness may exacerbate adverse selection. On the other hand, rules that restrict access to limit selection may seem unfair. It's rare for there to be easy have-your-cake-and-eat-it-too options. Usually there are only compromises and trade-offs.

Understanding the trade-offs — how promoting efficiency might reduce fairness and vice versa — can help us think more clearly about how to balance these two competing goals. This chapter is about exactly these difficult trade-offs and the results of the compromises that policy has struck.

What Happens in 23andMe Stays at 23andMe. Or Does It?

DNA testing is a boon for people digging into their origins. What amorous secrets might account for that blond-haired sibling? Is there any truth in your crazy grandmother's claim that she was descended from Genghis Khan?* Some of these mysteries can be at least partly resolved if you spit in a test tube and mail it off to one of the various companies that offer DNA analysis. The same analysis might also offer clues as to your genetic destiny — whether you're at higher risk for Parkinson's, Alzheimer's, and a number of other diseases.

So-called direct-to-consumer genetic-testing pioneer 23andMe

---

* It's entirely possible. According to a 2010 study, about one in two hundred people alive today can count him as an ancestor. Razib Khan, "1 in 200 Men Are Direct Descendants of Genghis Khan," *Discover*, August 5, 2010, https://www.discovermagazine.com/planet-earth/1-in-200-men-direct -descendants-of-genghis-khan.

charged $199 for its basic service in 2021.[2] If you're thinking of sending your saliva off for evaluation, you might want to know that the company also can make a bit extra by taking your information and selling it. Genetic codes are sold to pharmaceutical companies to help them develop new drugs. You can imagine that health insurers would love to get their hands on 23andMe data as well — it would be very useful to know who is most likely to get Parkinson's and other debilitating illnesses before they've signed up those people, so an insurer can charge higher prices or refuse coverage altogether.

But 23andMe and its competitors cannot, for the most part, sell information on Parkinson's or Alzheimer's risk to health insurers. It's forbidden under the 2008 Genetic Information Nondiscrimination Act (GINA), which prohibits the use of any genetic information as an input into a health insurer's decision of whether to offer coverage to an applicant or in setting customers' premiums. It's part of a wider patchwork of rules and regulations, some national, some that vary by state, that limit what insurers can learn about their prospective and existing customers and limit how they might use data that they *can* learn in setting their rates and rejection criteria. Companies can't offer coverage to a childless couple while rejecting a neighbor with half a dozen kids, even though the latter has at least half a dozen reasons why she's more likely to see her house burned down or otherwise damaged. California forbids auto insurers from pricing on *anything* that doesn't relate directly to an applicant's driving record; so zip-code-based pricing is a no-no, as is pricing on, say, credit ratings, which, it turns out, are correlated (for whatever reason) with someone's chances of a fender bender in the future. Insurance plans offered on Obamacare exchanges can't set different prices based on race or gender or charge more to people with preexisting health conditions.[3]

There's a clear case to be made for these laws on the grounds of fairness, which goes beyond questions of privacy and whether individuals should have a say in who sees their data. It seems unfair to reward those who already won the genetic lottery with lower life and health insurance premiums: Why should those who were born into genetic misfortune be further punished with extortionate prices for their health insurance coverage? Similarly, should those who live in poverty have their finances further strained by high auto premiums, just because auto theft may be more common in lower-income neighborhoods? If it doesn't seem right to set automobile insurance prices based on data that are not directly related to one's driving history — say, credit score, income of the neighborhood where you live, or gender or race — governments need to place limits on the data that are fed into auto insurers' rate-setting algorithms.

But if, in the name of fairness, we decide to prohibit companies from "punishing" people for bad luck or exacerbating inequities with their price-setting decisions, we take away a key instrument that insurers have for dealing with selection. We live in what may be a more just world but create selection problems in the process. Everything involves trade-offs.

What these trade-offs ultimately lead to with regard to policies can feel quite arbitrary. 23andMe can't sell your genetic data to health insurers. But it's free to sell that data to life, disability, and long-term-care insurance providers, for which information about future health risks is just as valuable.* Oh, and that rule about not

---

* Remember our discussion of Huntington's disease and long-term-care insurance from chapter 2. People at risk of Huntington's were overwhelmingly more likely to purchase long-term-care insurance, which served as clear evidence of selection. As best we can tell, since it isn't covered by GINA, insurers *could* do genetic testing to determine whether an applicant carries the Hun-

selling to health insurers? There's an exception for health insurance provided via employers with fifteen or fewer workers – for them, 23andMe can do what it wants.[4] This patchwork of regulation reflects the tug of conflicting interests and differing trade-offs in how one regulator or another thinks about issues of privacy, fairness, and efficiency and tries to reach a reasonable compromise for technologies that are new and probably changing too quickly for well-intentioned policy makers to keep up.

Once we appreciate the basic trade-off between equal treatment and selection, it's easier to see that a much wider set of government rules – while motivated by concerns that are entirely unrelated to insurance – nonetheless have a fundamental impact on the functioning of insurance markets. A notable example is the Civil Rights Act of 1964 and the subsequent legislation that reinforced and expanded the initial act. These laws aimed to fulfill President John F. Kennedy's goal of "giving all Americans the right to be served in facilities which are open to the public – hotels, restaurants, theaters, retail stores, and similar establishments."[5]

The right to be served also meant the right to be treated on an equal footing, regardless of race. Black Americans could no longer be sent to the back of the bus or put in a segregated section of a restaurant. Nor could they be charged different prices for the same bus ride or meal. (A two-sided Coke machine on display at the International Civil Rights Center and Museum lists a price of a nickel on the "white" side and a dime for the side available to Blacks.)[6]

These laws were influenced in part by the indelible images of the protests against such inequities: pictures of Black students –

---

tington mutation, but at the time the study was written, they had chosen not to do so.

sometimes accompanied by white supporters – sitting at whites-only lunch counters in Woolworth's stores across the South, with crowds of white hecklers looking on; the iconic photo of Rosa Parks calmly peering out a window from the front of a bus in Montgomery, Alabama, with a sullen white man seated just behind. (While it very much captured the era's tensions, the photo was staged – the white passenger was United Press International (UPI) journalist Nicholas Chriss, who was in Montgomery to cover the protests, and was asked by his UPI photographer to sit next to Ms. Parks on an otherwise empty bus.)[7]

With the passage of the Civil Rights Act, it was illegal to set prices that depended on a customer's race or ethnicity. It is hard to see a downside to giving everyone, regardless of race, the right to sit at a Woolworth's lunch counter and order an egg-salad sandwich for the same thirty-cent charge (the actual price of an egg-salad sandwich at the F. W. Woolworth's lunch counter in 1960, based on vintage menus posted on eBay).[8] However, edicts against higher prices for minorities have also been extended to cover markets in which they would be costlier to have as customers, as in insurance. And this is where regulation aimed at equal treatment may exacerbate problems in selection markets or even create selection problems in markets in which they otherwise wouldn't exist. If insurers can't charge higher prices for customers they know will be riskier or more expensive, it's as if they're setting prices blindfolded.

For example, injustices both past and present have resulted in lower life expectancies for Black Americans relative to White Americans, even after taking account of factors such as income and family medical history. If insurers were allowed to further refine their prices by taking account of race in setting premiums, white customers would get better rates since they would be expected to survive for longer before collecting any payout. However, in many states, insurers are forbidden from accounting for race in setting life insurance rates (similar prohibitions exist for incorporating race into pricing auto or homeowner's insurance). To return to the basic policy trade-off, we'd say this is a good policy, in the sense that it prevents insurers from setting higher prices for a historically disadvantaged group; in other words, it makes things (a bit) more equitable. But we have to at least acknowledge that there's a cost: insurers are prohibited from using relevant information on how costly a customer is likely to be, which would reduce selection problems in the marketplace.

Whether this is indeed fair is a question for philosophers of the marketplace. Still, given its immediate relevance for public policy, we'd be remiss if we failed to at least note some of the complications and uncomfortable ethical ambiguities that the same-price-for-all rule creates. On the one hand, it seems unjust that some customers should have to pay more than others simply because of circumstances that weren't of their making – arguably, institutionalized racism and centuries of discrimination are the root cause of Black drivers' high auto premiums. And in this case, the marketplace would exacerbate existing inequalities if left to its own devices, by extracting higher payments from the already poor. Then again, if one set of customers is more expensive to take care of than another, are the two groups really buying the same product?

Should one's view on fairness differ if pricing decisions work in favor of poorer or disadvantaged groups? A Black person is 35 percent more likely to die in a given year, relative to their white counterpart.[9] So if insurers are allowed to set race-specific annuity prices, it will lead to more generous payouts to Black annuitants, thus reducing – albeit by a small amount – existing racial inequities. As we noted earlier, however, by the same logic, insurers would – if allowed — set higher prices on life insurance for Black customers. Is it fair to allow race-specific pricing that favors a disadvantaged group but not if it reinforces existing inequities?

And what about laws that — in the name of "fairness" — end up destroying the market entirely? The end result is "fair" — everyone does have access to the same options for insurance, because there's absolutely nothing for anyone to choose from at all.

Not Having Your Cookie and Eating It Too

Before looking in greater detail at the fairness-selection trade-off for insurance specifically, let's first take a step back to consider the question of what's "fair." This is a much-explored topic in moral philosophy. And in parental disputes with their children. And in economics.

The Ultimatum Game is a classic experiment economists have used to study how people think about fairness.[10] One subject is assigned the role of "proposer," who makes an offer of how to split a sum of money — say $10 — with another subject, the "responder." The proposer can suggest a fifty-fifty split or that they, the proposer, keep everything for themselves, or anything in between. It's a take-it-or-leave-it offer — hence the name Ultimatum Game — which the responder either accepts or rejects. If the offer is accepted, each subject leaves the experiment with whatever amount of money they got under the proposed split. If the responder rejects the offer, both walk out with nothing.

The Ultimatum Game has been around for four decades; we have a lot of data on how people react to "unfair" divisions of a pie — for example, take a proposer who suggests that they keep $9, offering just $1 to the responder. These lowball offers are very often rejected, even if it means both parties get nothing at all. Apparently, most people think it's better to have fairness than a dollar or two.

If you have children or can think back to a childhood (or adulthood) with siblings, recall what happens if one child's share of a cookie is smaller than their brother's. "It's not fair!" If you ask them if they'd rather just eat their smaller piece of cookie while their brother enjoys his slightly larger share or have no dessert for anyone at all? They'll choose the no-dessert option. Trust us. We've run this experiment at home.

These aren't perfect analogies for the policy options we face in managing the efficiency-fairness trade-offs in regulating selection markets. An Ultimatum Game responder might lash out at an inequitable offer as a form of revenge on the proposer, rather than resenting the unequal split itself. And sibling relationships are, well, complicated. But they do capture an essential feature of the consequences of limiting how insurers set prices: we end up sacrificing a lot of cookie – perhaps the entire cookie – in the name of equal treatment.

The canonical example of fairness-motivated insurance regulation is "guaranteed issue, community rating" for health insurance. That's a lot of jargon for some very simple ideas. "Guaranteed issue" means that insurers are required to issue insurance to anyone who wants it, regardless of their medical condition. "Community rating" means that these insurers are also required to charge the same price of every customer from a given "community," defined by, say, age or geography, regardless of medical history or health status. The combination makes it as if, from an insurer's perspective, it knows nothing about anyone applying for coverage. Guaranteed issue with

—

community rating is "fair," in the sense of forcing the market to treat everyone the same, but it also risks undermining the market in the name of equal treatment.

This is roughly what happened in the individual market for health insurance in New Jersey in the 1990s. The state set up the Individual Health Coverage Program (IHCP) to be an insurer of last resort for residents who couldn't get health insurance coverage through their employer or via a federal program like Medicare. Any health insurance company that wanted to do any business of any kind in New Jersey was required to participate in the program. By ensuring broad participation, legislators hoped to foster healthy competition among insurers, with state residents reaping the benefits in the form of lower premiums.

To make sure that coverage was available to all on equal terms, all of the plans had to have both community rating and guaranteed issue — that is, insurers had to set the same price for all customers and were prohibited from turning anyone away. During the first few years of this program, it ended up being, in the words of the late health economist Uwe Reinhardt, "the poster child for [the community rating's] so-called death spiral."[11]

In the first eight years of the program, it experienced the hallmarks of a death spiral. Initially, the state's insurer of last resort experienced robust enrollments, particularly in its most generous plan, which peaked at seventy-five thousand enrollees in 1995. But it was downhill from there. Premiums in that plan just went up and up and up. In 1996, premiums for the most generous plan were a little under $350 per month. But the customers in that pool were sicker than expected. So prices had to rise to cover costs, at which point some of the healthiest customers weren't as interested in the product and dropped out. So began the cycle of higher prices, sicker

—

customers, and higher costs. By the end of 2001, premiums in the most generous plan were approaching $1,200, and enrollment had fallen to just five thousand.* Everyone had equal access to the same programs at the same price, but by the end, there were fewer plans, fewer customers, and exorbitant rates.

Reinhardt's assessment was perhaps a bit severe – the market for the generous coverage didn't spiral down to total collapse in New Jersey's state program the way Harvard's more generous coverage gave up the ghost, as we saw in chapter 2.† Rather, the result was what we'd describe in less melodramatic terms as a "downgrade spiral." The most generous plan's enrollees became increasingly limited to the sickest, most expensive customers, and its premiums increased fourfold in just a few years. Meanwhile, the next-most-generous plan also saw a substantial decline in take-up, falling by about 50 percent between 1997 (when it probably started attracting sicker, higher-cost enrollees from the top plan) and 2002. New Jersey residents continued to buy coverage through the program into the 2000s, but they mainly bought the bargain-basement lowest-tier option, which

* There were other factors at play that also may have contributed to these patterns, so we can't unambiguously pin the decline of IHCP on a death spiral. In the early years of the program, insurers were encouraged to set very low premiums, which led to losses and their exit from the market. Increasing access to employer-sponsored plans may also have contributed to declining enrollment. Alan C. Monheit, Joel C. Cantor, Margaret Koller, and Kimberley S. Fox, "Community Rating and Sustainable Individual Health Insurance Markets in New Jersey," *Health Affairs* 23, no. 4 (2004): 167–75; Katherine Swartz and Deborah W. Garnick, "Lessons from New Jersey," *Journal of Health Politics, Policy and Law* 25, no. 1 (2000): 45–70.

† In that case, Harvard wasn't concerned with fairness. Rather, the university was simply trying to save money by passing the higher costs of more generous coverage on to its employees; when only the very sickest and most expensive employees were willing to pay the high premiums, it simply withdrew the plan. In New Jersey, the state was trying to preserve coverage options in the name of "fairness" and never actually killed the most generous option.

—

offered much less flexibility to enrollees on the doctors they could visit: plans with more extensive coverage cost so much that almost no one wanted to enroll, not even those who might have put substantial value on its greater flexibility.

A similar story played out around the same time in neighboring New York State, which imposed an extreme form of community rating on insurers offering health insurance coverage to individuals and small businesses in the state: all applicants, young and old, had to be charged exactly the same price.[12] One year into the community-rating experiment, Arthur Ferrara, the chairman of the state's insurance trade association, expressed concern that the price hikes had led to "many young people [dropping] their coverage rather than pay the high costs associated with health insurance." It sounded very much like a death spiral in the making. This led to doomsday predictions from insurers, with Mutual of Omaha's chief actuary warning, "Younger people are bailing out. If you're going to have universal access to insurance . . . then you need some kind of mandate for people to buy." As with New Jersey, the full-on doomsday scenario never arrived. Rather, as the economists Thomas Buchmueller and John DiNardo found, New Yorkers also got hit with a downgrade spiral, as higher-cost plans that allowed customers to visit any doctor lost considerable ground to less generous plans.[13]

If New York and New Jersey met their fairness objectives, it came at a high cost. Because of the limits put on how insurers set prices, healthy residents who would have liked to buy more flexible, more generous coverage could only do so at a price that effectively assumed that all buyers were quite sick. Even in these cases, it's not clear we can invoke the "I'd rather no one gets a cookie" theory of fairness to justify the rules. For example, New Jersey residents who could buy insurance through their companies — who tended to be better-off financially than the typical enrollees in the state's insurer-of-last-resort pool — still had a range of coverage options, whereas those without employer-based options were stuck with the unpalatable choice between bargain-basement limited coverage or a high-end plan whose price was bloated by selection.[14] In this case, New Jersey chose to prioritize fairness rather than efficiency but got neither.

The health-policy wonks who set the rules in New York and New Jersey surely weren't blind to the possible problems from guaranteed issue with community rating and had various partial solutions they might have applied to allow markets to survive even with these restrictions in place. However, convincing the public that their fixes are a good idea can be an uphill battle, particularly because they require steps that roll back at least some of the equity benefits of the original policies.

The government's no-win position is vividly illustrated by the bad PR it gets in the market for the elderly's health insurance. Here, the government has tried to set the rules to achieve fairness but tempers that fairness somewhat to try to avoid the kind of market meltdown that New York and New Jersey experienced in the prime-age health insurance market. As we'll see, it's gotten little thanks for its largely sensible efforts.

Misunderstood

In 2020, the *New York Times* ran a blistering takedown of Medicare Advantage, the federal program that offers subsidies for privately provided insurance plans to American seniors. Nearly half of elderly

Americans are enrolled in these plans.[15] The rest are enrolled in the alternative – so-called traditional Medicare, in which insurance is managed by the government itself, rather than a private company.

The *Times* article took up the sad case of Denver retiree Ed Stein to illustrate what it saw as the problems baked into Medicare's design. Stein was healthy and active when he became Medicare-eligible at the age of sixty-five. Recall from chapter 5 that companies offering Medicare Advantage policies throw in perks like gym memberships that are apt to appeal to people who are healthy and thus cheaper to cover – people like Ed Stein. So it is no surprise that Stein found Medicare Advantage offerings to be more appealing than traditional Medicare because of such benefits. As he explained to the *Times* journalist Mark Miller, "The price was the same, I liked the access to gyms, and the drug plan was very good."[16]

Fast-forward seven years. The seventy-two-year-old Stein gets a grim diagnosis: aggressive bladder cancer, which will require chemotherapy as well as complicated surgery. Gym access is no longer as important as access to a local doctor who specializes in his particular condition. Unfortunately, that doctor isn't in his Advantage plan's network – a familiar predicament. Stein faces an unpleasant choice: getting lower-quality care or paying out of pocket.

Or, as the *Times* article argues, shouldn't there be a third option? Why not switch plans? Traditional Medicare, as some readers may know, is accepted by almost any doctor, including the one whom Stein wanted to oversee his care. But traditional Medicare tends toward barebones coverage (recall our discussion of minimalist mandates). So many enrollees pay for additional insurance – so-called Medigap coverage – provided by private insurers to take care of some of the costs not covered by Medicare.

Ed Stein – no doubt along with thousands of others each year –

—

was dismayed to learn that switching to traditional Medicare plus Medigap wasn't as easy as he'd imagined. As the *Times* spun it in its story, "[Stein] ran up against one of the least understood implications of selecting Advantage when you enroll in Medicare: The decision is effectively irrevocable."[17]

Stein's circumstances are described in the article as the kind of between-a-rock-and-hard-place choice — don't access the medical care you need or go bankrupt — that exemplifies all that's wrong with the U.S. health-care system. Stein made his initial decision to forgo Medigap coverage back in 2013, when he turned sixty-five. At that age — but *only* at that age — the government rules require that all Medigap plans accept all comers (guaranteed issue) and must offer all potential customers the same price, no matter what preexisting health conditions they may have (community rating). But this requirement is in effect only in the first six months after a person's sixty-fifth birthday.[18]

Why doesn't the government resolve Stein's dilemma by setting the rules so that seniors can switch plans when the need arises? Why is U.S. health-care policy seemingly designed to screw sick people like Stein?

It just doesn't seem fair!

While there is surely a lot wrong with U.S. health-care policy, this story (and many similar ones like it) misses the mark. Stein's situation, while tragic, is in part of his own making. And the particulars of Medicare regulation that created it aren't the result of policy makers' ignorance or corruption by insurance-industry lobbyists. Rather, they reflect what we would say is a reasonable compromise between providing equal access to the health insurance market — which we all might see as one aspect of fairness — while preventing selection problems from undermining the market entirely.

—

The *Times* article directed its frustration and vitriol at the government for trapping Stein in a health plan that no longer served his needs after he got his cancer diagnosis. Without denying the terrible misfortune confronting the article's protagonist, we'd like to make the case for why it makes sense for the government to impose the rules it does.

Recall that Stein had initially enrolled in a Medicare Advantage plan that suited his needs as a newly minted and healthy senior citizen — a plan that had perks like a gym membership, even if it limited his options of which doctors he could see. Seven years and a cancer diagnosis later, he wanted to switch to Medigap coverage, which had been available to him at sixty-five regardless of health status. Now, however, he found that insurers didn't *have* to take him, and certainly none wanted him — insuring a cancer patient can be a money-losing proposition at any price.

Think back to Stein's initial decision to enroll in Medicare Advantage and to take a pass on Medigap coverage in 2013, when he turned sixty-five. Back then, he could have enrolled in whatever plan he wanted. There is surely some selection across plans — as we explained in chapter 5, healthier seniors who value gym memberships over cancer specialists will flock to Medicare Advantage offerings designed to appeal to low-cost enrollees. But it's a cost we may be willing to accept in the name of equality, to ensure that everyone — at the moment they turn sixty-five and enter the Medicare marketplace — can select the type of coverage they want on equal terms.

For the *Times* to call Stein's decision "effectively irrevocable" involves, to put it kindly, journalistic license; we might say it's closer to breathless exaggeration. It *is* possible to switch Medicare plans (including enrollment in traditional Medicare plus a Medigap supplement) every year. Stein could in fact have switched from Medicare

Advantage to traditional Medicare anytime he wanted, before he'd gotten cancer. But good luck finding a Medigap plan that would be willing to take him on, now that he really needed the extra coverage — after an initial six-month shopping-around period, the federal government leaves insurers free to charge what they want of new applicants or reject them entirely.

This is the balance of equality and efficiency that the Medicare program's architects have settled on: everyone is treated equally at initial enrollment, but six months after that, the market gets to decide who gets what and for how much. Overall, this policy creates selection problems with initial coverage choices, since when everyone is treated equally by the insurers, you can bet that people don't all respond equally. Indeed, healthy individuals like Ed Stein at age sixty-five tend to avoid the Medicare-plus-Medigap option and flock to the Medicare Advantage plans dangling those gym memberships and other perks. But after this initial period, the pendulum swings away from equity; insurers are free to use whatever information they can uncover to decide who gets to be their customer and at what price. It's not the only balance one could strike between equality and efficiency, nor is it obviously the "right" one. But we can see how a sensible policy process could end up with this set of rules.

Policy makers might be able to make the current system at least a bit better by, say, pushing freshly minted seniors to make better, more forward-looking decisions. You can imagine every American getting a Medicare information packet with a boldfaced reminder: "Choose carefully: Your Medicare choices will matter for the rest of your life." Inevitably, though, even if such rules are well designed and well advertised, they can nonetheless lead to the after-the-fact tragic circumstances for seniors like Ed Stein, who are confronted with the choice between medical care and bankruptcy. The idea of letting people switch insurance whenever they want may seem fair: Why *shouldn't* someone be able to get coverage that suits their current circumstances? That was certainly how Amy's husband, Ben, thought the world should work (if you recall from chapter 5 his attempts to upgrade his towing insurance when his car broke down).

But, as you might guess by now, it would effectively undermine the basic purpose of insurance, which is to protect against unforeseen calamity. If you could switch to auto coverage with roadside assistance, you'd do it with a roadside phone call when your car breaks down and not a moment earlier. You'd get health insurance with gym memberships while you're healthy and switch to coverage with more generous medical benefits when you're sick and then switch back again after you recover. That sounds like a good deal from the perspective of the guy by the side of the road, but it's no longer insurance for the guy who might someday be by the side of the road.

This also drags us back into the morass of defining what's fair. On one's sixty-fifth birthday, everyone is free to get whatever coverage one likes, to hedge against whatever health risks the future holds. If you choose to get flimsy insurance because it's cheap and comes with a fitness membership, that's your choice. Why should the rest of us have to bail you out down the road? The whole purpose of insurance is that you're supposed to buy it to insure against a *possible* event or risk, not to pay for that eventuality *after* it happens. Viewed from this perspective, what Ed Stein wants isn't insurance; it's a bailout.

And whatever your notion of fairness, the unfortunate reality is that, while being able to switch to a policy that works better for you when you're sick might solve Stein's dilemma in the short run, it probably wouldn't take long before such a rule led to the collapse of the market entirely. The lock-in created by Medicare rules is a deliberate policy choice to keep the market from unraveling, not an ill-conceived misfire concocted by misguided bureaucrats. The Medicare rules are reminiscent of strategies that private companies deploy to limit selection problems.*

We know the Medicare lock-in rules are important for reducing selection because not all states have them. Ed Stein lived in Denver, Colorado, which abides by the federal government's standard rules for Medigap: community rating and guaranteed issuance, but just in the first six months after one's sixty-fifth birthday. But states were free to augment pricing regulation for their own residents, and many did. Connecticut, Maine, and New York chose to allow senior citizens to enroll in Medigap at any time, while forcing insurers not only to enroll them whenever they applied but also to charge the same price regardless of medical condition.[19] It's just what the *Times* and Ed Stein had wanted.

Unfortunately for these states' Medicare enrollees, the result was exactly what we just warned about: seniors waited till they were sick to enroll in Medigap. The result was substantially higher prices

---

* As we discussed in chapter 5, insurers impose waiting periods before a newly purchased insurance plan can pay benefits or only allow you to change your insurance plan once a year, precisely to prevent plan switching only when expensive costs are on the immediate horizon. The lock-in created by Medicare rules also parallels our discussion of life insurance in chapter 5. Recall that one impediment to the market was that businesses couldn't lock their customers into lifetime commitments. The solution, as you may recall, was to make new customers pay a fee up front, followed by guaranteed (lower) annual premiums. Because the cost of insurance is front-loaded, customers effectively commit themselves to staying with their initial provider. While healthier people might wish they could get a better deal once they learn of their good luck, the lock-in means that everyone gets to buy insurance at a fair price before the future reveals whether they'll be sick or healthy. And this is, after all, what insurance is really meant to do — at least partly cancel out future and as-yet-unknown risks.

---

for supplemental Medigap coverage. Faced with these higher prices, enrollment was lower—another win for the theory and a loss for insurance customers in community-rating states.

Those were the main findings of the economist Vilsa Curto's PhD dissertation: when states gave people the option of enrolling—at the same price—at any point no matter what their health conditions, there was less of a need for those in good health to sign up right when they turned sixty-five, before they got sick.[20] So seniors waited on average about one year longer before signing up for Medigap and signed up when they were sicker. The combination of the option to wait and the higher prices that insurers needed to charge because their customers tended to be unhealthy ones led to much-lower rates of Medigap enrollment—nearly 30 percent lower than in neighboring states.

If there's a broader lesson here, it may be that, while policy design involves trade-offs, some choices may end up looking better than others once one accounts for the full consequences of what might be well-meaning efforts at creating access and equity. It's easy to appreciate the impulse to allow for a "do-over" for those who are hit with debilitating and costly ailments like cancer or stroke. It's humane and straightforward to comprehend at the level of the individual tragedy. But it also messes with the functioning of the market and makes just about everyone else worse off for it.

This isn't to say that we should ignore the plight of the Ed Steins of America. But the solution taken up by Connecticut, Maine, and New York may not be the best alternative. The government might have, for example, forced *everyone* to opt into a Medigap plan at age sixty-five, which amounts to mandating more generous insurance for all American seniors. Who would pay for it? Well, we're back to the world of trade-offs—rather than observing the tragedy of

—

the underinsured seventy-two-year-old, we'd see people who would rather spend their money on food and housing forced into spending their nest egg on health insurance instead. Or, if the government paid the bills, there'd be less money for it to pay for schools, roads, and bridges.

Pity then the poor regulator who has only unpopular options: whatever balance between fairness and efficiency the government chooses, there will be winners and there will be losers. The losers will often have genuinely tragic stories to tell.

———

The way we've described it thus far, it sounds as if the government is merely playing against itself, in a sense: on top of guaranteed issue and community rating, which ensure fair and equitable access but create selection problems, policy makers then tacked on a set of further rules that govern switching among offerings, to ensure that selection problems weren't too severe. The government isn't the only player, though. At every step, Medicare's designers have to anticipate how program beneficiaries will respond to make the best use of the system—foreseeing, for example, that people will want to switch plans as their health conditions change. There's yet another set of players, though: insurance companies stand ready to create or adjust their coverage offerings to best profit from rules that the government might set.

It should not surprise you that businesses often come out on top. In chapter 8, we'll see that sometimes it's because businesses — with deep pockets and motivated by profit — come up with creative ways of gaming the rules. In other words, sometimes it's the inevitable consequence of businesses getting the last move.

Chapter 8

BUSINESS GETS THE LAST MOVE

In 1980, Mark DeFriest — out on probation after a year in prison — went to retrieve a set of tools that his recently deceased father had bequeathed him. DeFriest's stepmom called the cops, and since the will hadn't yet been processed, he was charged with robbery, along with possession of a firearm, which violated his parole. He was sent to Florida State Hospital, a psychiatric facility, because experts appointed by the court deemed him to be mentally ill (he was eventually diagnosed with schizophrenia and bipolar disorder).

It was there that DeFriest made his first attempt at a prison break. He pilfered blotter acid — commonly known as LSD-25 — from the hospital dispensary and sneaked a generous portion of it into the staff coffee pot just before a shift change. He planned on using a counterfeited master key he'd made to break out while the staff were in the midst of their collective drug-induced freak-out. Unfortunately, before he could act on his plan, some of the first in line at the LSD-laced coffee pot started to attract attention. A staff member attacked a washing machine with a broom; a psychologist sashayed provocatively through the halls yelling obscenities. It was

—

clear that something was up. The hospital was locked down and security summoned. According to DeFriest, he was never fingered as the culprit.

His next try went a bit better. He and some other patients made a run for a barbed-wire-topped fence; DeFriest was among those who made it over. He hot-wired a car and drove off but was quickly apprehended. Rather than send him back to the hospital, the authorities sent him to Bay County Jail.

And so began the back-and-forth between DeFriest and the Florida correctional system of stricter measures to prevent him from escaping and ever-more-elaborate schemes to elude whatever new restraints prison officials imposed. He had what the filmmaker Gabriel London, who made a documentary about DeFriest, called a "tragic gift" — a certain brilliance, which he devoted to the singular objective of making it to freedom. He could memorize the intricacies of keys hanging from a guard's belt and carved replicas from scraps of wood and metal; he constructed a rudimentary firearm out of a toothpaste tube. Were it not for his "gift," he might have walked out of prison in 1984. His original four-year sentence stretched to decades of lockup as a result of hundreds of prison rule violations, which included thirteen attempted escapes.

DeFriest did have his successes — he made it out seven times, an astounding record, particularly as with each try, he was put in ever-more-secure confinement. He was moved from Bay County Jail to Florida State Prison; once there, he was put in a secure, second-story lockup for prisoners who required extra scrutiny. Within a few years, DeFriest was put in solitary, which prison staff saw as the only way of containing the man known as the "prison Houdini."[1]

Anyone charged with making and enforcing a set of rules is familiar with the action-reaction problem confronting DeFriest's jailers. This includes the rule setters in government who endeavor to set public policy to address problems created by adverse selection. We looked at a number of these solutions in chapters 6 and 7. But the story rarely ends with the passage of a single rule. Indeed, the story never really ends at all, because insurers, like DeFriest, always respond to whatever set of shackles — literal or regulatory — constrains them. DeFriest always looked for a new path to freedom. Insurers will always look to figure out how they can work within the new rules to keep on attracting the cheapest possible customers.

The Whac-a-Mole Problem

Whether you're trying to keep a teenager from sneaking out at midnight or a multibillion-dollar company from fleecing investors, whatever answer you come up with is most likely the solution to yesterday's problem. You set an alarm to keep your child from leaving without permission, but she uncovers the alarm code and slips out anyway. So you change the code. Instead, she buys a rope and rappels out her window. You install window alarms. She finds a way of disabling them. If she's crafty enough, the best you can do is to make escape more difficult and perhaps less frequent, not stop it altogether. And enforcing the curfew is expensive, whether measured in out-of-pocket expenses or heartache.

It's what is referred to as the "Whac-a-Mole" problem, after the old-school arcade game in which a little furry creature (the mole) pops its head up out of various holes and you get points by whacking it back down with a mallet. But you can't make the mole disappear — the moment he's been smashed into one hole, he reappears in another. All you can do is keep whacking him back down as quickly as possible. And so it goes when dealing with errant teenagers or regulating insurance companies: you can't win. You just try to plug up whatever opening they've found in existing rules and wait for their next move.*

To continue with the errant-teenager analogy, now imagine that your daughter employed a team of lawyers to make her case for a later curfew and an army of engineers to devise ever-more-elaborate means of escape. Then you have some idea of what government rule makers are up against when they go toe-to-toe with Corporate America. Before legislation is even passed or regulations enacted, companies are working out how to best respond.

To stretch the comparison even further, imagine that you can only change the alarm passcode once a year. That's a decidedly optimistic time line for a governmental response to whatever workaround the lawyers and engineers have devised. It's like your teenager gets to make her move, and you have to stick to whatever constraints you've imposed until she goes to college.

To give you a feel for this game of Whac-a-Mole, we'll consider the case of Medicare, the government health insurance for the elderly. We'll see that the U.S. government has been playing – and mostly losing – the Whac-a-Mole game with private health insurers ever since it started outsourcing Medicare to private providers in the 1980s. That doesn't necessarily mean that the government should

---

* Struggling parents and government regulators alike can take some comfort from the fact that they are in good company: Sherlock Holmes also ended up on the losing end of the Whac-a-Mole game he played with Irene Adler, which we described in chapter 5. Recall that Holmes tricks Adler into revealing where she hid a potentially scandalous photo of herself with the King of Bohemia. However, when Holmes goes back to retrieve the photo, he finds instead a note from Adler, who had recognized Holmes's plan from the beginning. And so ends the tale of "how the best plans of Mr. Sherlock Holmes were beaten by a woman's wit." Arthur Conan Doyle, "A Scandal in Bohemia," in *The Adventures of Sherlock Holmes* (New York: A. L. Burt, 1920), 28.

throw up its hands and get out of the regulatory business – or that it should take over from the private sector entirely. But it does mean that sensible design of Medicare policy – or any public policy aimed at insurance, for that matter – needs to be always thinking about selection. It also means that when it comes to policy that attempts to regulate private insurance companies, the government needs to think not just about selection possibilities that currently exist but also about those that the private market might create in response to regulation.

The Insurer's Advantage

When Medicare was established in the mid-1960s, it provided U.S. seniors with basic health insurance, paid for and also administered by the government itself. Two decades later, spurred by the cost-cutting agenda that motivated much of U.S. government policy under then-President Ronald Reagan, private insurers were given a chance to get into the business of covering health insurance for Medicare-eligible Americans.[2] It's still paid for by the government but is now administered by the supposedly invisible hand of the market, to which many an economist attributes quasi-magical properties of efficiency.

Here's how it works: For each beneficiary an insurer takes off the government's hands, it gets a fixed payment from the government. In turn, the insurer is now on the hook for providing that beneficiary with Medicare coverage. By one measure, the program has been a huge success: by 2020, about a third of Medicare enrollees got their coverage from a private insurer, through a program that we've already encountered, Medicare Advantage.[3]

Champions of laissez-faire might see this growth as evidence of the market's inherent superiority. Motivated by profit, the private sector would service its Medicare clientele with such efficiency that the government could pay insurers less than the government would have had to spend on providing coverage itself and still leave businesses with a tidy profit. Because insurers could only profit by attracting enrollees, they'd have to keep their customers happy. It was to be a win-win-win: win (profits) for insurers, win (more options) for beneficiaries, and win (savings) for government.

But there's another way the private insurer could win that puts a very different perspective on the virtues of private versus government provision of insurance: private insurers can profit by making sure to attract only the healthiest and thus cheapest-to-manage customers. The amount they are paid for each individual they enroll is based on the government's best guess of how much it would have cost to cover that individual with Medicare. As a result (as we already discussed in chapter 5), insurers did what they could to attract those who were likely to be healthier than the government (or the insurer) could necessarily see — by offering gym memberships and other inducements that appealed primarily to healthy customers. And that came at the government's expense: the government had set a fixed per-enrollee payment to private insurers on the assumption that they would enroll a mix of sick and healthy people. Instead, insurers lured away mostly healthy ones, leaving the government with the mostly sicker — and costly to insure — leftovers.

The government was not entirely asleep at the wheel. It realized that insurers would design ploys to skim off the healthiest enrollees who promised the fattest profit margins. To entice insurers to also offer plans that might be attractive to less healthy seniors, Medicare set more generous reimbursements for insurers that took on expensive-to-serve customers. But initially, the government didn't have much to go on in deciding which seniors warranted these more generous payments. This was the early 1980s, after all, which was long before any readily accessible central patient database existed, digital or otherwise. The best regulators could do was to pay insurers different amounts based on customer demographics—giving, for example, a more generous payment to insurers for taking an eighty-year-old relative to someone ten years younger or for taking on customers in expensive health-care markets like Miami (relative to, say, rural Iowa). Of course, that didn't eliminate selection entirely. There are eighty-year-old Miami residents who munch on almonds all day and diligently attend their aquarobics classes and others who laze around on the beach downing Margaritas. The gap between the almond munchers and Margarita drinkers left plenty of room for insurers to pick the cheapest customers.

As we saw in chapter 5, insurers did exactly that. Even if they didn't have better data than the regulators, they were able to figure out creative ways (like those gym memberships) to attract the healthiest customers. As a result, according to a 2011 study by a trio of health economists, the government was losing money—paying private insurers more than it would have cost the government to simply cover the customers itself.[4] At least initially, Medicare Advantage was turning out to be, at best, a win-win-lose proposition.

For the government to make its next move to try to stop—or at least limit—insurers' ability to skim off the cheapest patients, it needed better data on enrollees to better adjust how much it paid insurers. If payments more accurately reflected the patients' health, insurers would have less of an incentive to try to attract the healthiest customers (or, if they did, they'd be paid less for taking them on).

It took a while, but by the late 1990s, Medicare administrators were able to access patients' hospital records to get a better read on their health problems, which gave them a view – albeit a partial one – of the chronic health conditions that each enrollee might suffer from.[5] An eighty-year-old in Miami with hypertension, for example, warranted higher reimbursement than an eighty-year-old in Miami who didn't suffer from high blood pressure.

But, as always, there was a catch: Medicare could only set reimbursements based on *measured* health problems, that is, the ones that showed up in hospital records. If, for example, you were diabetic or hypertensive – or both – but lucky enough never to be hospitalized, as far as the government knew, you were the very picture of eighty-year-old vigor. As is inherent to Whac-a-Mole regulation, this partial "solution" also caused other problems to pop up. In this case, because a patient had to be admitted to a hospital to get their diagnosis into Medicare's system, insurers had an incentive to hospitalize patients who might have been perfectly fine being treated in a doctor's office.[6]

The government's solution, naturally, was yet more data – to try to set reimbursements based on diagnoses made not just at the hospital but at the physician's office as well. Eventually, it was able to incorporate this broader set of patient characteristics into its pricing models, which curbed insurer incentives for excessive hospitalization.

As you probably can guess, though, the story didn't end there. The game of action-and-reaction continued. Private insurers now welcomed new enrollees to their plan with a free checkup – conducted at home for their convenience, no less.[7] This gave insurers a chance to diagnose any and all health problems that an enrollee might suffer from, including ones that previously went undetected – good for the patient and good for the insurer, which could then get paid more for its patient in subsequent years. Insurers were also accused of recording not only maladies that had been missed in the past but also some that didn't exist at all. The boundary between working within the system for maximum profit and outright fraud is sometimes a fuzzy one. Insurers in many cases were in fact turning up existing, previously undetected patient illnesses that warranted higher payments from Medicare; in others, auditors found that doctors had entered diagnoses without providing any evidence for them (to be fair, in some of these cases, the diagnoses were accurate, and the only "crime" was insufficient documentation). Regulators, your turn to respond. Whac-a-Mole isn't just a game of designing better rules; it also involves a back-and-forth in better enforcing the rules you have.

To be clear, the goal is not some regulatory nirvana in which Medicare comprises an impeccably designed and perfectly enforced set of regulations that leave no opening for exploitation or manipulation by insurers. Even if it were possible, it would probably end up being about as useful as buying a $20,000 lockbox to store a $20 necklace—a lot more trouble and expense than warranted. Rather, the hope is that with each round of action and reaction, the rules get a bit better at working in the interests of the U.S. government and the seniors whom Medicare is meant to serve, rather than those of the insurance industry. You can take steps toward salvation, but it's a journey, not a destination.

Still, there are some simple guiding principles on how best to whack a mole. First and foremost, don't just focus on whacking the current mole. You need to think ahead to where it will pop up next and have the mallet already at the ready, hovering over that hole.

"If there is any one secret of success," as Henry Ford remarked, "it lies in the ability to get the other person's point of view and see things from that person's angle as well as from your own." Ford followed his own advice, famously offering the "five-dollar day" for workers at his Highland Park factory in 1914—more than double the $2.30 wage that was previously the standard at Ford's own factory and others in the area.[8] Ford seemed to have correctly intuited that his workers were being driven mad by the tedium of assembly-line production and distracted by money problems at home. The higher wage would pay for itself through more productive workers and lower turnover; if not, at $5 a day, there were many well-motivated workers eager to fill any openings.

If you want to predict how factory workers respond to a wage increase, think like a factory worker. If teachers want to anticipate how students will game a take-home test or assignment (manipulating margins or font size; seeking expert assistance), they need to think like a student (take it from us!). And if your job is regulating the insurance industry, you need to think like an insurance executive. Otherwise, you end up with the regulated always one step ahead of the regulator, the all too common Houdini-like experience in which each attempt by the regulator to pin down the insurers' ability to cherry-pick its customers is parried with another escape hatch crafted by the insurer.

It's easy in hindsight to see where one side failed to think ahead. Surely Reagan's architects of privatization—particularly given their undying faith in the pursuit of profits as a driver of corporate creativity and innovation—could have foreseen that insurers would find a way of ferreting out healthy retirees and leaving the sick ones for the government to manage. Maybe. But even if you know that your counterpart will find *some* way of gaming the rules, you still (without the benefit of hindsight) might not know exactly how they'll do it, how to block it, or just how much their reaction will skew the game in their favor.

Or maybe Reagan's regulators anticipated how insurers would

react and went ahead with their plans anyway. They knew they were playing the long game. For the second guiding principle of Whac-a-Mole is that no matter how hard you slam the mallet, the mole always comes back for another round.

Whac-a-Mole Goes High(er)-Tech

What can make things even harder for the hapless regulator is that it is forced to play catch-up in an ever-changing world. It has to anticipate businesses' responses to the current game, while at the same time managing the shifting landscape – driven by, for example, changing technologies or an aging of the population – that can further push the rule setter off balance. A century ago, no one saw the need to regulate greenhouse-gas emissions. Now it's a global imperative.

Medicare regulators have likewise been caught flat-footed by technological progress. One recent example comes from the prescription-drug benefit that was added to Medicare coverage in 2006.[9] Indeed, it was a changing world that brought about Medicare's prescription-drug coverage in the first place.

For the first four decades of Medicare, it covered the cost of visiting a physician or hospital, as well as many of the expenses that might arise during such a visit. If the doctor ordered a colonoscopy, no problem – Medicare paid the hospital and gastroenterologist for the procedure on the patient's behalf. Similarly, government insurance would cover emergency treatment if, say, Grandpa collapsed from a heart attack and was rushed to the hospital in an ambulance.

What Medicare *didn't* cover, though, was prescription medication that might help prevent that visit to the emergency department. At first, that didn't matter much. When Medicare was introduced, there were relatively few prescription drugs, and most were cheap anyway. But there's been tremendous growth in the quantity and quality of available drugs. By the 2000s, spending on prescription drugs constituted a sizeable share of the elderly's overall health-care expenses. Something had to be done about Medicare's (lack of) coverage of these costs.[10]

To get a sense of how far we'd come, consider the advice offered to President Franklin Roosevelt, who was first diagnosed with hypertension in the late 1930s. At that point, it remained a medical controversy as to whether high blood pressure was a good or bad thing to have. A medical text in the 1940s described hypertension as "a natural response to guarantee a more normal circulation to the heart, brain and kidneys" and warned that "overzealous attempts to lower the pressure may do no good and often do harm." Roosevelt's personal physician, Dr. Howard Bruenn, recommended (after consultation with half a dozen other senior medical officers) that the president "curtail" his use of cigarettes, eat a low-fat diet, and take it easy ("a minimum of 10 hours of sleep; the use of mild laxatives to avoid strain; no swimming; avoid, if possible, tension and irritations of [being President]"). He was also prescribed a barbiturate to further help him relax.[11]

Today, if a hypothetical grandpa (or president) found out that his blood pressure was too high, he'd probably still be told to quit smoking, eat better, and avoid stress. But in the twenty-first century, he'd also have an array of drugs that his doctor might recommend to help manage his hypertension. Diuretics, ACE inhibitors, beta-blockers, calcium channel blockers — the pharma industry offers many options that, used alone or in combination, can keep blood pressure under control with a minimum of side effects.[12]

Low blood pressure doesn't necessarily come cheap. Suppose,

for example, the doctor prescribed a daily regimen of Zestril, an ACE inhibitor that in 2000 would have cost our friend about $500 per year. The government may have covered the checkup when the prescription was written, but for the prescription itself, you were on your own. And blood-pressure medication was cheap, relatively speaking. If the doctor had ordered a prescription for Repatha, a drug targeted at patients with extremely high cholesterol that was approved in 2015, the annual bill in 2021 would have topped $5,700.

Costs like these ultimately led the government to finally add prescription-drug coverage to Medicare in 2006. As with the Medicare Advantage program it had introduced in the early '80s, the government once again went the route of paying for the new coverage but outsourcing the actual provision of prescription-drug plans to the private sector. The idea once again was to get the best of both worlds: the market gets to work its wonders of efficiency, while at the same time, government funds ensure that drug plans are affordable for everyone — efficient *and* equitable.

One thing the market isn't good at, though, is telling the government how much it should pay as subsidies to make the market work for everyone. And therein lies the inherent tension between what policy makers and insurance companies aim to achieve in the Medicare prescription-drug market. It was Medicare Advantage redux but with a twist: drug development — and rising drug prices — didn't slow down just because Medicare added a drug plan. To stretch the metaphor, the government was playing regulatory Whac-a-Mole in an arcade in which the mole was popping up at the Pop-A-Shot or air-hockey table — options that never even existed in last year's Whac-a-Mole game.

To ensure that Medicare prescription-drug coverage is accessible to all seniors — both sick and healthy — the government requires that any private insurers participating in the market take all comers, whether a healthy sixty-five-year-old or a sick or a frail ninety-year-old taking a daily cocktail of high-priced drugs.[13] Because the latter would be far costlier for insurers to cover, the government sets reimbursements correspondingly higher for customers with conditions that require expensive prescriptions — the subsidy for, say, a cancer patient might be particularly generous, given the high cost of chemotherapy drugs. If the subsidies were set just right, insurers would have neither the ability nor the incentive to try to attract some program participants and avoid others.

If it sounds familiar, there's a reason. It's just what the government tried to do with Medicare Advantage. And just as in that case, if businesses are well behaved (with regard to following the assumptions laid out by economic theory), they will then scrutinize whatever rules are put in place and go about setting *their* policies and rates to squeeze whatever profits they can out of the government and their customers.

The first problem was the familiar one: despite the government's efforts, there were openings for businesses to exploit. While insurers couldn't turn anyone away, they had a lot of leeway in how they set up each plan. That was in fact the whole point — by outsourcing insurance provision to the private market, the almighty profit motive would spur insurers to develop and offer plans that matched their customers' needs in order to attract more business. For example, by limiting reimbursement for branded equivalents of the same drug, patients and their doctors would have incentives to cut costs with no obvious consequences for health outcomes.

—

But insurers were spurred to create more substantive gaps in coverage — some drugs might be completely absent from a plan's list of covered medications or require the patient to pay thousands of dollars of their own money — to try to avoid covering patients who were less profitable and to attract patients who were more profitable. And the fact that new drugs constantly appeared on the market gave quick-reacting insurers endless opportunities to circumvent the intentions of the much-slower-moving regulator.

This was all vividly on display in a 2008 *New York Times* article by the veteran health journalist Gina Kolata about some of the glaring gaps in Medicare's prescription-drug coverage. She described the heartbreaking case of Julie Bass of Orlando, whose doctor had prescribed Tykerb to combat her metastatic breast cancer. Medicare's prescription-drug plans required that she pay a third of the drug's cost, which was over $1,000 per week. For someone like Bass, who got by on Social Security disability benefits, it was literally a choice between eating and taking her cancer meds.

And it wasn't only Bass's Tykerb that created the agonizing choice between buying food and buying drugs. Indeed, Tykerb was just one of many drugs requiring $1,000 copays (the contributions that patients are required to pay out of pocket to complement insurers' own contributions). Insurers cut or skimped on coverage for certain drugs in order to avoid getting stuck with patients who were too costly relative to what the government would reimburse.

Of course, they all tried it a little differently. Each plan had its own set of prescriptions included in a list of covered drugs. Plans also created different tiers of coverage within the list — lists within lists, if you will, with higher or lower copays depending on the tier. We'll spare you the details — the minutiae of U.S. health-care regulations and policies is enough to drive you to, ahem, tiers — but hope-

—

fully you get the basic idea. The result, as Kolata put it: "The new system sticks seriously ill people with huge bills."[14]

Wait, you *must* be thinking, didn't the government set reimbursement rates differently across different patients depending on their existing health conditions precisely to avoid this situation? How had the designers of Medicare's drug plan failed Julie Bass? The short answer is that, despite the government's efforts at getting reimbursement rates right, inevitably it overshot on the expected costs of some conditions, so that the government subsidies were "too high" relative to expected treatment costs. For other cases — like that of Bass — average costs and thus subsidies were "too low." Insurers thus offered only miserly coverage of the latter group's needs, hoping to keep them away or limit the cost of covering them if they did enroll.

The more complete explanation is that the government's problem was made all the harder because the "right" subsidy was itself a moving target. Just as new drugs that could have treated Roosevelt's high blood pressure in the 1940s were later developed, so too were new drugs — a great many of them — developed *after* the government set up its initial schedule of subsidies. Every time a new drug comes out, the prescription costs associated with treating a particular disorder might go up — or down — as a result.

New drugs save lives but are often very expensive. Older drugs lose their patents and become cheaper as low-priced generic versions enter the market. Amid these changes, the government-designed payments — which were set depending on what health conditions an enrollee had — didn't budge. But insurers could, and did, calculate who was most desirable (given newer drug prices) and adjust their lists of covered drugs accordingly to try to attract the more desirable customers and deter the less desirable (from a profit perspective).

Take HIV/AIDS, the diagnosis with, by far, the highest reimbursement subsidy, over $1,900 per year, in 2009. While this may have been generous enough when the prescription-drug benefit was calculated in 2003, by 2009, a number of new drugs had been brought to market. The estimated drug expenses for an HIV/AIDS patient were now so high that they warranted a much higher subsidy — over $2,500 in fact, according to calculations by the health economist Colleen Carey.[15] The subsidy however, remained unchanged. Unsurprisingly, therefore, insurers tried to design their plans to discourage HIV-positive enrollees, for whom the subsidies weren't enough to cover their costs. One way to do that was to require very high copays for any AIDS medication.

The widest gap that Carey found was for the diagnosis for multiple sclerosis (MS), a degenerative neurological disease in which the body's own immune system breaks down the myelin sheaths that cover and insulate nerve fibers. As nerves' coverings break down, messages between the brain and the rest of the body get garbled or disrupted, leading to symptoms ranging from muscle spasms to memory loss to uncontrollable mood swings. Whereas insurers enrolling a customer who had an MS diagnosis would get an extra $330 per year from the government for prescription-drug coverage, Carey calculated that an MS sufferer enrolling in a prescription-drug plan would cost the insurer nearly $1,200 in additional prescription expenses. It's not that the government had messed up when it set the payment schedule; rather, the treatment of MS changed considerably — *after* those payments were set.

At the other extreme, sometimes changes in medicine mean that certain diagnoses become a real bargain to insurers. For example, high cholesterol was an expensive diagnosis for many elderly Americans in the early 2000s, in large part because of one expensive drug, Zetia, that was being taken for high cholesterol by many elderly

—

Americans at the time. As a result, when the prescription-drug program began, Medicare set payments to insurers substantially higher for customers with cholesterol problems, recognizing that they had a good chance of being on this expensive drug. But shortly thereafter, the drug's patent expired, and its generic, simvastatin, quickly appeared on the market, drastically reducing the cost of cholesterol treatment.

This made high cholesterol an extremely desirable diagnosis (from the insurer's perspective, that is). There were other high-value diagnoses that insurers were similarly motivated to go after, because of differences in drug costs in earlier years versus drug costs in the present. In 2009, the government was paying insurers an extra $207 for covering an enrollee with a diagnosis of hypertension, even though Carey estimates that the extra cost from a hypertensive customer was less than $150; an even bigger gap emerged for muscular dystrophy, which yielded a bonus payment of nearly $80, even though sufferers of the disease spent substantially less on prescription drugs than the average Medicare enrollee.

Insurers would have loved to have been able to pick and choose among insurance applicants, taking those with muscular dystrophy while avoiding the ones with multiple sclerosis. But they couldn't, by law. So, Carey shows, they more or less did the same thing by adjusting which drugs they covered and how generously they covered them.

As certain conditions became more or less profitable, companies did what they could to keep enrollees with multiple sclerosis or AIDS away, by requiring high copays or not covering their medications at all. At the same time, they competed fiercely for highly profitable hypertensive enrollees, who benefited from insurers' rivalries by getting access to generous coverage that paid more or less the entire cost

—

of their drugs. It's yet another take on the general theme we introduced in chapter 5: insurers design their policies to get profitable customers and keep the less desirable ones away. In this case, though, it's the result — perhaps an inevitable one — of government regulations that aim to both allow for equal access *and* limit adverse selection.

The government, as is often the case, found itself playing catch-up. In 2011, it revised the payments for different diagnoses to reflect more recent cost data and a more sophisticated pricing formula.[16] But, of course, technologies continue to change, creating new opportunities for insurers to game the new subsidies. It certainly wasn't the last regulatory response or the last corporate response to this response. Regulators are never done tweaking their rules, and insurers are never done figuring out how to game them.

It's the back-and-forth that we expect, with an ultimate outcome that may be the best we can hope for. Businesses look for weaknesses in policy design to exploit, and with time, policy makers realize the openings for manipulation and revise the rules to plug them up.

If governments aren't quite up for the "move fast and break things" Silicon Valley design philosophy, there is at least some element of this to regulatory rollout. The government puts a set of rules out there, sees how "customers" respond, and tweaks the product accordingly. If regulators instead insisted on developing a more-manipulation-free rulebook before making any new rules, we'd still be back in the 1960s pondering how best to provide government-funded insurance to aging Americans.

So where does this story, and our story, end? It's always tempting, when confronted with a hard problem, to throw up one's hands and say, "let the market take care of itself" or "let the government take care of insurance markets."

As we warned at the outset of the book, we're not going to have any such pat answers here. Just as you should be wary of anyone offering you the chance to invest in their divorce insurance start-up, you should view with skepticism anyone who is pitching an all-or-nothing approach to markets versus government provision of insurance. It's easy to be an armchair critic, enumerating the problems that emerge in insurance markets, as well as the inadequacies of government interventions to fix those shortcomings. It's much harder to come up with anything better. That's what keeps generations of entrepreneurs, economists, and policy wonks in business. Coming up with better ways of combating selection—whether by business or through government regulation—is a never-ending project.

Hopefully this book has made it clear that "let the market take care of itself" is usually the wrong response if insurance markets are going to realize their full potential to provide protection and security in an uncertain world. Without government intervention, selection can drive the price of insurance up and the extent of available coverage down, sometimes to nothing at all—the divorce insurance business took care of itself, all the way out of existence.

When markets don't work well on their own, it can be tempting to go to the other extreme: hand the whole thing over to the government to run. We don't need to raise the specter of inefficient government bureaucracy to see why this isn't a panacea either. We saw, for example, how government mandates are a mixed bag as an answer to selection. There's the question of how to enforce the mandate as well as what level of insurance to require; the latter issue still remains if the government decides to avoid having to enforce a man-

—

date by providing insurance directly. Then again, we've also seen that when the government tries to regulate private insurance, it can end up on the losing side of an endless game of Whac-a-Mole.

Just as with all the other sources of market frailties, the typical response tends to be a middle ground in which the government intervenes to put its thumb on the market scales—sometimes quite heavily—but doesn't take over the whole weighing operation itself. To return to where we started in chapter 1, governments intervene in markets for all sorts of reasons. They break up monopolies to keep them from charging extortionate prices, put limits on banks' lending practices to reduce the chances of another Great Depression, and make polluters pay for the costs they inflict on others.

In none of these cases is there a single, perfect policy, only trade-offs. When banks are forced to keep a lot of money in reserve to prevent a bank run, they're less able to hand out loans that would allow more people to get mortgages and more businesses to make investments. If and when regulators break up Facebook, it would give the company less of a lock on the online ad market, but users might not have the seamless experience they currently enjoy in using its constellation of social media products. So too with selection problems in insurance markets.

But to focus only on the problems with government solutions (as admittedly we've just spent chapters 6–8 doing) is the wrong standard. Judging the policy by whether it got rid of all problems is an impossible bar for success. A more useful standard is whether it's an improvement over the status quo. That applies whether policy making involves the seemingly hapless Medicare regulators we've discussed in this chapter or the architects of the mandates we discussed in chapter 6.

An even more useful standard to consider is: Is there another

—

policy that could do better? Even when there are "obvious" flaws, it's less obvious that there's a way to do better. Trade-offs inevitably introduce shortcomings, sometimes obvious ones, but fixing those obvious deficiencies can make things a whole lot worse. Just ask anyone in New Jersey or New York, after they'd "fixed" the problem of unequal access to health insurance.

This is where we hope our book comes in: we've explained the basics of the selection problem, what some of the policy levers are for addressing the problem, and why the problem defies any easy fix. Perhaps you'll have more patience than vitriol for policy makers and bureaucrats or even have some sympathy for insurance companies themselves. Maybe you'll even be inspired — armed with your new-found knowledge — to leap into the fray yourself to try to come up with better solutions.

At the same time, the possible consequences of adverse selection can be hard to fully grasp — that's why it's taken us centuries to come to understand them better, and we're still a ways off from reaching complete enlightenment. Speaking for ourselves, we're still actively engaged in research on the topic and expect to still be gainfully employed in this undertaking when we're old enough to start collecting Medicare senior-citizen benefits. If policy makers continue to make missteps and, we hope, learn from their mistakes — as with the initial design of Medicare Advantage — adverse selection will continue to provide us and other researchers with policies to study and postmortems to offer on what worked and what didn't. Next time you're inclined to criticize government officials for their ineptitude, remember that they're trying to solve hard problems and confront many trade-offs. Put yourself in their shoes and ask if you could really do better.

———

—

If the problem of selection is one of private information, will there come a day when technology has made the study of selection markets obsolete? When computers can literally read our minds? If so, it's a future that is perhaps even beyond science fiction.

In Liu Cixin's sci-fi classic *The Three Body Problem*, an invading force from a far-off planet hurtles toward Earth with the intention of taking our much-greener planet for themselves. These creatures from outer space, whom earthlings call Trisolarians, hold an immense technological advantage: they've mastered interstellar travel and spy on the comings and goings of earthlings via atom-sized supercomputers they've sent in advance of their attack. But the Trisolarians can't peer inside humans' brains to see what we're thinking (owing to a quirk of evolution, Trisolarians themselves can't have any private thoughts at all). At the risk of giving away a bit of the plot, it's this ability to maintain even a shred of private information that allows humanity to save itself from destruction.

Information technologies have vastly improved companies' abilities to collect and analyze our personal data. Yet even a society with the technological wherewithal to travel light-years across the galaxy couldn't solve the seemingly much simpler problem of private information. We also imagine that if the Trisolarians—or Google or Microsoft or Facebook—*could* read our minds, world governments would do what they could to stop them.

Which is all to say that private information—as well as limits on how information that's out there can be used—are sure to be with us for many, many years to come. And so will the problems of selection that result.

—

Epilogue

SELECTION MARKETS HERE,
THERE, AND EVERYWHERE

We hope this book has left you a bit wiser about the ways of the world, at least insofar as insurance is concerned. Hopefully, it has resolved some mysteries — many of which you may not have considered before reading our book — such as why you can't get divorce insurance, why you can typically only change health insurance once a year, and why insurance is so much more expensive than it "should" be.

It won't change the sometimes-maddening aspects of buying insurance — the inflexibility in changing policies, the waiting periods, or the endless fine print and limits on claims. But understanding that these features can serve the higher purpose of mitigating selection problems might help you to be at peace with the options that insurance markets provide. No, they aren't perfect. But then we don't live in a world of perfection; we live in a world of trade-offs. Nor do we live in a world in which we've always made the right trade-offs. But the understanding that economists have gained over the past half century about selection markets, which we have tried to communicate in the preceding pages, may help us make better ones going forward.

We hope that you no longer think health insurance is like broccoli. Both may leave a bad taste in your mouth, but the price of broccoli doesn't depend on who eats it. Should any of our readers ever find their way onto the Supreme Court, we hope that they will deploy this newfound wisdom and sophistication when (not if) insurance questions again come before the court.

For our more business-minded readers, we'd like to imagine that, had American Airlines CEO Bob Crandall (whom we met back in chapter 1) read our book, he might have reconsidered his company's decision to offer the all-you-can-fly AAirpass back in 1981. And if you ever open a restaurant, we hope you'll think twice about offering an all-you-can-eat special to fill empty seats on Sunday nights.

We've focused on insurance because it's a huge industry and one for which selection plays a very central role. It's also, admittedly, one that we find fascinating. We are not alone in this respect. Indeed, Franz Kafka, who generally held a distinctly glass-half-empty view of the world, nonetheless found insurance to be captivating. Kafka spent much of his career employed by the Austrian Workmen's Accident Insurance Institute. The fact that working for the insurance industry he came to see bureaucracy as composed of pointless rules administered by small-minded autocrats will not surprise anyone who has ever tried to appeal a rejected insurance claim. But as he wrote to a friend in 1907, "the whole world of insurance itself interests me greatly, though my present work is dreary."[1] We can only hope our book has made you a bit more interested (if not "greatly" interested) in insurance as well.

But there is a much wider set of markets that are vulnerable to selection. We'd like to whet your appetite for our sequel, *Riskier Business* (should we ever get around to writing it), or at least make you appreciate the ubiquity of the economic concepts that are the foundation of our book. Because once you think about the features that make a selection market a selection market, you realize they are everywhere. Many of the business and policy consequences of selection, as well as their implications for you, the consumer (or perhaps the seller), apply in much the same way to these other markets as they do to the insurance markets that this book has focused on.

A selection market requires two things: first, that a buyer has some self-knowledge that is unknown to the seller – probably that's almost always true; second, that this self-knowledge affects how good a customer this buyer will turn out to be. If you take the broadest of interpretations, really almost any market has at least a little bit of selection. You might think that a supermarket, for example, doesn't care who buys its apples or oranges, because once the customer has paid at the register, the money belongs to the company and the apples to the consumer, regardless of the buyer's identity. Even supermarkets, however, worry about those customers with sufficient time and sense of moral indignation that they will repatriate any blemished fruit and demand a refund. These bad (read: costly) customers know who they are; the supermarket doesn't. (On the other side, the supermarket might exploit its information to foist blemished fruit on its customers; private information among sellers will be a topic for the last book in our trilogy, *Riskiest Business*.)

In some markets, selection issues are really front and center for how the market operates (or fails to operate). Insurance – as we've hopefully convinced you in this book – is a prime example. Supermarkets probably are not.

In these last few pages, we'll highlight a few other examples of markets afflicted by selection that may be particularly relevant for the lives of our readers. We hope you'll finish by thinking, "Oh *that* would have been useful; now I understand why it doesn't really exist" or "I've *been* participating in this market for half my life but never really thought about how selection makes it the way it is."

These are markets that potentially matter to all of us. If you've struggled to finance higher education, your life has been affected by selection. If you've ever applied for a credit card or loan, the process was very likely affected by selection concerns. If you've ever looked for a job, again, selection plays a role in how the labor market works (and sometimes doesn't) to help laid-off workers find new jobs. Selection markets are everywhere. We didn't have to look hard to select these examples.

The Value of an Education

You can, to some extent, measure the value of a college degree in dollars and cents. College graduates earn about 50 percent more than high school grads and 80 percent more than high school drop-outs.[2] But—and this will surprise exactly no one—these averages obscure vast differences. Some college graduates earn a lot more than otherwise equally qualified college graduates. These differences are partly a matter of dumb luck. One kid might score a job at a high-paying quant fund; another might just miss the cut. One might find work at what turns out to be the next Facebook; another, at what becomes the next Pets.com (which, unless you remember the internet bubble and bust of the late '90s, you've probably never heard of). Some students are lucky enough to graduate during a boom; others, amid recessions.

So going to college is a bit of a gamble, in financial terms. And it's now an infamously expensive one. In 2020, the average cost of a four-year college was over $100,000 (far higher at high-end private schools); and this figure doesn't account for four years of foregone earnings — money that you could have made had you not been in school.[3] What if you spend six figures on a college education, then lose the job-search lottery?

There's an insurance-like solution to this problem: someone willing to front the cost of a student's education in exchange for a share of their income for, say, the first ten years after graduation. The person or organization that pays the up-front cost of tuition bears the risks of job-market success or failure. But if the risk is spread over enough student customers, it should all even out in the end. It's called an *income-share agreement*, an idea that traces its intellectual roots back to the iconic libertarian economist Milton Friedman, who first proposed it in 1955.[4]

You can think of Friedman's proposal as a form of insurance against ending up with a low income in the future and thus facing the headaches and heartache of making debt payments you can't possibly afford. It passes the risk of a low-income future onto a deep-pocketed institution that may expect that losses from its customers with unexpectedly low incomes are offset by extra profits from those who fare unexpectedly well.

It's an indication of the potential for both societal benefit and business profit that income-share agreements (or ISAs) have been tried many times over the years. In the 1970s, Yale University was among the first to try to offer an ISA as a way of trading tuition today for graduates' income a few years down the line; it was a short-lived effort that ended with a university-financed bailout. During the time we were writing this book, at least one other college tried to offer postgraduation income insurance to attract students.[5] It's never caught on at a larger scale, though.

As you might guess, selection is surely part of the reason why Milton Friedman's idea has not taken off. You'd think if anyone could overcome the problem of private information, it would be the colleges themselves. They certainly know a great deal about their students. If they couldn't do it on their own, surely they'd be able to do so in collaboration with for-profits run by entrepreneurs who are well motivated financially to find clever ways around selection problems. That's surely what has motivated many to try. But they have been no match for selection.

To understand the selection problem, ask yourself: What kind of freshman is going to accept a university's offer of free tuition for a percentage of income? It's true that success is partly a matter of luck — but only partly. What you choose to do with your life also matters for your income. Some students might choose to take jobs on Wall Street; others, at nonprofits. Some are eager to put in eighty-hour weeks to make their way up the corporate ladder; others are looking for a more balanced lifestyle. And incoming freshmen may have some idea of what kind of lifestyle they're hoping to have.

Colleges could try to account for some of these differences in student aspirations. They could, for example, agree to take a lower percentage of economics majors' salaries (who are more likely to be among those applying for Wall Street jobs) and demand a higher percentage for those studying to be (starving) artists. But it turns out that better information is only a partial fix — students still know plenty about what their future is likely to hold, beyond what's captured by students' test scores or choice of major or other demographics. We know this to be true because of work by Nathan Hendren

—

(whose work we already saw in chapter 4), in collaboration with Daniel Herbst.[6]

Hendren and Herbst studied data on students who first en-rolled in college in 2012. The information they got on each student is about what a college might hope to know about one of its new enrollees, including basic demographics like age, sex, and race; pa-rental income; and academic information like GPA and SAT scores as well as declared major. The pair then followed these students through to 2017, so they also know whether a student graduated on time and their starting salary after graduation. They then threw the latest machine-learning technology at the task of predicting income in 2017 from what might be known to an income-share sponsor in 2012.

Critically, the students in the sample were also asked—back in 2012—questions about what they expected in the years ahead. How likely were they to graduate? Would they find work in their desired occupation? And how much did they expect to earn?

Students are wildly overoptimistic about their futures—but then, aren't we all? On average, they predicted salaries of just over $64,000 at graduation, far higher than the average of $32,700 that they actually reported earning in their first jobs. There's nonetheless a lot of information about ultimate earnings in those freshman pre-dictions: the students who expect to earn more are in fact more likely to be high earners than are students who expect to earn less.

More importantly from the perspective of the market for ISAs, when Hendren and Herbst incorporated students' forecasts into their prediction model, they found that it makes the model substantially better at predicting actual incomes. That is, there is information in students' knowledge of their futures that isn't captured by their GPA, major, family background, and so forth, so that even if ISAs take into account these various factors in setting the terms of the tuition-for-income exchange, there is still plenty of room for students who know — privately — that they won't make much after graduation. Hendren and Herbst concluded that this private information — and the resultant selection problem — is sufficiently important that ISAs would have a hard time breaking even. And if any college tried, it'd probably experience the same death spiral that we described Harvard experiencing in chapter 2 when it tried to reprice its employees' health insurance. Selection messes with this potential win-win, destroying a market that might have otherwise helped lower-income students access a college education. Certainly that was the conclusion of Hendren and Herbst, who calculated that, given the extent of private information, ISAs would have to have markups of more than 60 percent over the *average* college grad's expected income to avoid losing money. The result: those who expect to be average won't bother to apply.

ISAs do exist. Purdue still has an ISA. Lumni, a South American start-up, offers ISAs in Colombia, Chile, Mexico, and Peru and still hopes to tap the mother of all student markets, the United States. A Silicon Valley start-up, Pando, helps MBA students and professional athletes build income-pooling groups, so if one member of the group makes it big, everyone shares in the spoils.[7]

But as best we can tell, customers of these various undertakings number in the thousands, the teensiest drop in the bucket of education financing. We can hope ISAs can make the numbers work to expand their businesses in the future — there is much social benefit to be had if they can — but in order to do so, they'll need some way of finding out what, to this point, only college students seem to know about their futures.

Layoffs and Lemons

Once our graduates make their way into the labor force, the forces of selection continue to complicate their work lives. Most students do a job search their senior year of college, so there's no stigma attached to being a fresh graduate looking for employment. (The ones who are unsuccessful in this endeavor may end up in graduate and professional schools.) But what of the 2021 graduate who is sending out résumés again in 2022? An employer looking for a sane, stable, easy-to-manage worker who will stick around for more than a few weeks might wonder why the applicant's previous boss didn't do more to retain them. If sane, stable, and easy-to-manage employees are the ones that companies try to keep, while happily letting go of the rest, job seekers suffer from a classic selection problem: only the insane, unstable, hard-to-manage "bad" types make their way onto the market.

The job seekers, of course, always have a story to tell. Their previous manager was the boss from hell; the company's finances took a turn for the worse, and some new hires had to be let go. Sometimes these claims are true, but it might be hard to verify with that boss from hell who of course won't give the kindest of references. Until the applicant gets on the payroll and starts punching the clock, the new employer is at a distinct informational disadvantage.

This information gap between applicant and employer, as well as between previous and future employers, doesn't mean that no one can ever make a move if they get fired or are dissatisfied with their current job. It does, however, lead to problems that are exactly analogous to the too-expensive, too-small insurance markets that we've looked at throughout the book. That is, too few people may leave jobs that are unsatisfying, underpaid, or overseen by the boss from hell, because if they do, they face a job market in which it's assumed that most people sending out résumés are out of work for good reason. Since they're assumed to be of lower quality, the "price" — which in this case is new hires' wages — ends up being "too low."

The too-low wage further discourages workers who were on the fence about sticking it out with their current jobs from looking for something else. And so the cycle begins of lower wages leading to a worse pool of job hunters, which, in turn, leads employers to offer even less generous wages to new hires. The gap in earnings between workers who are kept and those who are shed may be further exacerbated by the following: the very same businesses that are laying off bad employees may ratchet up the salaries of the ones they want to keep, precisely so they aren't forced to find replacements from the negatively selected pool of applicants.

"Layoffs and Lemons," a well-known study by the economists Bob Gibbons and Larry Katz, found evidence for this type of adverse selection among job seekers.[8] (Their title is a nod to the original formulation of the adverse-selection problem by George Akerlof, which was titled "The Market for 'Lemons.'" Akerlof's original paper described how selection problems would affect the used-car market, and the lemons in his title refer to the many lemons provided by owners wanting to unload their defective vehicles.)

Gibbons and Katz didn't just compare the wage gap between workers who have been at the same employer for a while and those who hop from job to job — there are many reasons why the job hoppers might, all else equal, earn less. Instead, they observed that people are unemployed for various reasons, and some of these reasons trigger greater selection concerns than others. If a plant shutters, sending its entire workforce into unemployment, it probably isn't the fault of any single worker — even Homer Simpson was never able to put Montgomery Burns's nuclear power plant permanently out of commission. The plant closure is more likely the result of larger market forces — it's becoming less profitable to make cars in Detroit, so Michigan auto plants are closing — or because of spectacular mismanagement that shutters the entire operation. None of this can be pinned on a single bookkeeper minding some tiny sliver of the company's accounts or a computer technician who provides tech support to the bookkeepers. However, if only one of a dozen bookkeepers is let go, you have to wonder what's wrong with that one, relative to the other eleven.

To test whether the job market is plagued by the types of selection issues we've described, Gibbons and Katz compared job-market outcomes for workers laid off because of plant closures — which are caused by company- or market-wide problems rather than employee-specific dysfunction — to workers laid off for other reasons. They found that those who were forced out of the labor force by plant closings found new jobs faster, and their wages at these new positions were about 6 percent higher, when compared to those who were laid off for other reasons.

None of this is to say that you should suffer depression and heartache in a dead-end job overseen by a sadistic manager. When you leave, however, you might want to find a way of credibly convincing future employers that you left for a good reason or accept a lower starting wage at the new job and hope your wages will improve as you prove your mettle.

Playing with the House Money

In early 2021, the hockey player Evander Kane filed for bankruptcy. The San Jose Sharks' star was more than $8 million in the hole to

Centennial Bank as a result of his regular gambling benders in Vegas. In the last month of 2020 alone, he'd reportedly blown through $1.5 million.[9]

While it's rare to gamble with the bank's money in so literal a sense, the Evander Kane story captures a central feature of many credit contracts: the bank's upside is limited. It earns at best a fixed return based on whatever interest rate is set in the credit agreement and less if the customer defaults. By contrast, the upside for the recipient of the loan is unlimited. If things go well at the casino, there's enough to pay the bank and have plenty left over. If the fates are less kind, the bank is left with nothing, while the borrower is simply back where they started. So it goes with, say, the owner of a start-up who runs up credit card debt with an upside of a billion-dollar payday if the business takes off; the downside is declaring bankruptcy, leaving the bank with a loss on the debt, and starting over.

Who, then, will be the bank's most eager borrowers? Gamblers and risk-takers — in other words, exactly the ones the bank, in its quest for modest yet reliable return, doesn't want. Credit markets have a selection problem.

And exactly as with the selection markets we've already considered, there is the same impulse to "solve" the problem by charging higher prices — in this case, by raising the interest rates on loans and credit card balances. Again, though, raising prices only makes the problem worse. Who will want a loan at interest rates of 50 percent? Only entrepreneurs with moon-shot business ideas, who think they'll either make a fortune or go bust.

This characterization of credit markets was developed by the economist Joseph Stiglitz, whom we met in chapter 5 with his Nobel Prize and apocryphal fifth-floor walk-up. Stiglitz was interested in understanding why, particularly in poorer countries, the demand for loans from borrowers exceeded the availability of loans that banks were willing to supply at prevailing interest rates. As he observed in his classic 1981 article with Andrew Weiss, this imbalance of demand and supply should put upward pressure on interest rates, that is, the price of a loan.[10] Yet instead of charging customers more, banks rationed credit. It wasn't how the neoclassical markets that economists had long studied should behave.

Yet it was probably how banks *should* behave if they realize they are operating in a selection market—raising interest rates would attract less-reliable customers, so better to charge a bit less and keep the borrower pool from deteriorating.

If at this point you are thinking, "This isn't really how credit markets work"—you might think, for example, that Evander Kane's bankruptcy would force him to pay back some of his outstanding debts—you'd be right. Kane had declared bankruptcy, which allowed the bank to sell off his rather-sizeable home and other assets to recover some of its losses. The bank had gone further, requiring that Kane guarantee the debt with his even-more-sizeable contract with the Sharks, which totaled $49 million over the next few years (at the time of writing, Kane and the Sharks were not allowing the bank to garnish his salary, however).[11] And after declaring bankruptcy, surely Kane's credit rating would be in tatters, so he'd also have a tough time borrowing money in the future.

These are all partway measures that limit the damage that selection does to credit markets that at the same time also limit the benefits of credit. If you need to pledge collateral that's equivalent to the value of a loan, that's not helpful for someone who needs to borrow now precisely because they haven't a penny to their name but expect to start earning more in the future. The bank is in the business of making loans, not holding estate sales, so it would be better if it wasn't put in the position of regularly seizing collateral to cover unpaid debts. Everyone would be better off in a world in which borrowers have no secrets.

The need to post collateral is just one of the many ways that banks endeavor to attract customers who are most likely to pay back their debts. In other words, they follow very much along the lines of the approaches we've seen firms taking in insurance markets throughout the book. Lenders insert features into loan contracts that aim to screen out the worst risks. To give just a couple of examples, you need to put money down on a vehicle in order to get a car loan, which increases the borrower's pain if the vehicle is repossessed; or the lender may require a cosigner, who is also on the hook in case of default.

And lenders put *a lot* of effort into collecting data to predict default. Collectively, these are captured in a credit score. By stiffing Continental for millions, for example, Evander Kane surely obliterated his credit rating. Long before you get to that point, though, the many decisions, large and small, you make in your financial life add up to a credit score that is a significant determinant of whether — and at what rate — you can get a mortgage, loan, or credit card. Taking out loans and then paying them back is a good sign. Applying for many credit cards simultaneously is a bad one. Paying on time is a plus. Defaulting is credit-score death.

Yet even armed with credit scores and other predictors of default, private information remains in the hands of borrowers. That's one of the many findings from a remarkable study by Larry Ausubel, authored in collaboration with a large U.S. bank (the bank isn't named in the study).[12] The bank ran an experiment in which it randomly varied the terms offered to different prospective customers via credit card solicitations.

You've probably gotten these types of solicitations in the mail. They all look kind of the same: "You've been preapproved for an Acme Credit Card—interest rate of only 2 percent on balances for the first six months!" (Then there's the finer print explaining that after six months, the interest rate jumps to 20 percent or something like that.)

In Ausubel's study, the terms the bank offered for the credit card were different on each solicitation. For example, one lucky household might have been offered a 2 percent "teaser" rate, while another, by chance, faced a 6 percent rate. The longer-term interest charge might be 10 percent for some and 20 percent for others. Ausubel could then analyze how these terms affected whether recipients accepted the offer and also *who* took the offer. Because of selection, the bank didn't just care how many customers it got; it also wanted to make sure it got the right ones.

Like every other bank, the credit card issuer had some idea of the riskiness of the various people who were getting its solicitations. So it could compare, for a given offer, whether it was accepted by recipients with worse credit scores and other markers for default. The ones flagged as risky were indeed more likely to take up the credit card. This gap in creditworthiness between recipients accepting the offer and those ignoring it was at its worst when the advertised interest rate was particularly high—people with decent credit scores aren't interested in credit cards that offer horrible terms.

Here was empirical proof of what Stiglitz and Weiss had theorized: even when there's excess demand for loans at the bank's interest rates, it may make sense to leave rates where they are. Raising them isn't a profitable strategy if doing so discourages the best customers from applying.

Stiglitz observed in his 2001 Nobel Prize address that the reason why economists in earlier generations had assumed away the problem of private information wasn't because they actually thought all relevant data were out in the public domain. Rather—as we've seen throughout the book—the problem is that it's a lot harder to model and analyze the behavior of markets in the presence of private information. It's better, perhaps, just to assume that it's not there and hope for the best. However, as the information economics revolution that Stiglitz helped to lead showed us, information matters in very fundamental ways for how markets work or don't.

Stiglitz went on to explain that the particular nature and consequences of private information surely differ from market to market—borrowers' secrets have different consequences from those of insurance customers, for example. Indeed, the very nature of these secrets may differ across markets and circumstance. As Stiglitz put it—(un?)knowingly repurposing Tolstoy's line about happy families—"while there was a single way in which information could be perfect, there are an infinite number of ways in which information can be imperfect."[13]

Thus, while there are indeed common features across all selection markets, understanding the effects of selection in credit markets needs a book in itself. Selection in labor markets too requires its own volume. We hope we've given you just a taste of what those volumes might have in store for you.

ACKNOWLEDGMENTS

This book benefited greatly from a number of generous friends, family members, and colleagues who read the draft. All three of our fathers—Roni Einav, Alan Finkelstein, and Michael Fisman—read early drafts and provided extensive comments as well as useful insights into how "real people" (or at least noneconomists) think. In addition, Gill Bejerano, Todd Fitch, Annabella Gong, Gail Marcus, Ben Olken, Maura O'Neill, Emily Oster, Jim Poterba, and Gina Wilson all provided extensive comments on the entire draft, sometimes multiple times.

We are also grateful to the following people who provided key feedback on specific parts of the draft: Ran Abramitzky, George Akerlof, Colleen Carey, Nathan Hendren, Damon Jones, Julian Reif, Steve Shebik, David Stuewe, and Mark Vonnahme.

We are enormously grateful to Connie Xu for her extraordinary research assistance. Connie was there from the very beginning and continued helping us even after she went from being an RA to a full-time PhD student. Her ability to take our vague requests and musings, dig into a topic, and return with both essential background information and delightful nuggets that fed directly into our book was invaluable. Her constant good cheer and (purported) enthusiasm for every request we threw at her—from automobile insurance mandates to tontines to genetic-testing regulation to pet health insurance—was also much appreciated. This book truly would not have been the same without her.

Finally, we would each like to acknowledge our families, albeit in different ways. Ray would like to thank—and apologize to—his wife and children, who have suffered through countless dinnertime conversations during which he recounted the many fascinating insurance-related facts and stories that fill this book. Amy is grateful to her husband, Ben, who, despite being a bad insurance customer (see chapter 5), has been a steadfast source of support and sage advice ever since he won her heart on their first date by commenting on the selection properties of the credit card he used to pay for (his portion of) their meal. Liran is still in the process of trying to convince his wife and kids that insurance is much more interesting than brown socks (see the Prologue).

NOTES

CHAPTER 1

1. "Company News: American to Offer Fixed-Fare Passes," *New York Times,* September 22, 1981, sec. Business, https://www.nytimes.com/1981/09/22 /business/company-news-american-to-offer-fixed-fare-passes.html; Ken Bensinger, "The Frequent Fliers Who Flew Too Much," *Los Angeles Times,* May 5, 2012, sec. Travel, https://www.latimes.com/travel/la-xpm-2012-may-05-la-fi-0506 -golden-ticket-20120506-story.html.

2. George A. Akerlof, "The Market for 'Lemons': Quality Uncertainty and the Market Mechanism," *Quarterly Journal of Economics* 84, no. 3 (1970): 488–500, https://doi.org/10.2307/1879431; Nobel Prize, "George A. Akerlof," accessed January 26, 2022, https://www.nobelprize.org/prizes/economic-sciences/2001 /akerlof/facts/.

3. GEICO, "Geico Pet Insurance Calculator," accessed February 1, 2022, https://www.geico.com/pet-insurance/.

4. Michael Isbell, "AIDS and Access to Care: Lessons for Health Care Reformers," *Cornell Journal of Law and Public Policy* 3, no. 1 (1993): 7–54; California Task Force on HIV/AIDS Insurance Issues, *Report to the Commissioner from the Task Force on HIV/AIDS Insurance Issues* (Sacramento: California Department of Insurance, 1992).

5. Society of Actuaries AIDS Task Force, "The Impact of Aids on Life and Health Insurance Companies: A Guide for Practicing Actuaries," *Transactions of Society of Actuaries* 40, pt. 2 (1988), https://www.soa.org/globalassets/assets/library /research/transactions-of-society-of-actuaries/1988/january/tsa88v40pt25.pdf;

—

Jane E. Sisk, "The Costs of Aids: A Review of the Estimates," *Health Affairs* 6, no. 2 (1987): 5–21.

6. World Health Organization, "HIV/AIDS," November 30, 2020, https://www.who.int/news-room/fact-sheets/detail/hiv-aids; Richard A. McKay, "'Patient Zero': The Absence of a Patient's View of the Early North American AIDS Epidemic," *Bulletin of the History of Medicine* 88, no. 1 (2014): 161–94.

7. Transcript of Oral Argument, Department of Health and Human Services, et al., v. Florida, et al., No. 11-398 (Supreme Court of the United States March 27, 2012).

8. Holly Wood, "Unless You've Lived without Health Insurance, You Have No Idea How Scary It Is," *Vox*, March 14, 2017, https://www.vox.com/first-person/2017/3/14/14907348/health-insurance-uninsured-ahca-obamacare.

9. Kaitlyn Wells and Mark Smirniotis, "How to Shop for the Best Pet Insurance," *Wirecutter, New York Times*, August 25, 2021, https://www.nytimes.com/wirecutter/reviews/best-pet-insurance/.

10. Timothy Snyder, *Our Malady: Lessons in Liberty from a Hospital Diary* (New York: Crown, 2020), 138.

11. Anne B. Martin, Micah Hartman, David Lassman, and Aaron Catlin, "National Health Care Spending in 2019: Steady Growth for the Fourth Consecutive Year," *Health Affairs* 40, no. 1 (December 16, 2020): 14–24, https://doi.org/10.1377/hlthaff.2020.02022; Insurance Information Institute, "Facts + Statistics: Industry Overview," accessed September 13, 2021, https://www.iii.org/fact-statistic/facts-statistics-industry-overview; U.S. Bureau of Economic Analysis, "Gross Domestic Product, Fourth Quarter and Year 2019 (Third Estimate); Corporate Profits, Fourth Quarter and Year 2019," March 26, 2020, https://www.bea.gov/news/2020/gross-domestic-product-fourth-quarter-and-year-2019-third-estimate-corporate-profits.

12. Congressional Budget Office, "The Federal Budget in 2019: An Infographic," April 15, 2020, https://www.cbo.gov/publication/56324; U.S. Department of the Treasury, "Remarks of Under Secretary of the Treasury Peter R. Fisher to the Columbus Council on World Affairs Columbus, Ohio Beyond Borrowing: Meeting the Government's Financial Challenges in the 21st Century," press release, November 14, 2002, https://www.treasury.gov/press-center/press-releases/Pages/po3622.aspx.

13. Center for Responsive Politics, "Defense PACs Contributions to Candidates," OpenSecrets, 2020, https://www.opensecrets.org/political-action-committees-pacs/industry-detail/D/2020; Insurance Information Institute, "Facts + Statistics"; Center for Responsive Politics, "Industry Breakdown," OpenSecrets, 2020, https://www.opensecrets.org/political-action-committees-pacs/industry-breakdown/2020.

CHAPTER 2

1. Mark Leland, "FOX 11 Investigates Layoff Insurance," Fox 11 News, November 11, 2018, https://fox11online.com/news/fox-11-investigates/fox-11 -investigates-layoff-insurance.

2. Jackson, comment on "Good Luck Getting Private Insurance for Unemployment," *New York Times,* August 7, 2009, sec. Your Money, https://www.nytimes .com/2009/08/08/your-money/08money.html; Ron Lieber, "Finally, Private Unemployment Insurance. But Will Anyone Buy It?," *New York Times,* May 27, 2016, sec. Your Money, https://www.nytimes.com/2016/05/28/your-money/finally -private-unemployment-insurance-but-will-anyone-buy-it.html.

3. Jackson, comment on "Good Luck Getting Private Insurance"; Relaxed_ Meat, "IncomeAssure Supplemental Unemployment Insurance," *R/Personalfinance,* Reddit, May 4, 2016, http://www.reddit.com/r/personalfinance/comments /4hwzx8/incomeassure_supplemental_unemployment_insurance/.

4. Erin McDowell, "The Average Cost of Getting Divorced Is $15,000 in the US—but Here's Why It Can Be Much Higher," *Business Insider,* August 1, 2019, https://www.businessinsider.com/average-cost-divorce-getting-divorced-us -2019-7.

5. National Center for Health Statistics, Center for Disease Control and Prevention, "National Marriage and Divorce Rate Trends," 2021, https://www.cdc .gov/nchs/data/dvs/national-marriage-divorce-rates-00-19.pdf.

6. Monica Scherer, "Divorce Insurance?," *Maryland Divorce Lawyer Blog,* November 2, 2012, https://www.marylanddivorcelawyerblog.com/divorce_insurance/; Jennifer Saranow Schultz, "Divorce Insurance (Yes, Divorce Insurance)," *Bucks* (blog), *New York Times,* August 6, 2010, https://bucks.blogs.nytimes.com/2010 /08/06/divorce-insurance-yes-divorce-insurance/.

7. Schultz, "Divorce Insurance."

8. Doug Kenney, "A Dog Named Buffy Launches Pet Health Insurance," Your Pet Insurance Guide, February 24, 2009, https://www.petinsuranceguideus.com /2009/02/a-.html.

9. Statista, "Pet Insurance Premium Volume in the U.S. 2013–2019," November 5, 2020, https://www.statista.com/statistics/606279/total-premium-volume -for-pet-insurance-usa/; Susan Jenks, "Pet Insurance Is the Latest Work Perk," *New York Times,* June 7, 2017, https://www.nytimes.com/2017/06/07/well/family /pet-insurance-is-the-latest-work-perk.html.

10. Petplan, "Start Quote," December 2020, https://www.gopetplan.com /mypet.

11. Embrace Pet Insurance, "Comprehensive Pet Insurance Coverage," 2021, https://www.embracepetinsurance.com/coverage/pet-insurance-plan; Trupanion, "Is Your Pet Eligible for Pet Health Insurance?," 2021, https://trupanion.com/pet-insurance/is-your-pet-eligible.

12. Kaitlyn Wells and Mark Smirniotis, "How to Shop for the Best Pet Insurance," *Wirecutter, New York Times*, August 25, 2021, https://www.nytimes.com/wirecutter/reviews/best-pet-insurance/.

13. Marika Cabral, "Claim Timing and Ex Post Adverse Selection," *Review of Economic Studies* 84, no. 1 (January 2017): 1–44, https://doi.org/10.1093/restud/rdw022.

14. David M. Cutler and Sarah J. Reber, "Paying for Health Insurance: The Trade-Off between Competition and Adverse Selection," *Quarterly Journal of Economics* 113, no. 2 (1998): 433–66.

15. Thomas C. Buchmueller and Paul J. Feldstein, "The Effect of Price on Switching among Health Plans," *Journal of Health Economics* 16, no. 2 (April 1, 1997): 231–47, https://doi.org/10.1016/S0167-6296(96)00531-0.

16. Charles Kelley Knight, *The History of Life Insurance in the United States to 1870* (Philadelphia: University of Pennsylvania, 1920).

17. Gerard Malynes, *Consuetudo; Vel, Lex Mercatoria; or, The Ancient Law-Merchant, in Three Parts, According to the Essentials of Traffick* (London: Basset, 1622); Knight, *History of Life Insurance.*

18. Geoffrey Clark, "Life Insurance in the Society and Culture of London, 1700–75," *Urban History* 24, no. 1 (1997): 17–36.

19. Knight, *History of Life Insurance;* Cornelius Walford, "History of Life Assurance in the United Kingdom (Continued)," *Journal of the Institute of Actuaries and Assurance Magazine* 25, no. 3 (1885): 207–16; Clark, "Life Insurance in the Society and Culture of London."

20. Mila Araujo and Julius Mansa, "What to Expect from a Life Insurance Medical Exam," *The Balance*, April 1, 2021, https://www.thebalance.com/what-to-expect-your-life-insurance-medical-exam-2645799.

21. Daifeng He, "The Life Insurance Market: Asymmetric Information Revisited," *Journal of Public Economics* 93, no. 9 (October 1, 2009): 1090–97, https://doi.org/10.1016/j.jpubeco.2009.07.001.

22. Logan Sachon, "What Happens If You Lie on Your Life Insurance Application," *Policygenius*, August 2, 2019, https://www.policygenius.com/blog/what-happens-if-you-lie-on-your-life-insurance-application/.

23. Northwestern Mutual Life Insurance Company, "Form of Life Insurance Application," accessed April 20, 2021, https://www.sec.gov/Archives/edgar/data/742277/000119312505088510/dex99e.htm; Andrew P. Tobias, *The Invisible Bankers* (Markham, Ont.: PaperJacks, 1983); Aubrey Cohen, "How DUIs Can

Wreck Your Chance to Buy Life Insurance," *USA Today,* September 26, 2015, https://www.usatoday.com/story/money/personalfinance/2015/09/26/nerdwallet -life-insurance-drunk-driving/72825260/.

24. Victoria Divino, Mitch DeKoven, John H. Warner, Joseph Guiliano, Karen E. Anderson, Douglas Langbehn, and Won Chan Lee, "The Direct Medical Costs of Huntington's Disease by Stage: A Retrospective Commercial and Medicaid Claims Data Analysis," *Journal of Medical Economics* 16, no. 8 (August 2013): 1043–50, https://doi.org/10.3111/13696998.2013.818545.

25. Huntington's Disease Collaborative Research Group, "A Novel Gene Containing a Trinucleotide Repeat That Is Expanded and Unstable on Huntington's Disease Chromosomes," *Cell* 72, no. 6 (1993): 971–83.

26. Kalyan B. Bhattacharyya, "The Story of George Huntington and His Disease," *Annals of Indian Academy of Neurology* 19, no. 1 (2016): 25–28, https://doi .org/10.4103/0972-2327.175425; Chuck Dinerstein, "The Hamptons, Huntington's & Hope," American Council on Science and Health, May 22, 2019, https:// www.acsh.org/news/2019/05/22/hamptons-huntingtons-hope-14047.

27. Howard Markel, "This Genetic Brain Disorder Turned Woody Guthrie's Life from Songs to Suffering," *PBS.org,* July 14, 2019, https://www.pbs.org/news hour/health/this-genetic-brain-disorder-turned-woody-guthries-life-from-songs -to-suffering; Judity Dobrzynski, "The Lost Years of Woody Guthrie: The Singer's Life in Greystone Hospital," *Aljazeera America,* January 12, 2014, http://america .aljazeera.com/features/2014/1/when-the-hard-travelinawasoverwoodyguth rieatgreystonehospital.html; Woody Guthrie Publications, "The Hospital Years (1954–1967)," accessed October 29, 2020, https://www.woodyguthrie.org/biog raphy/biography8.htm.

28. Jeff Wallenfeldt, "Woody Guthrie | Biography, Music, & Facts," *Britannica,* accessed April 9, 2021, https://www.britannica.com/biography/Woody-Guthrie; Huntington's Disease Society of America, "Long-Term Care Huntington's Disease," Family Guide Series booklet, 2009.

29. Emily Oster, Ira Shoulson, Kimberly Quaid, and E. Ray Dorsey, "Genetic Adverse Selection: Evidence from Long-Term Care Insurance and Huntington Disease," *Journal of Public Economics* 94, no. 11 (December 1, 2010): 1041–50, https:// doi.org/10.1016/j.jpubeco.2010.06.009.

30. "For Arlo Guthrie, 'Alice' Brought What He Wanted," *New York Times,* August 8, 2007, sec. Arts, https://www.nytimes.com/2007/08/08/arts/08iht -guthrie.1.7034904.html; Emily Oster, Ira Shoulson, and E. Ray Dorsey, "Optimal Expectations and Limited Medical Testing: Evidence from Huntington Disease," *American Economic Review* 103, no. 2 (2013): 804–30, https://doi.org/10.1257 /aer.103.2.804.

31. National Human Genome Research Institute, "Genetic Discrimination," accessed April 9, 2021, https://www.genome.gov/about-genomics/policy-issues/Genetic-Discrimination.

32. Kira Peikoff, "Fearing Punishment for Bad Genes," *New York Times*, April 7, 2014, https://www.nytimes.com/2014/04/08/science/fearing-punishment-for-bad-genes.html?searchResultPosition=6.

CHAPTER 3

1. Craig R. Whitney, "Jeanne Calment, World's Elder, Dies at 122," *New York Times*, August 5, 1997, sec. World, https://www.nytimes.com/1997/08/05/world/jeanne-calment-world-s-elder-dies-at-122.html; Lucinda Smyth, "Jeanne Calment: The Supercentenarian Who Met Van Gogh and Lived to See Tony Blair Elected PM," *Prospect*, August 21, 2018, https://www.prospectmagazine.co.uk/arts-and-books/jeanne-calment-the-supercentenarian-who-met-van-gogh-and-lived-to-see-tony-blair-elected-pm; Jason Daley, "Was the World's Oldest Person Ever Actually Her 99-Year-Old Daughter?," *Smithsonian Magazine*, January 2, 2019, https://www.smithsonianmag.com/smart-news/study-questions-age-worlds-oldest-woman-180971153/; Lauren Collins, "Was Jeanne Calment the Oldest Person Who Ever Lived — or a Fraud?," *New Yorker*, February 10, 2020, https://www.newyorker.com/magazine/2020/02/17/was-jeanne-calment-the-oldest-person-who-ever-lived-or-a-fraud.

2. "A 120-Year Lease on Life Outlasts Apartment Heir," *New York Times*, December 29, 1995, sec. A.

3. Social Security Administration, "Actuarial Life Table," 2017, https://www.ssa.gov/oact/STATS/table4c6.html.

4. Smyth, "Jeanne Calment."

5. Social Security Administration, "Actuarial Life Table," 2017, https://www.ssa.gov/oact/STATS/table4c6.html.

6. Anders Hald, *A History of Probability and Statistics and Their Applications before 1750* (Hoboken, N.J.: Wiley, 1990); Poterba, "Annuities in Early Modern Europe."

7. Murphy, *Sale of Annuities by Governments;* Aquinas, *Summa Theologiae;* Poterba, "Annuities in Early Modern Europe"; Usury Act, 13 Ann., c. 15 (1714).

8. Sybil Campbell, "Usury and Annuities of the Eighteenth Century," *Law Quarterly Review* 44, no. 4 (1928): 473.

9. Geoffrey Poitras, *The Early History of Financial Economics, 1478–1776* (Northampton, Mass.: Elgar, 2000); François R. Velde and David R. Weir, "The Financial Market and Government Debt Policy in France, 1746–1793," *Journal of Economic History* 52, no. 1 (1992): 1–39; Poterba, "Annuities in Early Modern Europe"; Michael Wolfe, *Walled Towns and the Shaping of France: From the Medieval* *to the Early Modern Era* (New York: Palgrave Macmillan, 2009); Nicolas De Vijlder and Michael Limberger, "Public or Private Interests? The Investment Behaviour of Public Officials in Antwerp during the Early Modern Period," *Financial History Review* 21, no. 3 (2014): 301-26; Murphy, *Sale of Annuities by Governments;* John Briscoe, "An Abstract of the Discourse on the Late Funds of the Million-Act, Lottery-Act, and Bank of England" (London, 1694); George Alter and James C. Riley, "How to Bet on Lives: A Guide to Life Contingent Contracts in Early Modern Europe," *Research in Economic History* 10 (1986): 1-53.

10. Poterba, "Annuities in Early Modern Europe."

11. Poterba, "Annuities in Early Modern Europe"; Murphy, *Sale of Annuities by Governments.*

12. Poterba, "Annuities in Early Modern Europe"; Alter and Riley, "How to Bet on Lives"; Velde and Weir, "Financial Market and Government Debt Policy"; George V. Taylor, "The Paris Bourse on the Eve of the Revolution, 1781-1789," *American Historical Review* 67, no. 4 (1962): 951-77.

13. Alter and Riley, "How to Bet on Lives"; Poterba, "Annuities in Early Modern Europe."

14. John Francis, *Annals, Anecdotes and Legends: A Chronicle of Life Assurance* (London: Longman, Brown, Green, and Longmans, 1853); Murphy, *Sale of Annuities by Governments;* Poterba, "Annuities in Early Modern Europe."

15. Hald, *History of Probability and Statistics.*

16. Edmond Halley, "An Estimate of the Degrees of the Mortality of Mankind: Drawn from Curious Tables of the Births and Funerals at the City of Breslaw; with an Attempt to Ascertain the Price of Annuities upon Lives," *Philosophical Transactions of the Royal Society of London* 17, no. 196 (January 1, 1693): 596-610, https://doi.org/10.1098/rstl.1693.0007; Geoffrey Heywood, "Edmond Halley – Actuary," *Quarterly Journal of the Royal Astronomical Society* 35, no. 1 (1994): 151; Poitras, "Early History of Financial Economics."

17. Marquis James, *The Metropolitan Life: A Study in Business Growth* (New York: Viking, 1947).

18. Jan de Witt, *Value of Life Annuities in Proportion to Redeemable Annuities* (1671); Wade Pfau, "Annuity Pricing 101," *Forbes,* August 13, 2015, https://www.forbes.com/sites/wadepfau/2015/08/13/annuity-pricing-101/.

19. Poterba, "Annuities in Early Modern Europe"; Velde and Weir, "Financial Market and Government Debt Policy."

20. Menahem E. Yaari, "Uncertain Lifetime, Life Insurance, and the Theory of the Consumer," *Review of Economic Studies* 32, no. 2 (April 1, 1965): 137-50, https://doi.org/10.2307/2296058; Thomas Davidoff, Jeffrey R. Brown, and Peter A. Diamond, "Annuities and Individual Welfare," *American Economic Review*

95, no. 5 (December 2005): 1573–90, https://doi.org/10.1257/000282805 775014281.

21. Jeffrey R. Brown, "Rational and Behavioral Perspectives on the Role of Annuities in Retirement Planning" (NBER Working Paper 13537, National Bureau of Economic Research, Cambridge, Mass., October 23, 2007), https://doi .org/10.3386/w13537; Davidoff, Brown, and Diamond, "Annuities and Individual Welfare"; Jeffrey R. Brown, Jeffrey R. King, Sendhil Mullainathan, and Marian V. Wrobel, "Why Don't People Insure Late-Life Consumption? A Framing Explanation of the Under-Annuitization Puzzle," *American Economic Review* 98, no. 2 (May 2008): 304–9, https://doi.org/10.1257/aer.98.2.304.

22. Ron Lieber, "We Went to a Steak Dinner Annuity Pitch. The Salesman Wasn't Pleased," *New York Times,* November 30, 2018, sec. Your Money, https:// www.nytimes.com/2018/11/30/your-money/retirement-annuities-steak-dinner .html; FBI, "Elder Fraud," accessed January 26, 2022, https://www.fbi.gov/scams -and-safety/common-scams-and-crimes/elder-fraud.

23. Lawrence Pines, "Understanding the Rules for Defined-Benefit Pension Plans," *Investopedia,* May 31, 2021, https://www.investopedia.com/articles/credit -loans-mortgages/090816/understanding-rules-defined-benefit-pension-plans.asp.

24. Halley, "Estimate of the Degrees of the Mortality"; Heywood, "Edmond Halley," 151.

25. Rabah Kamal, Julie Hudman, and Daniel McDermott, "What Do We Know about Infant Mortality in the U.S. and Comparable Countries?," Peterson-KFF Health System Tracker, October 18, 2019, https://www.healthsystemtracker .org/chart-collection/infant-mortality-u-s-compare-countries/#item-start; Social Security Administration, "Actuarial Life Table," 2017, https://www.ssa.gov/oact /STATS/table4c6.html.

26. Congressional Budget Office, "The Federal Budget in 2019: An Infographic," April 15, 2020, https://www.cbo.gov/publication/56324.

27. Society of Actuaries, "Mortality and Other Rate Tables," accessed April 27, 2021, https://mort.soa.org/.

28. James Poterba and Adam Solomon, "Discount Rates, Mortality Projections, and Money's Worth Calculations for US Individual Annuities" (NBER Working Paper 28557, National Bureau of Economic Research, Cambridge, Mass., March 2021), https://doi.org/10.3386/w28557.

CHAPTER 4

1. Andrew McFarlane, "How the UK's First Fatal Car Accident Unfolded," *BBC News Magazine,* August 17, 2010, https://www.bbc.com/news/magazine

-10987606; Fredrick Kunkle, "121 Years Ago Bridget Driscoll Was the First Pedestrian to Be Killed by an Automobile," *Washington Post,* March 22, 2018, https://www.washingtonpost.com/news/tripping/wp/2018/03/22/fatal-crash-with-self-driving-car-was-a-first-like-bridget-driscolls-was-121-years-ago-with-one-of-the-first-cars/.

2. Roger Roots, "The Dangers of Automobile Travel: A Reconsideration," *American Journal of Economics and Sociology* 66, no. 5 (2007): 959–76; Federal Highway Administration, "Motor Vehicle Traffic Fatalities, 1900–2007," 2007, https://www.fhwa.dot.gov/policyinformation/statistics/2007/pdf/fi200.pdf.

3. Patrick Robertson, *Robertson's Book of Firsts: Who Did What for the First Time* (London: Bloomsbury, 2011); "Perils of Automobile Manipulation – What Experience Is Teaching – Necessity for Insurance of Machines and against Personal Accidents – New Policy Forms Issued by the Travelers Insurance Company," *The Spectator,* April 15, 1909.

4. "Gilbert Loomis, 90, an Inventor of Cars," *New York Times,* October 27, 1961.

5. Allstate Insurance, "Allstate Online Shopping," accessed February 2, 2022, https://purchase.allstate.com/onlineshopping/welcome; Nationwide, "Auto Insurance – Get a Free Car Insurance Quote," accessed February 2, 2022, https://www.nationwide.com/personal/insurance/auto/.

6. U.S. Department of State, "Vehicle Liability Insurance Requirements," accessed April 29, 2021, https://www.state.gov/vehicle-liability-insurance-requirements/.

7. Eric J. Holweg, "Mariner's Guide for Hurricane Awareness in the North Atlantic Basin," National Oceanic and Atmospheric Administration, Silver Spring, Md., August 2000.

8. Christopher Kingston, "Governance and Institutional Change in Marine Insurance, 1350–1850," *European Review of Economic History* 18, no. 1 (February 1, 2014): 4, https://doi.org/10.1093/ereh/het019.

9. Christopher Kingston, "Adverse Selection and Institutional Change in Eighteenth Century Marine Insurance" (unpublished working paper, Amherst College, Amherst, Mass., November 17, 2016).

10. U.S. Federal Highway Administration, *Driver License Administration Requirements and Fees* (Washington, D.C.: U.S. Department of Transportation, Federal Highway Administration, 1967).

11. "Perils of Automobile Manipulation"; U.S. Federal Highway Administration, *Driver License Administration Requirements and Fees;* U.S. Senate Subcommittee on Antitrust and Monopoly, *The Insurance Industry: Hearings Before the United States Senate, Senate Subcommittee on Antitrust and Monopoly* (1971); Dorothy Barclay, "A

Boy, a Car: A Problem," *New York Times,* November 22, 1959, https://www.ny times.com/1959/11/22/archives/a-boy-a-car-a-problem.html.

12. "Telling the Risky from the Reliable," *Businessweek,* August 1, 2005.

13. Allstate Insurance, "Allstate Online Shopping"; Nationwide, "Auto Insurance"; State Farm, "Car Insurance Quote Checklist — State Farm," accessed February 2, 2022, https://www.statefarm.com/insurance/auto/resources/auto-insurance -checklist.

14. Federal Trade Commission, "Credit-Based Insurance Scores: Impacts on Consumers of Automobile Insurance," July 2007; Jane Birnbaum, "A Poor Credit Rating May Affect Auto Policy," *New York Times,* August 27, 1994, sec. 1.

15. Alma Cohen, "Asymmetric Information and Learning: Evidence from the Automobile Insurance Market," *Review of Economics and Statistics* 87, no. 2 (2005): 197–207; Hyojoung Kim, Doyoung Kim, Subin Im, and James W. Hardin, "Evidence of Asymmetric Information in the Automobile Insurance Market: Dichotomous versus Multinomial Measurement of Insurance Coverage," *Journal of Risk and Insurance* 76, no. 2 (2009): 343–66; Peng Shi, Wei Zhang, and Emiliano A. Valdez, "Testing Adverse Selection with Two-Dimensional Information: Evidence from the Singapore Auto Insurance Market," *Journal of Risk and Insurance* 79, no. 4 (2012): 1077–1114.

16. Cohen, "Asymmetric Information and Learning."

17. Ralph Nader, *Unsafe at Any Speed* (New York: Pocket Books, 1966).

18. Nathaniel Hendren, "Private Information and Insurance Rejections," *Econometrica* 81, no. 5 (September 2013): 1713–62.

19. William Vickrey, "Automobile Accidents, Tort Law, Externalities, and Insurance: An Economist's Critique," *Law and Contemporary Problems* 33, no. 3 (July 1, 1968): 464–87; Nobel Prize, "William Vickrey," accessed January 26, 2022, https:// www.nobelprize.org/prizes/economic-sciences/1996/vickrey/biographical/.

20. Progressive, "Our History," accessed April 30, 2021, https://www.pro gressive.com/about/history/; Adam Tanner, "Data Monitoring Saves Some People Money on Car Insurance, but Some Will Pay More," *Forbes,* August 14, 2013, https://www.forbes.com/sites/adamtanner/2013/08/14/data-monitoring-saves -some-people-money-on-car-insurance-but-some-will-pay-more/#28f33a3 e2334; Steve O'Hear, "Cuvva Raises £15M Series A to Launch Flexible Monthly Car Insurance," *TechCrunch,* December 3, 2019, https://techcrunch.com/2019/12 /03/cuvva-raises-15m/.

21. Ptolemus Consulting Group, "UBI Infographic 2018," 2018, https:// www.ptolemus.com/ubi-infographic-2018/.

22. timberwolvesguy, comment on "Don't Use Insurance Tracking Devices to

Get a Discount!," *r/cars*, Reddit, August 7, 2018, https://www.reddit.com/r/cars /comments/957a7w/dont_use_insurance_tracking_devices_to_get_a/.

23. Yizhou Jin and Shoshana Vasserman, "Buying Data from Consumers: The Impact of Monitoring Programs in U.S. Auto Insurance" (NBER Working Paper 29096, National Bureau of Economic Research, Cambridge, Mass., 2021), https:// doi.org/10.3386/w29096; Lee Rainie and Maeve Duggan, "Auto Insurance Discounts and Monitoring," Pew Research Center, January 14, 2016, https://www .pewresearch.org/internet/2016/01/14/scenario-auto-insurance-discounts-and -monitoring/.

24. Amy Finkelstein and James Poterba, "Testing for Asymmetric Information Using 'Unused Observables' in Insurance Markets: Evidence from the UK Annuity Market," *Journal of Risk and Insurance* 81, no. 4 (2014): 709–34.

25. Halley, "Estimate of the Degrees of the Mortality of Mankind."

26. Aquinas, *Summa Theologiae;* Bernard W. Dempsey, "Just Price in a Functional Economy," *American Economic Review* 25, no. 3 (1935): 471–86.

27. Virginia Heffernan, "Amazon's Prime Suspect," *New York Times Magazine,* August 6, 2010, https://www.nytimes.com/2010/08/08/magazine/08FOB -medium-t.html; David Streitfeld, "On the Web, Price Tags Blur," *Washington Post,* September 27, 2000, https://www.washingtonpost.com/archive/politics/2000 /09/27/on-the-web-price-tags-blur/14daea51-3a64-488f-8e6b-c1a3654773da/.

28. Daniel Kahneman, Jack L. Knetsch, and Richard Thaler, "Fairness as a Constraint on Profit Seeking: Entitlements in the Market," *American Economic Review* 76, no. 4 (1986): 728–41.

29. Judity Dobrzynski, "The Lost Years of Woody Guthrie: The Singer's Life in Greystone Hospital," *Aljazeera America,* January 12, 2014, http://america.aljazeera .com/features/2014/1/when-the-hard-travelinawasoverwoodyguthrieatgreystone hospital.html.

30. Julia Angwin, Jeff Larson, Lauren Kirchner, and Surya Mattu, "Minority Neighborhoods Pay Higher Car Insurance Premiums than White Areas with the Same Risk," ProPublica, April 5, 2017, https://www.propublica.org/article /minority-neighborhoods-higher-car-insurance-premiums-white-areas-same -risk?token=MZ4huG2khovdFzdzgBUWYctqeKrXQgA5.

31. Teresa Hunter, "Your Pension Will Depend on Your Postcode: Norwich Union Will Base Annuities on Location and Socio-economic Status," *Sunday Telegraph,* July 6, 2003; Naomi Caine, "Postcode Prejudice," *Sunday Times,* July 13, 2003.

32. Kahneman, Knetsch, and Thaler, "Fairness as a Constraint on Profit Seeking," 732–33.

33. Maddy Varner and Aaron Sankin, "Suckers List: How Allstate's Secret Auto

Insurance Algorithm Squeezes Big Spenders," The Markup, February 25, 2020, https://themarkup.org/allstates-algorithm/2020/02/25/car-insurance-suckers-list.

34. Varner and Sankin.

35. John Rawls, *A Theory of Justice* (Cambridge, Mass.: Harvard University Press, 1971).

CHAPTER 5

1. Arthur Conan Doyle, "A Scandal in Bohemia," in *The Adventures of Sherlock Holmes* (New York: A. L. Burt, 1920), 12.

2. Doyle, 21.

3. Doyle, 24.

4. Mila Araujo and Thomas Catalano, "What Is the Dental Insurance Waiting Period and How Does It Work?," *The Balance*, August 7, 2020, https://www.the balance.com/dental-insurance-waiting-period-2645722; Centers for Medicare and Medicaid Services, "Gym Membership Coverage," accessed October 28, 2020, https://www.medicare.gov/coverage/gym-memberships-fitness-programs; Gary Schuman, "Suicide and the Life Insurance Contract: Was the Insured Sane or Insane? That Is the Question—or Is It?," *Tort and Insurance Law Journal* 28 (1993): 745–77.

5. Joseph E. Stiglitz, "Information and the Change in the Paradigm in Economics," *American Economic Review* 92, no. 3 (2002): 472.

6. Kaiser Family Foundation, "Medicare Advantage," June 6, 2019, https://www.kff.org/medicare/fact-sheet/medicare-advantage/.

7. Centers for Medicare and Medicaid Services, "Gym Membership Coverage"; Alicia L. Cooper and Amal N. Trivedi, "Fitness Memberships and Favorable Selection in Medicare Advantage Plans," *New England Journal of Medicine* 366, no. 2 (January 12, 2012): 150–57, https://doi.org/10.1056/NEJMsa1104273.

8. Meredith Freed, Anthony Damico, and Tricia Neuman, "A Dozen Facts about Medicare Advantage in 2020," Kaiser Family Foundation, January 13, 2021, https://www.kff.org/medicare/issue-brief/a-dozen-facts-about-medicare-advantage-in-2020/.

9. Damon Jones, David Molitor, and Julian Reif, "What Do Workplace Wellness Programs Do? Evidence from the Illinois Workplace Wellness Study," *Quarterly Journal of Economics* 134, no. 4 (November 1, 2019): 1747–91, https://doi.org/10.1093/qje/qjz023.

10. Charlotte Lieberman, "What Wellness Programs Don't Do for Workers," *Harvard Business Review,* August 14, 2019, https://hbr.org/2019/08/what-wellness-programs-dont-do-for-workers.

11. Arthur Miller, *Death of a Salesman* (New York: Penguin Books, 1998), 99–100.

12. Sandra G. Boodman, "The Dilemma of AZT: Who Can Afford It?," *South Florida Sun-Sentinel,* August 10, 1989, https://www.sun-sentinel.com/news/fl-xpm -1989-08-10-8902250304-story.html; "AZT's Inhuman Cost," *New York Times,* August 28, 1989, sec. A.

13. Rebecca Shoenthal and Amanda Shih, "Does Life Insurance Cover Suicide?," *Policygenius,* November 10, 2020, https://www.policygenius.com/life -insurance/does-life-insurance-cover-suicide/.

14. AAA Northeast, "Membership Terms," accessed April 20, 2021, https:// northeast.aaa.com/membership/my-aaa/membership-terms.html.

15. Mila Araujo and Julius Mansa, "What to Expect from a Life Insurance Medical Exam," *The Balance,* April 1, 2021, https://www.thebalance.com/what -to-expect-your-life-insurance-medical-exam-2645799; Kaitlyn Wells and Mark Smirniotis, "How to Shop for the Best Pet Insurance," *Wirecutter, New York Times,* August 25, 2021, https://www.nytimes.com/wirecutter/reviews/best-pet -insurance/.

16. Samuel Hsin-yu Tseng, "Three Essays on Empirical Applications of Contract Theory" (University of Chicago, 2006); Yun Jeong Choi, Joe Chen, and Yasuyuki Sawada, "Life Insurance and Suicide: Asymmetric Information Revisited," *B.E. Journal of Economic Analysis & Policy* 15, no. 3 (July 1, 2015): 1127–49, https://doi.org/10.1515/bejeap-2014-0081.

17. Neil D. Weinstein, "Unrealistic Optimism about Future Life Events," *Journal of Personality and Social Psychology* 39, no. 5 (1980): 806–20.

18. Marika Cabral, "Claim Timing and Ex Post Adverse Selection," *Review of Economic Studies* 84, no. 1 (January 2017): 1–44, https://doi.org/10.1093/restud /rdw022.

19. Ran Abramitzky, *The Mystery of the Kibbutz,* Princeton Economic History of the Western World (Princeton, N.J.: Princeton University Press, 2018).

20. Wells and Smirniotis, "How to Shop for the Best Pet Insurance."

21. Igal Hendel and Alessandro Lizzeri, "The Role of Commitment in Dynamic Contracts: Evidence from Life Insurance," *Quarterly Journal of Economics* 118, no. 1 (2003): 299–327.

CHAPTER 6

1. Patient Protection and Affordable Care Act, Pub. L. No. 111-148, 42 U.S. Code (2010), https://www.congress.gov/bill/111th-congress/house-bill/3590

—

/text; Matthew Rae, Anthony Damico, Cynthia Cox, Gary Claxton, and Larry Levitt, "The Cost of the Individual Mandate Penalty for the Remaining Uninsured," Kaiser Family Foundation, December 9, 2015, https://www.kff.org/health-reform/issue-brief/the-cost-of-the-individual-mandate-penalty-for-the-remaining-uninsured/.

2. Patient Protection and Affordable Care Act.

3. Transcript of Oral Argument, Department of Health and Human Services, et al., v. Florida, et al., No. 11-398 (Supreme Court of the United States March 27, 2012).

4. George A. Akerlof, "The Market for 'Lemons': Quality Uncertainty and the Market Mechanism," *Quarterly Journal of Economics* 84, no. 3 (1970): 488–500, https://doi.org/10.2307/1879431.

5. American Association for Labor Legislation, "Brief for Health Insurance," *American Labor Legislation Review* 6 (1916): 212.

6. Commonwealth of Massachusetts, chapter 58 of the Acts of 2006 (2006), https://malegislature.gov/Laws/SessionLaws/Acts/2006/Chapter58; Commonwealth of Massachusetts, 830 CMR 111M.2.1: Health Insurance Individual Mandate; Personal Income Tax Return Requirements (2006), https://www.mass.gov/regulations/830-CMR-111m21-health-insurance-individual-mandate-personal-income-tax-return.

7. Amitabh Chandra, Jonathan Gruber, and Robin McKnight, "The Importance of the Individual Mandate—Evidence from Massachusetts," *New England Journal of Medicine* 364, no. 4 (January 12, 2011): 293–95, https://doi.org/10.1056/NEJMp1013067.

8. National Federation of Independent Business, et al., v. Sebelius, Secretary of Health and Human Services, et al., 567 U.S. 519 (2012).

9. National Highway Traffic Safety Administration, "Summary of State Speed Laws," August 2007, https://www.ems.gov/pdf/HS810826.pdf.

10. Emanuel Ezekiel, *Which Country Has the World's Best Health Care?* (New York: PublicAffairs, 2020); Bruce Gowers, dir., *Robin Williams: An Evening at the Met* (HBO, 1986).

11. Tax Cuts and Jobs Act, Pub. L. No. 115-97 (2017).

12. Massachusetts Department of Revenue, "TIR 09-25: Individual Mandate Penalties for Tax Year 2010," Technical Information Release (December 30, 2009), https://www.mass.gov/technical-information-release/tir-09-25-individual-mandate-penalties-for-tax-year-2010; U.S. Census Bureau, "HIC-6_ACS. Health Insurance Coverage Status and Type of Coverage by State—Persons under 65: 2008 to 2019," 2008, 6, https://www.census.gov/data/tables/time-series/demo/health-insurance/historical-series/hic.html; U.S. Census Bureau, "HIB-6. Health Insurance Coverage Status and Type of Coverage by State—Persons under 65: 1999 to

2012," 2006, 6, https://www.census.gov/data/tables/time-series/demo/health-insurance/historical-series/hib.html; Lisa Zamosky, "Do We Need a Stiffer Individual Mandate Penalty?," *HealthInsurance.org Blog*, September 14, 2016, https://www.healthinsurance.org/blog/do-we-need-a-stiffer-individual-mandate-penalty/.

13. "Text – H.R. 3590 – 111th Congress (2009–2010): Patient Protection and Affordable Care Act," March 23, 2010, https://www.congress.gov/bill/111th-congress/house-bill/3590/text; Kaiser Family Foundation, "Marketplace Average Benchmark Premiums," October 2020, https://www.kff.org/health-reform/state-indicator/marketplace-average-benchmark-premiums/; U.S. Census Bureau, "HIB-6," 6.

14. Kaiser Family Foundation, "An Overview of Medicare," February 13, 2019, https://www.kff.org/medicare/issue-brief/an-overview-of-medicare/.

15. Florida Department of Highway Safety and Motor Vehicles, "Florida Insurance Requirements," accessed October 30, 2020, https://www.flhsmv.gov/insurance/; Mark Fitzpatrick, "Cost of SR-22 & FR-44 Insurance in Florida and How Coverage Works," ValuePenguin, March 5, 2021, https://www.valuepenguin.com/car-insurance/sr22-fr44-florida; Kara McGinley and Stephanie Nieves, "How Much Car Insurance Is Required in Every State," *Policygenius*, April 21, 2021, https://www.policygenius.com/auto-insurance/car-insurance-required-in-every-state/.

16. Pietro Tebaldi, "Estimating Equilibrium in Health Insurance Exchanges: Price Competition and Subsidy Design under the ACA" (PhD diss., Stanford University, 2016), 78.

17. Insurance Information Institute, "Automobile Financial Responsibility Laws by State," 2019, https://www.iii.org/automobile-financial-responsibility-laws-by-state; McGinley and Nieves, "How Much Car Insurance Is Required in Every State."

18. The Right Honorable George Osborne and Her Majesty's Treasury, "Chancellor George Osborne's Budget 2014 Speech," March 19, 2014, https://www.gov.uk/government/speeches/chancellor-george-osbornes-budget-2014-speech; Djuna Thurley, "Pensions: Annuities" (House of Commons Library, June 29, 2015); Finance Act (1921), https://www.legislation.gov.uk/ukpga/1921/32/pdfs/ukpga_19210032_en.pdf; Finance Act, 4 & 5 Eliz. 2 (Parliament of the United Kingdom, 1956), https://www.legislation.gov.uk/ukpga/1956/54/pdfs/ukpga_19560054_en.pdf; Finance Act (1976), https://www.legislation.gov.uk/ukpga/1976/40/pdfs/ukpga_19760040_en.pdf.

19. Edmund Cannon, Ian Tonks, and Rob Yuille, "The Effect of the Reforms to Compulsion on Annuity Demand," *National Institute Economic Review* 237, no. 1 (August 1, 2016): R47–54, https://doi.org/10.1177/002795011623700116.

20. Mark Bowden, *Killing Pablo: The Hunt for the Richest, Most Powerful Criminal in History* (New York: Atlantic Monthly Press, 2001).

21. Amitabh Chandra, Jonathan Gruber, and Robin McKnight, "The Impact of Patient Cost-Sharing on Low-Income Populations: Evidence from Massachusetts," *Journal of Health Economics* 33 (January 1, 2014): 57–66, https://doi.org/10.1016/j.jhealeco.2013.10.008; Matthew Panhans, "Adverse Selection in ACA Exchange Markets: Evidence from Colorado," *American Economic Journal: Applied Economics* 11, no. 2 (April 2019): 1–36, https://doi.org/10.1257/app.20170117.

22. Tebaldi, "Estimating Equilibrium," 78.

23. Panhans, "Adverse Selection in ACA Exchange Markets."

24. National Flood Insurance Act, Pub. L. No. 90-448, 42 U.S.C. (1968), https://www.govinfo.gov/content/pkg/STATUTE-82/pdf/STATUTE-82-Pg476.pdf.

CHAPTER 7

1. Alisha Haridasani Gupta and Natasha Singer, "Your App Knows You Got Your Period. Guess Who It Told?," *New York Times,* January 28, 2021, sec. U.S., https://www.nytimes.com/2021/01/28/us/period-apps-health-technology-women-privacy.html; Arthur Holland Michel, "There Are Spying Eyes Everywhere—and Now They Share a Brain," *Wired,* February 4, 2021, https://www.wired.com/story/there-are-spying-eyes-everywhere-and-now-they-share-a-brain/.

2. 23andMe, "Our Health + Ancestry DNA Service," accessed February 2, 2022, https://www.23andme.com/dna-health-ancestry.

3. National Human Genome Research Institute, "Genetic Discrimination," accessed April 9, 2021, https://www.genome.gov/about-genomics/policy-issues/Genetic-Discrimination; Article 10. Reduction and Control of Insurance Rates, California Insurance Code, § 1861 (1988), https://leginfo.legislature.ca.gov/faces/codes_displayText.xhtml?lawCode=INS&division=1.&title=&part=2.&chapter=9.&article=10.

4. National Human Genome Research Institute, "Genetic Discrimination."

5. Civil Rights Act, Pub. L. No. 88-352, 42 U.S. (1964), https://www.govinfo.gov/content/pkg/STATUTE-78/pdf/STATUTE-78-Pg241.pdf; John F. Kennedy, "Civil Rights Message," June 11, 1963, http://www.presidentialrhetoric.com/historicspeeches/kennedy/civilrightsmessage.html.

6. Civil Rights Act; Memsy Price, "To Buy the World a Coke," *Indy Week,* February 15, 2012, https://indyweek.com/news/archives/buy-world-coke/.

7. Library of Congress, "Greensboro Lunch Counter Sit-In," accessed January 26, 2022, https://www.loc.gov/exhibits/odyssey/educate/lunch.html; Peter Applebome, "The Man Behind Rosa Parks," *New York Times,* December 7, 2005, sec. New York, https://www.nytimes.com/2005/12/07/nyregion/the-man-behind -rosa-parks.html.

8. eBay, "Sept. 1960 F W Woolworth Colorado Lunch Counter Laminate Digital Menu Reprint," accessed January 26, 2022, https://www.ebay.com/itm /133720536369?hash=item1f225d7531:g:vbQAAOSwE~xgcIBS.

9. Robert A. Hummer and Juanita J. Chinn, "Race/Ethnicity and U.S. Adult Mortality," *Du Bois Review: Social Science Research on Race* 8, no. 1 (2011): 5–24, https://doi.org/10.1017/S1742058X11000051.

10. Werner Güth, Rolf Schmittberger, and Bernd Schwarze, "An Experimental Analysis of Ultimatum Bargaining," *Journal of Economic Behavior & Organization* 3, no. 4 (December 1, 1982): 367–88, https://doi.org/10.1016/0167-2681(82) 90011-7.

11. Alan C. Monheit, Joel C. Cantor, Margaret Koller, and Kimberley S. Fox, "Community Rating and Sustainable Individual Health Insurance Markets in New Jersey," *Health Affairs* 23, no. 4 (2004): 167–75; Katherine Swartz and Deborah W. Garnick, "Lessons from New Jersey," *Journal of Health Politics, Policy and Law* 25, no. 1 (2000): 45–70; Uwe Reinhardt, "The Case for Mandating Health Insurance," *Economix* (blog), *New York Times,* October 23, 2009, https://economix .blogs.nytimes.com/2009/10/23/the-case-for-mandating-health-insurance /?searchResultPosition=10; Jonathan Cohn, "The New Jersey Experience: Do Insurance Reforms Unravel without an Individual Mandate?," *Kaiser Health News,* March 20, 2012, https://khn.org/news/nj-ind-mandate-case-study/; Larry Levitt and Gary Claxton, "Is a Death Spiral Inevitable If There Is No Mandate?," Kaiser Family Foundation, June 19, 2012, https://www.kff.org/health-reform/perspec tive/is-a-death-spiral-inevitable-if-there-is-no-mandate/.

12. Thomas Buchmueller and John DiNardo, "Did Community Rating Induce an Adverse Selection Death Spiral? Evidence from New York, Pennsylvania, and Connecticut," *American Economic Review* 92, no. 1 (2002): 280–94; Leigh Wachenheim and Hans Leida, "The Impact of Guaranteed Issue and Community Rating Reforms on States' Individual Insurance Markets," Miliman, March 2012, http:// www.statecoverage.org/files/Updated-Milliman-Report_GI_and_Comm_Rating _March_2012.pdf.

13. Robert Pear, "Pooling Risks and Sharing Costs in Effort to Gain Stable Insurance Rates," *New York Times,* May 22, 1994; Buchmueller and DiNardo, "Did Community Rating Induce an Adverse Selection Death Spiral?"

14. Katherine Swartz and Deborah W. Garnick, "Can Adverse Selection Be Avoided in a Market for Individual Health Insurance?," *Medical Care Research and*

Review 56, no. 3 (September 1, 1999): 373–88, https://doi.org/10.1177/1077 55879905600306.

15. Mark Miller, "Medicare's Private Option Is Gaining Popularity, and Critics," *New York Times,* September 18, 2020, sec. Business, https://www.nytimes.com /2020/02/21/business/medicare-advantage-retirement.html; Centers for Medicare and Medicaid Services, "Medicare Enrollment Dashboard," accessed January 22, 2021, https://www.cms.gov/Research-Statistics-Data-and-Systems/Statistics -Trends-and-Reports/CMSProgramStatistics/Dashboard; Meredith Freed, Anthony Damico, and Tricia Neuman, "A Dozen Facts about Medicare Advantage in 2020," Kaiser Family Foundation, January 13, 2021, https://www.kff.org/medicare/issue -brief/a-dozen-facts-about-medicare-advantage-in-2020/.

16. Miller, "Medicare's Private Option."

17. Miller.

18. Centers for Medicare and Medicaid Services, "When Can I Buy Medigap?," accessed April 26, 2021, https://www.medicare.gov/supplements-other-insurance /when-can-i-buy-medigap.

19. Cristina Boccuti, Gretchen Jacobson, Kendal Orgera, and Tricia Neuman, "Medigap Enrollment and Consumer Protections Vary across States," Kaiser Family Foundation, July 11, 2018, https://www.kff.org/medicare/issue-brief/medigap -enrollment-and-consumer-protections-vary-across-states/.

20. Vilsa Curto, "Pricing Regulations in Individual Health Insurance: Evidence from Medigap" (PhD diss., Stanford University, 2016).

CHAPTER 8

1. Gabriel London, dir., *The Life and Mind of Mark DeFriest* (Naked Edge Films, Thought Café, 2014).

2. Thomas G. McGuire, Joseph P. Newhouse, and Anna D. Sinaiko, "An Economic History of Medicare Part C," *Milbank Quarterly* 89, no. 2 (2011): 289–332.

3. Gretchen Jacobson, Meredith Freed, Anthony Damico, and Tricia Neuman, "A Dozen Facts about Medicare Advantage in 2019," Kaiser Family Foundation, June 6, 2019, https://www.kff.org/medicare/issue-brief/a-dozen-facts-about -medicare-advantage-in-2019/.

4. McGuire, Newhouse, and Sinaiko, "Economic History of Medicare Part C."

5. McGuire, Newhouse, and Sinaiko; Gregory C. Pope, Randall P. Ellis, Arlene S. Ash, et al., "Principal Inpatient Diagnostic Cost Group Model for Medicare Risk Adjustment," *Health Care Financing Review* 21, no. 3 (2000): 93–118.

6. McGuire, Newhouse, and Sinaiko, "Economic History of Medicare Part C"; Joseph Newhouse, Melinda Beeuwkes Buntin, and John Chapman, "Risk Adjustment and Medicare," Commonwealth Fund, June 1999.

7. John Tozzi, "Insurers Gaming Medicare Might Cost Washington Billions a Year," *Bloomberg,* June 23, 2015, https://www.bloomberg.com/news/articles /2015-06-23/insurers-gaming-medicare-might-cost-washington-billions-a-year; Michael Geruso and Timothy Layton, "Upcoding: Evidence from Medicare on Squishy Risk Adjustment," *Journal of Political Economy* 128, no. 3 (2020), https:// doi.org/10.1086/704756.

8. "'Gold Rush' Is Started by Ford's \$5 Offer," *Ford Times,* January 7, 1914, https://www.thehenryford.org/collections-and-research/digital-collections/arti fact/99336/#slide=gs-216532.

9. Medicare Prescription Drug, Improvement, and Modernization Act, Pub. L. No. 108-182, § 1305, 42 U.S.C. (2003), https://www.congress.gov/108/plaws /publ173/PLAW-108publ173.htm.

10. Ben Franklin, "The Good, the Bad, and the Ugly," *Washington Spectator,* January 15, 2004; Jessie X. Fan, Deanna L. Sharpe, and Goog-Soog Hong, "Health Care and Prescription Drug Spending by Seniors," *Monthly Labor Review,* March 2003.

11. Marvin Moser, "Historical Perspectives on the Management of Hypertension," *Journal of Clinical Hypertension* 8, no. 8 (August 2006): 15–20; R. W. Scott, "Clinical Blood Pressure," in *Practice of Medicine,* ed. Frederick Tice (Hagerstown, Md.: W. F. Prior, 1946), 93–114; Howard Bruenn, "Clinical Notes on the Illness and Death of President Franklin D. Roosevelt," *Annals of Internal Medicine* 72, no. 4 (1970): 579–91.

12. Harvard Health, "Medications for Treating Hypertension," August 1, 2009, https://www.health.harvard.edu/heart-health/medications-for-treating -hypertension.

13. Kaiser Family Foundation, "An Overview of the Medicare Part D Prescription Drug Benefit," October 14, 2020, https://www.kff.org/medicare/fact-sheet /an-overview-of-the-medicare-part-d-prescription-drug-benefit/.

14. Gina Kolata, "Co-Payments for Expensive Drugs Soar," *New York Times,* April 4, 2008, https://www.nytimes.com/2008/04/14/us/14drug.html.

15. Colleen Carey, "Technological Change and Risk Adjustment: Benefit Design Incentives in Medicare Part D," *American Economic Journal: Economic Policy* 9, no. 1 (2017): 38–73.

16. John Kautter, Melvin Ingber, Gregory C. Pope, and Sara Freeman, "Improvements in Medicare Part D Risk Adjustment: Beneficiary Access and Payment Accuracy," *Medical Care* 50, no. 12 (December 2012): 1102–8, https://doi.org/10 .1097/MLR.0b013e318269eb20.

EPILOGUE

1. Franz Kafka, *The Office Writings*, ed. Stanley Corngold, Jack Greenberg, and Benno Wagner (Princeton, N.J.: Princeton University Press, 2015), 20.

2. National Center for Education Statistics, "Economic Outcomes," in *The Condition of Education*, 2020, https://nces.ed.gov/programs/coe/pdf/coe_cba.pdf.

3. Jaleesa Bustamante, "Average Cost of College [2021]: Yearly Tuition + Expenses," EducationData, June 7, 2019, https://educationdata.org/average-cost-of-college.

4. Milton Friedman, "Economics and the Public Interest," in *The Role of Government in Education*, ed. Robert Solo (New Brunswick, N.J.: Rutgers University Press, 1955), http://la.utexas.edu/users/hcleaver/330T/350kPEEFriedmanRole OfGovttable.pdf.

5. Bret Ladine, "'70s Debt Program Finally Ending," *Yale Daily News*, March 27, 2001, https://yaledailynews.com/blog/2001/03/27/70s-debt-program -finally-ending/; Elaine Fong, "New Model an Alternative for Financing Education," *Daily Northwestern*, January 28, 2002, https://dailynorthwestern.com/2002 /01/28/archive-manual/new-model-an-alternative-for-financing-education/; Michael T. Nietzel, "Augustana College Will Be First in U.S. to Test Income Insurance for Graduates," *Forbes*, July 21, 2021, https://www.forbes.com/sites/michaelt nietzel/2021/07/21/augustana-college-will-be-first-college-to-offer-income -insurance-to-graduates/.

6. Daniel Herbst and Nathaniel Hendren, "Opportunity Unraveled: Private Information and the Missing Markets for Financing Human Capital" (NBER Working Paper 29214, National Bureau of Economic Research, Cambridge, Mass., September 2021), https://doi.org/10.3386/w29214.

7. Purdue University, Division of Financial Aid, "Income Share Agreements," accessed May 24, 2021, https://www.purdue.edu/dfa/types-of-aid/income-share -agreement/index.html; lumni, "Students," accessed May 24, 2021, https://www .lumni.net/students/; Pando, "Income Pooling," accessed May 24, 2021, https:// www.pandopooling.com/.

8. Robert Gibbons and Lawrence F. Katz, "Layoffs and Lemons," *Journal of Labor Economics* 9, no. 4 (October 1, 1991): 351–80, https://doi.org/10.1086 /298273.

9. Matt Bonesteel, "Evander Kane, Who Has Made More than $50 Million in His NHL Career, Files for Bankruptcy," *Washington Post*, January 12, 2021, https:// www.washingtonpost.com/sports/2021/01/12/evander-kane-bankruptcy/.

10. Joseph E. Stiglitz and Andrew Weiss, "Credit Rationing in Markets with Imperfect Information," *American Economic Review* 71, no. 3 (1981): 393–410.

—

11. Marcus White, "Report: Sharks' Kane, $27 Million in Debt, Files for Bankruptcy," NBC Sports, January 11, 2021, https://www.nbcsports.com/bayarea/sharks/report-sharks-evander-kane-27-million-debt-declares-bankruptcy.

12. Lawrence Ausubel, "Adverse Selection in the Credit Card Market" (unpublished paper, June 17, 1999), https://jfhoude.wiscweb.wisc.edu/wp-content/uploads/sites/769/2019/09/Asubel_wp1999.pdf.

13. Joseph E. Stiglitz, "Information and the Change in the Paradigm in Economics," *American Economic Review* 92, no. 3 (2002): 468.

INDEX

INDEX

INDEX